The College of Law
of England and Wales

LIBRARY & INFORMATION SERVICES

The College of Law, Bishopthorpe Road, York YO23 2GA
Telephone: 01904 682054

**This book MUST be returned on or before the last date stamped below.
Failure to do so will result in a fine.**

Library Phone No
01483 216169

Birmingham • Chester • Guildford • London • York

Guide to Occupational Illness Claims

Second Edition

General Editor
Christopher Goddard

Published by
Jordan Publishing Limited
21 St Thomas Street
Bristol BS1 6JS

British Library Cataloguing-in-Publication Data

A catalogue record for this book is available from the British Library.

ISBN 978 1 84661 311 1

Typeset by Letterpart Ltd, Reigate, Surrey

Printed in Great Britain by CPI Antony Rowe, Chippenham and Eastbourne

LIST OF CONTRIBUTORS

Catherine Atkinson
Barrister, 9 Gough Square, London

Laura Elfield
Barrister, 9 Gough Square, London

Chris Fry
Solicitor and Managing Partner, Unity Law, Sheffield

Christopher Goddard
Barrister, 9 Gough Square, London

Giles Mooney
Barrister, 9 Gough Square, London

Gaurang Naik
Barrister, 9 Gough Square, London

Rajeev Shetty
Barrister, 9 Gough Square, London

Chris Stephenson
Barrister, 9 Gough Square, London

PREFACE

'The vast majority of personal injury cases are not difficult. The evidence may be complicated, witnesses may be confused or unreliable and the expert opinions may be contradictory or incomprehensible. ... Usually it is a matter of applying some well settled principles to the facts found.'

Baroness Hale in *Gregg v Scott* [2005] UKHL 2 at para 192

That neatly describes the theme of this book. It is an attempt to take an overall view so that the principles could be seen and applied. The principles are illustrated by consideration of the main five occupational illnesses, but the hope is that the principles can be seen not only in application to these five but to other occupational illnesses which may arise for consideration. The evidence in a dermatitis case or a Legionnaire's Disease case may be different and technical, but the principles should still be the beacons which guide the preparation for the case and help to control the evidence and keep the case focused.

Since the first edition in 2005 there have been many very important decisions of principle. In this second edition, the opportunity has been taken, not only to update the law, but to refresh and expand much of the text and to bring greater clarity to the matters discussed. For that purpose, a number of professional colleagues have taken over individual sections and brought their experience and expertise to rewriting the original. I am very grateful to them all. They have carried out the main tasks, politely adjusting, amending and correcting the original. A big thank you to all: Chris Fry, solicitor from Unity Law in Sheffield, and my colleagues from chambers at 9 Gough Square: Catherine Atkinson, Laura Elfield, Giles Mooney, Gaurang Naik, Raj Shetty and Chris Stephenson.

We hope this will be of assistance to you in applying the principles as they are now. However, do bear in mind the words of the Red Queen to Alice:

'Now, here, you see, it takes all the running you can do, to keep in the same place. If you want to get somewhere else, you must run at least twice as fast as that!'

Through the Looking-Glass, and What Alice Found There

Christopher Goddard

January 2012

ASSOCIATION OF PERSONAL INJURY LAWYERS (APIL)

APIL is the UK's leading association of claimant personal injury lawyers, dedicated to protecting the rights of injured people.

Formed in 1990, APIL now represents around 5,000 solicitors, barristers, academics and students in the UK, Republic of Ireland and overseas.

APIL's objectives are:

- to promote full and just compensation for all types of personal injury;
- to promote and develop expertise in the practice of personal injury law;
- to promote wider redress for personal injury in the legal system;
- to campaign for improvements in personal injury law;
- to promote safety and alert the public to hazards;
- to provide a communication network for members.

APIL is a growing and influential forum pushing for law reform, and improvements, which will benefit injured people.

APIL has been running CPD training events, accredited by the Solicitors Regulation Authority and Bar Standards Board, for nearly 20 years and has a wealth of experience in developing the most practical up-to-date courses, delivered by eminent leading speakers, either publicly or in-house.

APIL training now runs almost 200 personal injury training events nationally each year, plus up to a further 100 meetings of our regional and special interest groups. Topics cover a wide range of subjects and are geared towards giving personal injury lawyers a thorough grounding in the core areas of personal injury law, whilst keeping lawyers thoroughly up to date in all subjects.

APIL is also an authoritative information source for personal injury lawyers, providing up-to-the-minute PI bulletins, regular newsletters and publications, information databases and online services.

For further information contact:

APIL
3 Alder Court
Rennie Hogg Road
Nottingham NG2 1RX
DX 716208 Nottingham 42
Tel 0115 9580585
Email mail@apil.org.uk
Website www.apil.org.uk

CONTENTS

List of Contributors	v
Preface	vii
Association of Personal Injury Lawyers (APIL)	ix
Table of Cases	xxi
Table of Statutes	xxix
Table of Statutory Instruments	xxxi
Glossary	xxxv

Part 1
General Principles

Chapter 1
Occupational Illness — 3
Definition of occupational illness — 3
Common conditions — 4
Identifying the issues — 4
Basic principles — 5

Chapter 2
Duty and Foreseeability — 7
To whom is the duty of care owed? — 7
Foreseeability – extent of duty — 8
Foreseeability in specific occupational diseases — 10
    Asbestos — 10
    Noise — 12
    Work-related upper limb disorders — 13
    Vibration white finger (VWF) — 14
    Work-related stress — 15
Causation — 18
Expert evidence and foreseeability — 18

Chapter 3
Causation, Apportionment and Contributory Negligence — 19
Divisible and indivisible disease — 19
    The distinction — 19
    Why the distinction between divisible and indivisible disease
        matters — 19
Causation: the standard test — 20

Material cause   21
Increasing the risk – a new tort?   22
Epidemiological evidence and 'doubling the risk'   25
Mesothelioma and the Compensation Act 2006   27
Lung cancer   29
  Other causes   29
  Lung cancer plus asbestosis   29
  Lung cancer without asbestosis   29
  Smoking and other causes   30
De minimis exposure   32
Asymptomatic asbestos conditions   33
  Pleural plaques   33
  The decision in *Johnston*   33
Apportionment of damages in divisible disease cases   37
  The basis   37
  Apportionment in practice   38
  Expert evidence   39
  Does the defendant have to plead and prove apportionment?   39
  Death from asbestosis – is an apportionment exercise
     necessary?   39
Contributory negligence   40

Chapter 4
Limitation   **43**
Why have limitation of actions?   43
Personal injury claims   43
Intentional tort or breach of duty?   44
Does expiry of the limitation period prevent a claim being
     brought?   44
When time begins to run   45
Accrual of a cause of action   45
Knowledge under section 14   45
Onus of proof   46
'Knowledge'   46
Constructive knowledge   46
'Knowledge that the injury in question was significant'
     (section 14(1)(a))   48
'Knowledge that the injury was attributable in whole or in part to
     the act or omission which is alleged to constitute negligence,
     nuisance or breach of duty' (section 14(1)(b))   50
'Knowledge of the identity of the defendant' (section14(1)(c))   53
'Act or omission ... by a person other than the defendant'
     (section 14(1)(d))   53
When does the limitation period expire?   54
Can the period be extended by agreement etc?   54
The court's discretion under section 33   55
Previous proceedings   56
Considerations in exercising the discretion   56

Onus under section 33   58
Section 33(3)(a): the length of and reasons for the delay   58
Section 33(3)(b): the extent to which the evidence is likely to be
    less cogent   60
Section 33(3)(c): the conduct of the defendant after the cause of
    action arose   61
Section 33(3)(d): the duration of any disability of the claimant   62
Section 33(3)(e): the extent to which the claimant acted promptly
    and reasonably once he had 'knowledge'   62
Section 33(3)(f): the steps taken by the claimant to obtain
    medical, legal or other expert advice   62
Setting aside the discretion   63
Costs   63
Claims following death   63
    Law Reform (Miscellaneous Provisions) Act 1934 claim   63
    Fatal Accident Act 1976 claim   64
Section 33 and claims following death   64
Disability   65
    Who is under a disability?   65
    The effect of disability   65

Part 2
Types of Occupational Illnesses

Chapter 5
Asbestos-related Illnesses   69
Types of asbestos and its uses   69
Exposure to asbestos   70
Asbestos diseases   71
    Pleural plaques   71
    Pleural thickening   72
    Pleural effusion   72
    Asbestosis   72
    Lung cancer   73
    Mesothelioma   74
Breach of duty   74
    Date of knowledge   75
    Causation   79
    Apportionment of damages   80
    Contributory negligence   80
Specific considerations for asbestos-related claims   80
    Medical diagnosis   80
    Applicable law   81
    Exposure   81
    Causation   82
    Apportionment of damages   82
    Limitation   82
    Medical prognosis   82

Damages   82

Chapter 6
Noise-related Conditions   **83**
Introduction   83
The audiogram   85
Interpretation   86
Calculating the hearing loss   87
    Example   88
Awareness of data-collection methods   88
Hearing protection   89
Specific considerations for noise-related claims   90
  Medical diagnosis   90
    Typical audiogram pattern with 'notch' at 3–4, or 6Khz,
      Symmetrical shape to both ears, history of noise
      damage.   90
  Applicable law   90
  Exposure   90
    Type of noise source   90
  Causation   91
  Apportionment of damages   91
  Limitation   91
  Medical prognosis   91
  Damages   91

Chapter 7
Work-related Upper Limb Disorder   **93**
Introduction   93
Foreseeability and breach   94
Causation   95
A defined medical condition   96
Specific considerations for WRULD claims   97
  Medical diagnosis   97
  Applicable law   98
  Exposure   98
  Causation   99
  Apportionment of damages   99
  Limitation   99
  Medical prognosis   99
  Damages   99

Chapter 8
Vibration White Finger   **101**
Introduction   101
Causes of VWF   103
Prescribed disease   104
Vibration dose   104
Common law duty   107

Statutory duty   108
Specific considerations for VWF claims   109
  Medical diagnosis   109
  Applicable law   109
  Exposure   109
    Type of work and machinery and tools used   109
  Causation   109
  Apportionment of damages   110
  Limitation   110
  Medical prognosis   110
  Damages   110

Chapter 9
Occupational Stress Claims   **111**
Defining 'stress'   111
General principles   112
The guidance   113
Foreseeability   115
  Knowledge about employee   115
  Evidential value of a GP certificate   116
  Inherently stressful occupations   116
  The Management Standards   117
Breach of duty   118
  The test of reasonableness   118
  Provision of occupational health or counselling service   119
  Demotion/leaving the job   119
Causation and apportionment   120
Alternative causes of action   121
  Protection from Harassment Act 1997   121
  Breach of contract/implied duty of trust and confidence   122
  Disability discrimination   122
Specific considerations for work-related stress claims   123
  Medical diagnosis   123
  Applicable law   123
  Exposure   123
  Causation   124
  Apportionment of damages   124
  Limitation   124
  Medical prognosis   124
  Damages   124
  Alternatives to common law claim   124

Part 3
Statutory Basis of Claim

Chapter 10
General Statutory Duty   **127**
Introduction   127

Statutes of general application   129
  Shipbuilding Regulations 1931, reg 18   129
  Factories Act 1937   129
  Building (Safety, Health and Welfare) Regulations 1948   132
  Shipbuilding and Ship-Repairing Regulations 1960   133
  Factories Act 1961   133
  Construction (General Provisions) Regulations 1961   134
  Construction (Working Places) Regulations 1966   135
  Control of Substances Hazardous to Health Regulations 1988,
      1994, 1999 and 2002   135
  Management of Health and Safety at Work Regulations 1992
      and 1999   140
  Workplace (Health, Safety and Welfare) Regulations 1992   143
  Provision and Use of Work Equipment Regulations 1992 and
      1998   144

Chapter 11
Regulations with Specific Application   **147**
At a glance   147
The Regulations   148
  Asbestos Industry Regulations 1931   148
    Exhaust draughts   149
    Storage   150
    Containment   150
    Cleaning   150
    Breathing apparatus   150
    Persons employed   151
  Asbestos Regulations 1969   151
  The Control of Asbestos at Work Regulations 1987   151
  The Control of Asbestos at Work Regulations 2002   152
  Woodworking Machines Regulations 1974   156
  Noise at Work Regulations 1989   157
  Health and Safety (Display Screen Equipment)
      Regulations 1992   158
    Overlap with other Regulations   158
    Users   158
    Self-employed   159
    Assessments   159
    Reassessments   159
    Training   161
    Provision of information   161
    Breaks   161
  Control of Substances Hazardous to Health Regulations 1988,
      1994, 1999 and 2002   162
  Manual Handling Operations Regulations 1992   162
    Regulation 4 – duties of employers   162
  The Control of Vibration at Work Regulations 2005   165
  Control of Noise at Work Regulations 2005   165

Part 4
Practical Matters

Chapter 12
Practical Matters **169**
Which employers to sue 169
Does the employer exist now? 169
Restoration under the Companies Act 2006 (the 2006 Act) 170
   The application 171
   The procedure 171
   The hearing and the order 172
   Limitation 172
Companies in receivership 173
   Retrospective permission to sue 173
Third Parties (Rights Against Insurers) Act 2010 (the 2010 Act) 174
   How does it work? 174
   When will the Act apply? 175
   Who is a relevant person? 175
   Defences and limitations 176
   Obtaining disclosure from the insurer and third parties 177
   Insurer's concession 177
Is the employer worth suing? 177
Finding the insurer 180

Chapter 13
Pre-action Protocol for Disease and Illness Claims **181**
Introduction 181
Obtaining health and other occupational records 182
Where the defendant has difficulty providing information 183
Failure to comply with a request for information 183
Third parties holding records 183
Letter of claim 183
Defendant's response to letter of claim 184
Schedule of special damage 185
Experts 185
Resolution of issues 187
Starting proceedings 187

Chapter 14
Evidential Matters **189**
Witness statement 189
Claimant's evidence 190
Required details 191
   Asbestos 192
      Where he worked 192
      When he worked there 192
      The type of product or substance used 192
      What work he did 193

What work others did in proximity to him   193
How long during each day he was exposed   193
Whether protective measures were taken   193
Whether protective equipment was provided and when   193
Whether there were any other sources or potential sources
    of exposure   194
Noise   194
Where he worked   194
When he worked there   194
The type of tools and machines used   194
What work he did   195
What work others did in proximity to him   195
How long during each day he was exposed   195
Whether protective measures were taken   195
Whether protective equipment was provided and when   195
Whether there were any other sources or potential sources
    of exposure   196
Work-related upper limb disorders (WRULDs)   196
Where he worked   196
When he worked there   196
What work he did   196
How long during each day he carried out the work   196
Whether protective measures were taken   197
Whether there were any other sources or potential sources
    of exposure   197
Vibration white finger (VWF)   197
Where he worked   197
When he worked with vibratory tools or machinery   197
The type of tools or machinery used   198
Whether protective measures were taken   198
Whether protective equipment was provided and when   198
Whether warnings and instructions were given   198
Whether there were any other sources or potential sources
    of exposure   198
Work-related stress   198
What work he did   198
What the defendant knew   198
What could have been done to avoid the stresses imposed
    on the claimant?   199
Causation   199
Investigating the circumstances of the claim   199
Defences   200
Documentary evidence   201

Part 5
Valuing the Claim

Chapter 15
General Damages **205**
Introduction 205
Provisional damages 205
Asbestos-related disease 207
    Pain, suffering and disability 207
    Mesothelioma 207
    Lung cancer 208
    Asbestosis 208
    Pleural thickening 209
    Pleural plaques 209
    Handicap on the labour market 210
    Loss of congenial employment 210
Asthma 210
    Pain, suffering and disability 210
    Handicap on the labour market 211
    Loss of congenial employment 211
Hearing loss 211
    Handicap on the labour market 212
    Loss of congenial employment 212
Work-related upper limb disorders (WRULDs) 212
    Handicap in the labour market 213
    Loss of congenial employment 213
Vibration white finger (VWF) 213
    Handicap on the labour market 215
    Loss of congenial employment 215
Work-related stress 216
    Handicap on the labour market 216
    Loss of congenial employment 217

Chapter 16
Special Damages **219**
Loss of earnings 219
Future effect on employment 219
Medical expenses 220
Fatal Accidents Act claims 221

Chapter 17
Settlement **223**
Introduction 223
When to negotiate 223
Know the issues 224
Part 36 offers 225
Part 36 offers and liability 225
Part 36 offers and quantum 225

Appendix 1
Pleadings   227

Appendix 2
Sample Schedule   261

Appendix 3
Restoring a Company to the Register   265

Appendix 4
Checklists   267

Appendix 5
Pre-action Protocol for Disease and Illness Claims   271

Index   289

TABLE OF CASES

References are to paragraph numbers.

A v Hoare and other appeals [2008] UKHL 6, [2008] 1 AC 844, [2008] 2 All ER 1,
[2008] 2 WLR 311, [2008] Fam Law 402, 100 BMLR 1, [2008] NLJR 218,
(2008) *Times*, 31 January, [2008] All ER (D) 251 (Jan)   4.3, 4.11, 4.21
AB and others v Ministry of Defence [2010] EWCA Civ 1317, 117 BMLR 101,
[2010] NLJR 1686, (2011) *Times*, 19 January, [2010] All ER (D) 252 (Nov)   3.3
AB v Nugent Care Society (formerly Catholic Social Services (Liverpool)) [2010]
EWHC 1005 (QB), 116 BMLR 84, [2010] All ER (D) 55 (May)   4.22
AB v Nugent Care Society; R v Wirral Metropolitan Borough Council [2009]
EWCA Civ 827, [2010] 1 FLR 707, [2009] Fam Law 1045, 153 Sol Jo (no 30)
28, [2009] All ER (D) 308 (Jul)   4.21, 4.22
Adams v Bracknell Forest Borough Council [2004] UKHL 29, [2005] 1 AC 76,
[2004] 3 All ER 897, [2004] ELR 459, [2005] PIQR 11   4.10, 4.19
Aktas v Adepta (a registered charity); Dixie v British Polythene Industries plc
[2010] EWCA Civ 1170, [2011] QB 894, [2011] 2 All ER 536, [2011] 2 WLR
945, [2010] NLJR 1532, [2010] All ER (D) 223 (Oct)   4.18
Albonetti v Wirral MBC [2008] EWHC 3523 (QB)   4.9
Allen v British Rail Engineering Ltd (1998) (unreported) 7 October   8.1
Allison v London Underground Ltd [2008] EWCA Civ 71, [2008] ICR 719, [2008]
IRLR 440, [2008] PIQR P185, 152 Sol Jo (no 8) 34, [2008] All ER (D) 185
(Feb), CA   7.2
Anderson v RWE Npower plc (2010) (unreported) 20 May   10.2.2
Armstrong and Others v British Coal [1997] 8 Med LR 259, (1996) *The Times*, 6
December, LTL 12/5/98   2.3.4, 8.1
Arnold v CEGB [1988] AC 228, [1987] 3 WLR 1009, [1987] 3 All ER 694   1.3
Asmussen v Filtrona United Kingdom Ltd [2011] EWHC 1734 (QB), [2011] All ER
(D) 42 (Jul)   2.2, 10.2.5
Atlantic Computer Systems plc, Re [1992] Ch 505, [1992] 1 All ER 476, [1992] 2
WLR 367, [1991] BCLC 606, [1990] BCC 859   12.4

Badger v Ministry of Defence [2005] EWHC 2941 (QB), [2006] 3 All ER 173, 91
BMLR 1, [2006] NLJR 65, (2005) *Times*, 30 December, [2005] All ER (D) 248
(Dec)   3.11, 5.4.4
Bailey (by her father and litigation friend) v Ministry of Defence [2008] EWCA Civ
883, [2009] 1 WLR 1052, 103 BMLR 134, (2008) *Times*, 26 August, [2008] All
ER (D) 382 (Jul)   3.3
Banks v Woodhall Duckham Limited (Unreported) 30 November 1995, CA   10.2.2,
10.2.5
Barber v Somerset County Council [2004] UKHL 13, [2004] 2 All ER 385, [2004] 1
WLR 1089, [2004] ICR 457, [2004] IRLR 475, 77 BMLR 219, 148 Sol Jo LB
419, [2004] All ER (D) 07 (Apr), HL   2.3.5, 9.3, 9.6, 14.3.5.3
Barker v Corus UK Ltd; Murray v British Shipbuilders (Hydrodynamics) Ltd;
Patterson v Smiths Dock Ltd [2006] UKHL 20, [2006] 2 AC 572, [2006] 3 All
ER 785, [2006] 2 WLR 1027, [2006] ICR 809, 89 BMLR 1, [2006] NLJR 796,
[2006] PIQR P390, (2006) *Times*, 4 May, [2006] 5 LRC 271, [2006] All ER (D)
23 (May)   3.1.2, 3.4, 3.6, 3.7.4, 3.10.2, 3.10.5, 3.11, 5.4, 5.4.2
Barlow v Borough of Broxborne [2003] EWHC 50, QB   2.3.5

Barnett v Chelsea and Kensington Hospital Management Committee [1969] 1 QB
    428, [1968] 1 All ER 1068, [1968] 2 WLR 422, 111 Sol Jo 912   3.2
Bateman v Danks Holdings Ltd and Bristol & Babcock Ltd [2009] EWHC 2082
    (QB), [2009] All ER (D) 66 (Aug)   12.6
Baxter v Harland & Wolff [1990] IRLR 516, CA   2.3.2
Beddoes and others v Vintners Defence Systems Ltd and Others (2009) Newcastle
    County Court, unreported   3.9.2
Bentley v Bristol & Western HA [1991] 2 Med LR 359   4.12
Berry v Stone Manganese Marine (1971) 12 KIR 13, (1971) 115 SJ 966, [1972] 1
    Lloyd's Rep 182   2.3.2
Bonnington Castings Ltd v Wardlaw [1956] AC 613, [1956] 2 WLR 707, [1956] 1
    All ER 615, HL   2.4, 3.3, 3.4, 3.5, 3.7.4
Bowes v Sedgefield District Council [1981] ICR 234, (1980) 125 SJ 80, CA   10.2.2,
    10.2.3, 10.2.4, 10.2.5, 10.2.6
Broadley v Guy Clapham & Co [1994] 4 All ER 439, [1993] 4 Med LR 328, 17
    BMLR 56   4.12
Brown v Corus (UK) Ltd [2004] EWCA Civ 374, [2004] PIQR P476, (2004) *The
    Times*, 27 May, 148 Sol Jo LB 418, [2004] All ER (D) 551, Mar   8.5
Bryce v Swan Hunter Group plc [1988] 1 All ER 659, [1987] 2 Lloyd's Rep 426   10.2.2
Buck v English Electric Co Ltd [1977] 1 WLR 806, [1978] 1 All ER 271, [1977] ICR
    629, QBD   4.22
Buckler v Sheffield City Council [2004] EWCA Civ 920, [2004] All ER (D) 214
    (Jun)   4.21
Burgin v Sheffield City Council [2005] EWCA Civ 482, 149 Sol Jo LB 480, [2005]
    All ER (D) 166 (Apr)   4.22

Caparo Industries plc v Dickman [1990] 2 AC 605, [1990] 1 All ER 568, [1990] 2
    WLR 358, [1990] BCLC 273, [1990] BCC 164, 11 LDAB 563, 134 Sol Jo 494,
    [1990] 12 LS Gaz R 42, [1990] NLJR 248, [1991] LRC (Comm) 460   5.4
Cartledge v E Jopling & Sons Ltd [1963] AC 758, [1963] 1 All ER 341, [1963] 2
    WLR 210, [1963] 1 Lloyd's Rep 1, 107 Sol Jo 73   3.9.2
Charles v Preston and Thomas Limited (Unreported) 14 May 1993   10.2.2
Coad v Cornwall and Scilly Isles Health Authority [1997] 1 WLR 189, [1997] 8
    Med LR 154, 33 BMLR 168, [1996] 27 LS Gaz R 29, [1997] PIQR P 92, 140
    Sol Jo LB 168   4.21
Conn v Sunderland City Council [2007] EWCA Civ 1492, [2008] IRLR 324, [2007]
    All ER (D) 99 (Nov)   9.7.1
Cookson v Novartis Grimsby Ltd [2007] EWCA Civ 1261, [2007] All ER (D) 465
    (Nov)   3.5
Copeland v Smith [2000] 1 All ER 457, [2000] 1 WLR 1371, 143 Sol Jo LB 276   4.14
Corbin v Penfold Metallising Co Ltd [2000] All ER (D) 2060; (2000) *The Times*, 2
    May, CA   4.21
Cressey v E Timm & Son Ltd [2005] EWCA Civ 763, [2005] 1 WLR 3926, [2006]
    ICR 282, [2005] 28 LS Gaz R 33, (2005) *Times*, 25 July, [2005] All ER (D) 295
    (Jun)   4.13

Deerness v John R Keeble & Son (Brantham) Ltd [1983] 2 Lloyd's Rep 260, [1983]
    Com LR 221, 133 NLJ 641, HL, *Affirming* (1982) 126 Sol Jo 729, CA   4.16
Dickins v O2 plc [2008] EWCA Civ 1144, [2009] IRLR 58, [2008] All ER (D) 154
    (Oct)   9.4, 9.5.1, 9.6
Doherty and Others v Rugby Joinery (UK) Ltd [2004] EWCA Civ 147, CA   2.3.4
Donachie v Chief Constable of Greater Manchester Police [2004] EWCA Civ 405,
    (2004) *The Times*, 6 May   2.3.5
Donoghue v Stevenson [1932] AC 562, 101 LJPC 119, 37 Com Cas 350, [1932] All
    ER Rep 1, 76 Sol Jo 396, 147 LT 281, 48 TLR 494, 1932 SC (HL) 31, 1932
    SLT 317   2.1
Donovan v Gwentoys Ltd [1990] 1 WLR 472, [1990] 1 All ER 1018, HL   4.21
Dugmore v Swansea NHS Trust & Morriston NHS Trust [2003] 1 All ER 33, [2003]
    ICR 574, [2002] EWCA Civ 1689   10.2.8, 11.2.4

Durham v BAI (Run Off) Ltd (In Scheme of Arrangement); Employers' Liability
Policy 'Trigger' Litigation, Re [2010] EWCA Civ 1096, [2011] 1 All ER 605,
[2011] 1 All ER (Comm) 811, [2011] Lloyd's Rep IR 1, [2010] All ER (D) 88
(Oct)   12.6

Eastwood v Magnox Electric Plc; McCabe v Cornwall CC [2004] UKHL 35, [2005]
1 AC 503, [2004] 3 WLR 322, HL   9.7.2
Ellis v The State of South Australia [2006] WASC 270   3.7.4
England v Foster Wheeler (2009) unreported, LTL 2 October   3.9.2
Estate of Trevor Owen Deceased v IMI Yorkshire Copper (unreported) 15 June
1995   10.2.5

Fairchild v Glenhaven Funeral Services Ltd (t/a Dovener & Son); Babcock
International Ltd v National Grid Co plc; Fox v Spousal (Midlands) Ltd;
Matthews v Associated Portland Cement Manufacturers (1978) Ltd; Dyson v
Leeds City Council (No 2); Pendleton v Stone & Webster Engineering Ltd;
Matthews v British Uralite plc [2003] 1 AC 32, [2002] UKHL 22, [2002] 3
WLR 89, [2002] 3 All ER 305, [2002] PIQR P28, HL   3.4, 3.5, 3.6, 3.7.4, 5.4,
                                                                                                                                          5.4.2
Firman v Ellis [1978] QB 886, [1987] 2 All ER 851, [1987] 3 WLR 1, CA   4.17
Fitzgerald v Lane [1989] AC 328, [1988] 2 All ER 961, [1988] 3 WLR 356, [1990]
RTR 133, 132 Sol Jo 1064, [1988] NLJR 209   3.11
Forbes v Wandsworth Health Authority [1997] QB 402, [1996] 4 All ER 881, [1996]
3 WLR 1108, [1996] 7 Med LR 175, 36 BMLR 1, [1996] 15 LS Gaz R 32,
[1996] NLJR 477, 140 Sol Jo LB 85   4.10
Foumeny v University of Leeds [2003] EWCA Civ 557   2.3.5

Garrett v Camden LBC [2001] EWCA Civ 395   2.4
Godfrey v Gloucestershire Royal Infirmary NHS Trust [2003] EWHC 549 (QB),
[2003] All ER (D) 346 (Mar)   4.12
Gogay v Hertfordshire County Council [2000] IRLR 703, (2000) IDS Brief B672/5,
CA   9.7.2
Gregg v Scott [2005] UKHL 2, [2005] 2 AC 176, [2005] 4 All ER 812, [2005] 2
WLR 268, 82 BMLR 52, *Times*, 28 January, 149 Sol Jo LB 145, [2005] 5 LRC
408, [2005] All ER (D) 269, Jan   3.9.2
Griggs v Transco plc [2003] EWCA Civ 564, 147 Sol Jo LB 507, [2003] All ER (D)
298 (Apr), CA   8.1
Guidera v NEI Projects (India) Ltd (Unreported) McCullough J 1988,   1.3
Gunn v Wallsend Slipway and Engineering Company Ltd (1989) *Times*, 23
January   2.1

Hall v British Gas (1998) (unreported) 7 April   8.1
Hare v Personal Representatives of Malik (1980) 124 Sol Jo 328, 131 NLJ 341   4.16
Hartley v Birmingham City District Council [1992] 1 WLR 968, [1992] 2 All ER
213, CA   4.19, 4.21
Haward v Fawcetts (a firm) [2006] UKHL 9, [2006] 3 All ER 497, [2006] 1 WLR
682, [2006] 10 EG 154 (CS), (2006) *Times*, 3 March, [2006] All ER (D) 07
(Mar)   4.9
Headford v Bristol and District Health Authority [1995] 6 Med LR 1, 24 BMLR
20, [1995] PIQR P 180   4.31.2
Heal v Garringtons Ltd (1982) (26 May 1982, unreported)   2.3.4
Heil v Rankin and Others [2001] QB 272, [2000] 2 WLR 1173, [2000] 3 All ER 138,
CA   15.3.2
Henderson v Temple Pier Co Ltd [1998] 3 All ER 324, [1998] 1 WLR 1540, [1998]
20 LS Gaz R 35, 142 Sol Jo LB 156, [1998] All ER (D) 143   4.13, 4.14
Hendy v Milton Keynes Health Authority [1992] 3 Med LR 114, [1992] PIQR P
281   4.21
Hewett v Alf Brown's Transport Ltd [1992] ICR 530, [1992] 15 LS Gaz R 33   2.1
Heyes v Pilkington Glass Ltd [1998] PIQR P303, CA   2.3.4
Hirst v William Procter [1882] WN 12   3.9.2

Holtby v Brigham & Cowan (Hull) Ltd [2000] 3 All ER 421, [2000] ICR 1086,
    [2000] NLJR 544, 144 Sol Jo LB 212, CA   3.1.2, 3.6, 3.10.1, 3.10.2, 3.10.4, 5.4.3,
                                                                                    15.3.4
Horton v Sadler [2006] UKHL 27, [2007] 1 AC 307, [2006] 3 All ER 1177, [2006] 2
    WLR 1346, [2006] RTR 330, 91 BMLR 60, [2006] NLJR 1024, (2006) *Times*,
    19 June, 150 Sol Jo LB 808, [2007] 3 LRC 146, [2006] All ER (D) 130
    (Jun)   4.18
Hughes v Lord Advocate [1963] AC 837, [1963] 2 WLR 779, [1963] 1 All ER 705   2.2

Intel Corporation (UK) Ltd v Daw [2007] EWCA Civ 70, [2007] 2 All ER 126,
    [2007] ICR 1318, [2007] IRLR 355, [2007] NLJR 259, [2007] All ER (D) 96
    (Feb)   9.5.2, 9.5.3

Johnson v Unisys Ltd [2001] UKHL 13, [2003] 1 AC 518, [2001] 2 WLR 1076,
    2001] ICR 480, HL   9.7.2
Johnston v NEI International Combustion Ltd; Rothwell v Chemical and
    Insulating Co Ltd; Topping v Benchtown Ltd (formerly Jones Bros Preston
    Ltd), *sub nom* Grieves v FT Everard & Sons Ltd [2007] UKHL 39, [2007] 4
    All ER 1047, [2007] 3 WLR 876, [2007] ICR 1745, 99 BMLR 139, [2007]
    NLJR 1542, [2008] PIQR P95, (2007) *Times*, 24 October, 151 Sol Jo LB 1366,
    [2007] All ER (D) 224 (Oct), HL, *Affirming* [2006] EWCA Civ 27, [2006] 4 All
    ER 1161, [2006] ICR 1458, 90 BMLR 88, [2006] 07 LS Gaz R 25, [2006]
    NLJR 185, 150 Sol Jo LB 164, [2006] All ER (D) 187 (Jan), CA   3.9.2, 4.6, 4.21,
                                                                                    5.3.1
Jones v Liverpool Health Authority (1995) 30 BMLR 1, [1996] PIQR P 251   4.12

Keenan v Miller Insulation and Engineering Ltd (Unreported) 8 December 1987   1.3
Kellett v British Rail Engineering Ltd (Unreported) 3 May 1984   2.3.2
Kew v Bettamix Ltd (formerly Tarmac Roadstone Southern Ltd) [2006] EWCA Civ
    1535, [2009] PIQR P210, (2006) *Times*, 4 December, 150 Sol Jo LB 1534,
    [2007] 4 Costs LR 527, [2006] All ER (D) 173 (Nov)   4.20, 4.28
Kill v Coastline Buses Ltd Current Law Digest, December 2000   2.3.2
Koonjul v Thameslink Healthcare Services NHS Trust [2000] PIQR P 123, (2000)
    Times, 19 May   11.2.9.1
KR v Bryn Alyn Community (Holdings) Ltd (in liq) [2003] EWCA Civ 85, [2003]
    QB 1441, [2004] 2 All ER 716, [2003] 3 WLR 107, [2003] 1 FCR 385, [2003] 1
    FLR 1203, (2003) *Times*, 17 February, [2003] All ER (D) 162 (Feb)   4.19, 4.20,
                                                                                    4.21

Lokumal (K) & Sons (London) Ltd v Lotte Shipping Co Pte Ltd, *The August
    Leonhardt* [1985] 2 Lloyd's Rep 28, CA, *Reversing* [1984] 1 Lloyd's Rep 322,
    Comml Ct   4.16
Long v Tolchard & Sons Ltd [1990] EWCA Civ 987, [1999] All ER (D) 1303, (2000)
    Times, 5 January   4.27
Lubovsky v Snelling [1944] KB 44, [1943] 2 All ER 577, 113 LJKB 14, 170 LT 2, 60
    TLR 52   4.16

Maguire v Harland & Wolff [2005] EWCA Civ 01   2.1
Mahmud v BCCI SA (in liq); Malik v BCCI SA (in liq) [1998] AC 20, [1997] 3 All
    ER 1, [1997] 3 WLR 95, [1997] ICR 606, [1997] IRLR 462, [1997] 94 LS Gaz
    R 33, [1997] NLJR 917   9.7.2
Majrowski v Guy's and St Thomas' NHS Trust [2006] UKHL 34, [2007] 1 AC 224,
    [2006] 4 All ER 395, [2006] 3 WLR 125, [2006] ICR 1199, [2006] IRLR 695,
    91 BMLR 85, [2006] NLJR 1173, (2006) *Times*, 13 July, 150 Sol Jo LB 986,
    [2006] All ER (D) 146 (Jul)   9.7.1
Margerson and Hancock v JW Roberts Limited [1996] PIQR P358, [1996] Env LR
    304, CA, [1996] PIQR P154, QBD   2.1, 2.2
Marren v Dawson Bentley & Co Ltd [1961] 2 QB 135, [1961] 2 All ER 270, [1961] 2
    WLR 679, 105 Sol Jo 383   4.15

Martin v Kaisary [2005] EWHC 531 (QB), [2005] All ER (D) 144 (Apr)   4.12

Matthews v Associated Portland Cement Manufacturers (1978) Ltd and one other
[2002] UKHL 22, [2003] 1 AC 32, [2002] 3 All ER 305, [2002] ICR 798, [2002]
IRLR 533, 67 BMLR 90, [2002] NLJR 998, (2002) *Times*, 21 June, [2003] 1
LRC 674, [2002] All ER (D) 139 (Jun)   3.10.2

McAnerney v Scott (1990) (unreported) 21 December   5.3.5

McGhee v National Coal Board [1973] 1 WLR 1, [1972] 3 All ER 1008, 13 KIR
471, [1973] 116 SJ 967, HL   3.4

McManus v Mannings Maine Ltd [2001] EWCA Civ 1668, [2001] All ER (D) 426
(Oct)   4.11

Middleton v Elliott Turbomachinery Ltd (1990) *Times*, 29 October   15.2

Miller v London Electrical Manufacturing Co Ltd [1976] 2 Lloyd's Rep 284, 120
Sol Jo 80   4.11

Ministry of Defence v AB & Others [2010] EWCA Civ 1317, 117 BMLR 101,
[2010] NLJR 1686, (2011) *Times*, 19 January, [2010] All ER (D) 252 (Nov)   4.19

Morris v West Hartlepool Steam Navigation Company Limited [1956] AC 552,
[1956] 1 WLR 177, [1956] 1 All ER 385, HL   2.2

Morrison v Central Electricity Generating Board and Babcock & Wilcox Limited
(Unreported) 15 March 1986,   2.5, 10.2.3

Moses v County Durham Health Authority and Others (2002) (unreported) 25
June   15.2

Mughal v Reuters Ltd [1993] IRLR 571, 16 BMLR 127, 137 Sol Jo LB 275   7.4

Murgai v The Home Office [2003] EWHC 1870, QB [2003] EWCA Civ 546, CA   2.3.5

Mustoe v Saunders Valve Co Ltd (Unreported) 1979,   2.3.4

Nash v Eli Lilly & Co; Berger v Eli Lilly & Co [1993] 4 All ER 383, [1993] 1 WLR
782, [1992] 3 Med LR 353, 14 BMLR 1   4.8, 4.9, 4.10

Naylor v Volex Group [2003] EWCA Civ 222, QBD, LTL 14/2/2003   10.2.8, 11.2.4

Nimmo v Alexander Cowan & Sons Ltd [1968] AC 107, [1967] 3 All ER 187, [1967]
3 WLR 1169, 111 Sol Jo 668, 1967 SC (HL) 79, 1967 SLT 277   10.2.2, 10.2.3,
10.2.4, 10.2.5, 10.2.6

Nurse v Morganite Crucible Limited [1989] AC 692, [1989] 2 WLR 82, [1989] 1 All
ER 113, HL   11.2.2

Owen v Esso Exploration and Production UK Ltd (2006) Liverpool CC,
unreported, 16 November   3.9.2

Page v Smith [1996] AC 155, [1995] 2 All ER 736, [1995] 2 WLR 644, [1995] RTR
210, [1995] 2 Lloyd's Rep 95, 28 BMLR 133, [1995] 23 LS Gaz R 33, [1995]
NLJR 723, [1995] PIQR P 329   2.2, 3.9.2, 5.4

Pakenham-Walsh v Connell Residential [2006] EWCA Civ 90, [2006] 11 LS Gaz R
25, [2006] All ER (D) 275 (Feb)   9.2

Parkes v PLA (1983) (unreported) 3 December   5.3.5

Pickford v Imperial Chemical Industries plc [1996] IRLR 622, [1996] ICR 566,
[1997] 8 Med LR 270, CA   11.2.7.8

Pinder v Cape plc [2006] EWHC 3630 (QB)   2.1

Poyner v Linde Heavy Truck Division Ltd LTL 9/1/2004   8.5

Price v United Engineering Steels Ltd. and another (1997) Transcript 12
December   4.21

Pritam Kaur v S Russell & Sons Ltd [1973] QB 336, [1973] 1 All ER 617, [1973] 2
WLR 147, 117 Sol Jo 91, CA, *On appeal from* [1973] QB 336, [1972] 3 All ER
305, [1972] 3 WLR 663, 116 Sol Jo 446, QBD   4.15

Raggett v Society of Jesus Trust of 1929 for Roman Catholic Purposes [2010]
EWCA Civ 1002, 154 Sol Jo (no 34) 30, [2010] NLJR 1228, [2010] All ER (D)
116 (Aug)   4.19

Robinson v St Helens Metropolitan Borough Council [2002] EWCA Civ 1099,
[2002] ELR 681, [2003] PIQR P 128, [2002] All ER (D) 388 (Jul)   4.1, 4.19

Rothwell v Chemical & Insulating Co Ltd; Re Pleural Plaques Litigation, *sub nom*
    Grieves v FT Everard & Sons, Re Pleural Plaques Litigation [2006] EWCA
    Civ 27, [2006] 4 All ER 1161, [2006] ICR 1458, 90 BMLR 88, [2006] 07 LS
    Gaz R 25, [2006] NLJR 185, 150 Sol Jo LB 164, [2006] All ER (D) 187 (Jan),
    CA, *Reversing* [2005] EWHC 88 (QB), (2005) *Times*, 22 March, [2005] All ER
    (D) 219 (Feb), QBD   4.6, 4.21
Rowbottom v Royal Masonic Hospital [2002] EWCA Civ 87, 65 BMLR 103, [2003]
    PIQR P 1, [2002] All ER (D) 148 (Feb)   4.12

Saunders (a bankrupt), Re; Re Bearman (a bankrupt), Bristol and West BS v
    Saunders [1997] Ch 60, [1997] 3 All ER 992, [1996] 3 WLR 473, [1996] BPIR
    355   12.4.1
Shell Tankers and Another v Jeromson and Another (2001) *The Times*, 2 March   2.3.1
Shepard and Others v Firth Brown Ltd (1985) (unreported) 17 April   2.3.4
Shortell v BICAL Construction Ltd [2008] Lawtel, Unreported, Liverpool District
    Registry, 16 May 2008   3.5, 3.7.4, 5.3.5
Sienkiewicz (Administratrix of the Estate of Enid Costello Deceased) v Greif (UK)
    Ltd; Willmore v Knowsley Metropolitan Borough Council [2011] UKSC 10,
    [2011] 2 AC 229, [2011] 2 All ER 857, [2011] 2 WLR 523, [2011] ICR 391, 119
    BMLR 54, (2011) *Times*, 10 March, 155 Sol Jo (no 10) 30, [2011] All ER (D)
    107 (Mar), SC, *Affirming* [2009] EWCA Civ 1159, [2010] QB 370, [2010] 2
    WLR 951, (2009) *Times*, 13 November, 153 Sol Jo (no 44) 34, [2009] All ER
    (D) 84 (Nov), CA   3.2, 3.4, 3.5, 3.7.4, 3.8, 5.4.2
Sir Robert Lloyd & Co Ltd & Ors v Bernard Hoey [2011] EWCA Civ 1060, 155 Sol
    Jo (no 35) 31, [2011] All ER (D) 36 (Sep)   4.11, 4.12
Skerratt v Linfax Ltd (t/a Go Karting For Fun) [2003] EWCA Civ 695, [2003] All
    ER (D) 49 (May)   4.21
Smith v Leech Brain & Co Ltd [1962] 2 QB 405, [1962] 2 WLR 148, [1961] 3 All
    ER 1159   6.4
Smith v Manchester Corporation (1974) 17 KIR 1; *sub nom* Smith v Manchester
    City Council (1974) 118 SJ 597, CA   15.3.7, 15.4.2
Smith v Ministry of Defence [2005] EWHC 682 (QB), [2005] All ER (D) 254
    (Apr)   4.19, 4.26
Smith v P & O Bulk Shipping Ltd [1998] 2 Lloyd's Rep 81, QBD   2.3.1
Smith v White Knight Laundry Ltd [2001] EWCA Civ 660, [2001] 3 All ER 862,
    [2002] 1 WLR 616, [2001] 2 BCLC 206, [2003] BCC 319, [2001] All ER (D)
    152 (May)   12.3.4
Sniezek v Bundy (Letchworth) Ltd [2000] All ER (D) 942   4.21
Spargo v North Essex District Health Authority [1997] 8 Med LR 125, 37 BMLR
    99, [1997] 15 LS Gaz R 26, [1997] PIQR P 235, (1997) *Times*, 21 March, 141
    Sol Jo LB 90   4.11, 4.12
St Helens MBC v Barnes [2006] EWCA Civ 1372, [2007] 3 All ER 525, [2007]
    PIQR P118, [2006] All ER (D) 303 (Oct)   4.15
Stokes v Guest, Keen and Nettlefold (Bolts and Nuts) Ltd [1968] 1 WLR 1776, 5
    KIR 401, 112 Sol Jo 821   2.2, 5.4.1, 8.5, 9.5.1
Stubbings v Webb and Another [1993] AC 498, [1993] 2 WLR 120, [1993] 1 FLR
    714, [1993] 1 All ER 322, HL; reversing [1992] QB 197, [1991] 3 WLR 383,
    [1992] 1 FLR 296, [1991] 3 All ER 949, CA   4.3
Sutherland v Hatton; *sub nom* Jones v Sandwell MBC; Hatton v Sutherland; Barber
    v Sutherland CC; Bishop v Baker Refractories Ltd; Somerset CC v Barber;
    Sandwell MBC v Jones; Baker Refractories Ltd v Bishop [2002] EWCA Civ
    76, [2002] 2 All ER 1, [2002] ICR 613, [2002] PIQR P21, CA   2.3.5, 9.1, 9.2, 9.3,
                                      9.4, 9.4.1, 9.4.2, 9.4.3, 9.5.1, 9.5.2, 9.5.3, 9.6, 14.3.5.3
Swain v Denso Martin Ltd [2000] PIQR P 51, (2000) *Times*, 24 April   11.2.9.1

T & N Limited, Re [2005] EWHC 2870 (Ch), [2006] 3 All ER 697, [2006] 1 WLR
    1728, [2006] 2 BCLC 374, [2006] BPIR 532, [2005] All ER (D) 211 (Dec)   12.3.4
Taylor (a bankrupt), Re [2006] EWHC 3029 (Ch), [2007] Ch 150, [2007] 3 All ER
    638, [2007] 2 WLR 148, [2006] All ER (D) 288 (Nov)   12.4.1
Thomas v Plaistow [1997] 17 LS Gaz R 25, [1997] PIQR P 540   4.24

Thompson v Smiths Shiprepairers (North Shields) Ltd; Mitchell v Vickers [1984]
 QB 405, [1984] 2 WLR 522, [1984] 1 All ER 881   2.2, 2.3.2, 3.10.1

Veakins v Kier Islington Ltd [2009] EWCA Civ 1288, [2010] IRLR 132, (2010)
 Times, 13 January, [2009] All ER (D) 34 (Dec)   9.7.1

Walker v Wabco Automotive UK Ltd (Unreported) 11 May 1999, CA   2.2, 2.3.4
Walkley v Precision Forgings Ltd [1979] 1 WLR 606, [1979] 2 All ER 548, (1979)
 123 SJ 354, HL   4.18
Warner v Huntingdon District Council [2002] EWCA Civ 791, [2002] All ER (D)
 233 (May)   11.2.9.1
Whalley v Montracon Ltd [2005] EWCA Civ 1383, [2005] All ER (D) 269 (Nov)   8.1
Whiston v London Strategic Health Authority [2010] EWCA Civ 195, [2010] 3 All
 ER 452, [2010] 1 WLR 1582, 113 BMLR 110, (2010) *Times*, 4 May, [2010] All
 ER (D) 56 (Mar)   4.10, 4.12, 4.22
Wilkinson v Ancliff (BLT) Ltd [1986] 3 All ER 427, [1986] 1 WLR 1352, 130 Sol Jo
 766, [1986] LS Gaz R 3248   4.12
Willmore v Knowsley Metropolitan BC [2009] EWCA Civ 1211, [2010] ELR 227,
 [2009] All ER (D) 209 (Nov)   3.8
Wilsher v Essex Area Health Authority [1988] AC 1074, [1988] 2 WLR 557, [1988] 1
 All ER 871, HL   2.4, 3.3, 3.7.4
Wilsons and Clyde Coal Company Limited v English [1938] AC 57, [1937] 3 All ER
 628, (1938) 157 LT 406, HL   2.1
Withers v Perry Chain Co Ltd [1961] 1 WLR 1314, [1961] 3 All ER 676, (1961) 105
 SJ 648, CA   9.5.3
Workvale Ltd (in dissolution), Re [1992] 1 WLR 416, [1991] BCLC 528, [1992] BCC
 349, CA, *Affirming* [1991] 1 WLR 294, [1991] BCLC 528, [1991] BCC 109,
 [1991] 22 LS Gaz R 35, Cd D   12.3.2, 12.3.4

XYZ and others v Schering Health Care Ltd and others [2002] EWHC 1420 (QB),
 70 BMLR 88, [2002] All ER (D) 437 (Jul)   3.5

TABLE OF STATUTES

References are to paragraph numbers.

Companies Act 1985	12.3, 12.3.1, 12.3.4
s 651	12.3, 12.3.1
Companies Act 2006	12.2, 12.3, 12.3.1, 12.3.2
Pt 8	12.3.2
s 1025	12.5.3
s 1029	12.3, 12.3.4
ss 1029–1032	12.3
s 1029(1)	12.3.1
s 1029(2)(f)	12.3.1
s 1030(3)	12.3.1
s 1031	12.5.3
s 1032	12.3.1
s 1032(3)	12.3.4
Compensation Act 2006	3.1.2, 3.5, 3.6, 3.10.5, 5.4.2, 15.3.2
s 3	3.1.2, 3.4, 3.6, 5.4, 5.4.2
s 3(2)	3.4
s 16	3.6
Consumer Protection Act 1987	4.17
Employers' Liability (Compulsory Insurance) Act 1969	12.6
s 1(1)	12.6
Equality Act 2010	9.7.3, 9.8.9
Factories Act 1937	5.4.1, 10.2.2
s 4	5.4.1, 10.2.2
s 4(1)	5.5.2, 10.1, 10.2.2
s 47	2.3.1, 5.4.1, 10.2.2
s 47(1)	5.5.2, 10.1, 10.2.2
s 151	10.2.2
Factories Act 1961	5.4.1, 8.7.2, 10.2.2, 10.2.5, 10.2.10
s 4	5.4.1
s 29(1)	5.5.2, 10.1, 10.2.5
s 30	10.2.10
s 41(1)	5.5.2, 10.1, 10.2.5
s 47	10.2.5
s 63	5.4.1, 5.5.2, 10.1, 10.2.5
Fatal Accidents Act 1976	4.17, 4.29.2, 4.30, 13.1, 13.6, 15.1, 16.4
Insolvency Act 1986	12.4.1
s 130	12.4
s 285(3)(b)	12.4.1
Sch B1	12.4
Law Reform (Miscellaneous Provisions) Act 1934	4.29.1, 4.30, 13.6
s 1	4.29.1
Law Reform (Personal Injuries) Act 1948	16.4
s 2(4)	16.3
Limitation Act 1954	1.3, 4.1
Limitation Act 1980	3.9.2, 3.11, 4.1, 4.4, 4.31.2, 6.7.6, 8.7.6, 9.8.6, 12.3.4
s 2	4.2, 4.3
s 11	4.3, 4.4, 4.5, 4.10, 4.17, 4.19, 4.29.2, 4.30, 4.31.2, 5.5.6, 6.7.6, 7.5.6, 8.7.6, 9.8.6
s 11(1)	4.2
s 11(3)	4.2
s 11(4)	4.2, 4.29.1
s 11(5)	4.29.1
s 11A	4.17, 4.19
s 12	4.17, 4.19, 4.30
s 12(1)	4.29.2
s 12(2)	4.29.2, 4.31.2
s 13	4.29.2
s 14	4.4, 4.7, 4.9, 4.12, 4.17, 4.25, 5.5.6, 6.7.6, 7.5.6, 8.7.6, 9.8.6
s 14(1)	4.7, 4.10, 4.12
s 14(1)(a)	4.11
s 14(1)(b)	4.12
s 14(1)(c)	4.13
s 14(1)(d)	4.14
s 14(2)	4.11
s 14(3)	4.10, 4.11, 4.13
s 14(3)(a)	4.17
s 28	4.29.2, 4.31.2
s 28(1)	4.31.2
s 28(6)	4.31.2
s 33	4.4, 4.10, 4.17, 4.18, 4.19, 4.20, 4.21, 4.22, 4.28, 4.29.2, 4.30, 4.31.2, 5.5.6, 6.7.6, 7.5.6, 8.7.6, 9.8.6, 12.3.4
s 33(1)	4.30
s 33(3)	4.19, 4.30
s 33(3)(a)	4.21
s 33(3)(b)	4.22
s 33(3)(c)	4.23
s 33(3)(d)	4.24, 4.31.2
s 33(3)(e)	4.25
s 33(3)(f)	4.26
s 33(4)	4.30

Limitation Act 1980—*continued*
  s 33(5)   4.30
  s 38   4.2
  s 38(1)   2.2
  s 38(2)   4.31.1

Mental Capacity Act 2005   4.24
  s 2(1)   4.31.1
Mental Health Act 1983   4.24
Mines and Quarries Act 1954   10.2.8,
                                           11.2.4

National Health Services Act
  1977   16.3

Protection from Harassment Act
  1997   9.7.1, 9.8.9

Senior Courts Act 1981
  s 31(a)   15.2

Third Parties (Rights against
  Insurers) Act 1930   12.5, 12.5.2
Third Parties (Rights Against
  Insurers) Act 2010   12.2, 12.5,
                        12.5.2, 12.5.4, 12.5.5, 12.5.6
  s 1(1)   12.5.3
  s 1(2)   12.5.3
  s 1(3)   12.5
  s 1(4)   12.5.3
  s 2(2)   12.5.1
  s 2(3)   12.5.1
  s 2(4)   12.5.4
  s 2(6)   12.5.1
  s 6   12.5.3
  s 8   12.5.4
  s 9   12.5.4
  s 10   12.5.4
  s 12(1)   12.5.4
  s 12(2)   12.5.4
  s 12(4)   12.5.4
  Sch 1   12.5.5
  Sch 3, para 3   12.5, 12.5.2
  Sch 4   12.5.2

TABLE OF STATUTORY INSTRUMENTS

References are to paragraph numbers.

Access for Community Air Carriers
to Intra-Community Air
Routes Regulations 1992,
SI 1992/2993 — 10.1

Asbestos Industry Regulations
1931, SI 1931/1140 — 2.3.1, 5.4.1,
5.5.2, 11.1, 11.2.1, 11.2.1.1,
11.2.1.6

reg 1 — 11.2.1.1, 11.2.1.3
reg 2 — 11.2.1.1
reg 3 — 11.2.1.1
reg 4 — 11.2.1.2
reg 5 — 11.2.1.3
reg 6 — 11.2.1.4
reg 7 — 11.2.1.4
reg 8 — 11.2.1.4
reg 9 — 11.2.1.1
reg 10 — 11.2.1.5
reg 13 — 11.2.1.6
reg 14 — 11.2.1.6
reg 15 — 11.2.1.6
reg 17 — 11.2.1.4

Asbestos (Prohibitions) Regulations
1985, SI 1985/910 — 5.1

Asbestos Regulations 1969,
SI 1969/690 — 5.4.1, 5.5.2, 11.1,
11.2.1, 11.2.2, 11.2.3

reg 3 — 11.2.2

Building (Safety, Health and
Welfare Regulations) 1948,
SI 1948/1145 — 5.4.1, 10.2.3
reg 2 — 10.2.3
reg 82 — 5.4.1, 5.5.2, 10.1, 10.2.3,
10.2.6

Carriage of Dangerous Goods
(Classification, Packaging and
Labelling) and Use of
Transportable Pressure
Receptacles Regulations 1996,
SI 1996/2092 — 11.1

Chemicals (Hazard Information
and Packaging for Supply)
Regulations 1994,
SI 1994/3247 — 10.2.8, 11.1,
11.2.4

Chemicals (Hazard Information
and Packaging) Regulations
1993, SI 1993/1746 — 11.1

Civil Procedure Rules 1998,
SI 1998/3132 — 4.4, 4.19, 13.5
PD7, para 5.1 — 4.15
PD7, para 5.2 — 4.15
PD7, para 5.4 — 4.15
Pt 32 — 14.1
PD32 — 14.1
Pt 36 — 13.10, 17.4, 17.5, 17.6

Coal Mines (Respirable Dust)
Regulations 1975,
SI 1975/1433 — 10.2.8, 11.2.4

Companies Act 2006
(Commencement No 8,
Transitional Provisions and
Savings) Order 2008,
SI 2008/2860
art 5 — 12.3
Sch 2, para 1 — 12.3
Sch 2, para 90 — 12.3
Sch 2, para 91 — 12.3
Sch 2, para 91(4) — 12.3

Construction (General Provisions)
Regulations 1961,
SI 1961/1580 — 5.4.1, 10.2.6
reg 20 — 5.4.1, 5.5.2, 10.1, 10.2.6
reg 21 — 10.2.10

Construction (Health, Safety and
Welfare) Regulations 1996,
SI 1996/1592 — 10.1

Construction (Metrication)
Regulations 1984,
SI 1984/1593 — 10.1

Construction (Working Places)
Regulations 1966,
SI 1966/94 — 5.4.1, 10.1, 10.2.7
reg 6(2) — 5.4.1, 10.2.7

Control of Asbestos at Work
(Amendment) Regulations
1992, SI 1992/3068 — 11.1, 11.2.3

Control of Asbestos at Work
(Amendment) Regulations
1998, SI 1998/3235 — 11.1, 11.2.3

Control of Asbestos at Work
Regulations 1987,
SI 1987/2115   5.4.1, 5.5.2,
     10.2.8, 11.2.3, 11.2.4
Control of Asbestos at Work
Regulations 2002,
SI 2002/2675   5.5.2, 10.2.8, 11.1,
     11.2.4
reg 2   11.2.4
reg 3   11.2.4
reg 6   11.2.4
reg 7   11.2.4
reg 8   11.2.4
reg 8(2)   11.2.4
reg 9   11.2.4
reg 10   11.2.4
reg 11   11.2.4
reg 12   11.2.4
reg 13   11.2.4
Sch 1   11.2.4
Sch 4   11.2.4
Control of Lead at Work
Regulations 1998,
SI 1998/543   10.2.8, 11.2.4
Control of Lead at Work
Regulations 2002,
SI 2002/2676   10.2.8, 11.2.4
Control of Noise at Work
Regulations 2005,
SI 2005/1643   6.7.2, 11.1,
     11.2.11
reg 7   11.2.11
Control of Substances Hazardous
to Health (Amendment)
Regulations 2003,
SI 2003/978   10.1
Control of Substances Hazardous
to Health Regulations 1988,
SI 1988/1657   10.1, 10.2.8, 11.1,
     11.2.8, 14.6
Control of Substances Hazardous
to Health Regulations 1994,
SI 1994/3246   10.1, 10.2.8, 11.1,
     11.2.4, 11.2.8, 14.6
Control of Substances Hazardous
to Health Regulations 1999,
SI 1999/437   10.1, 10.2.8, 11.1,
     11.2.4, 11.2.8, 14.6
Control of Substances Hazardous
to Health Regulations 2002,
SI 2002/2677   10.1, 10.2.8,
     10.2.9, 11.1, 11.2.4, 11.2.8, 14.6
reg 2   10.2.8
reg 3   10.2.8
reg 6   10.2.8
reg 7   10.2.8
reg 8   10.2.8
reg 8(2)   10.2.8
reg 9   10.2.8
reg 10   10.2.8
reg 11   10.2.8
reg 12   10.2.8

Control of Substances Hazardous to
Health Regulations 2002,
SI 2002/2677—*continued*
reg 13   10.2.8
Sch 1   10.2.8
Sch 4   10.2.8
Sch 8   10.2.8
Control of Vibration at Work
Regulations 2005,
SI 2005/1093   8.6, 8.7.2, 11.1,
     11.2.10
reg 5   8.6
reg 6(1)   8.6
reg 7   8.6
reg 8   8.6, 11.2.10

Docks Regulations 1988,
SI 1988/1655
reg 18   10.2.10

Electricity at Work Regulations
1989, SI 1989/635   10.1

Genetically Modified Organisms
(Contained Use) Regulations
2000, SI 2000/2831   11.1

Health and Safety (Display Screen
Equipment) Regulations 1992,
SI 1992/2792   7.5.2, 11.1, 11.2.7,
     11.2.7.1, 11.2.7.2, 11.2.7.3,
     11.2.7.4
reg 1   11.2.7.2
reg 2   11.2.7.8
reg 3   11.2.7.5
reg 4   11.2.7.7, 11.2.7.8
reg 6(1)   11.2.7.7
reg 7   11.2.7.7
Sch   11.2.7.5, 11.2.7.7
Health and Safety (Fees)
Regulations 1988,
SI 1988/712   11.1
Health and Safety Information for
Employees Regulations 1989,
SI 1989/682   10.1
Health and Safety (Safety Signs
and Signals) Regulations
1996, SI 1996/341   11.1

Insolvency (Amendment) Rules
2006, SI 2006/1272   12.3.4

Management of Health and Safety
at Work and Fire Precautions
(Workplace) (Amendment)
Regulations 2003,
SI 2003/2457
reg 6   10.2.9

Management of Health and Safety
at Work Regulations 1992,
SI 1992/2051   5.5.2, 7.5.2, 8.7.2,
          9.2, 10.1, 10.2.9, 11.2.9.1, 14.6
reg 3(1)(a)   9.2
reg 3(4)   14.6
reg 4   10.2.9
reg 6   9.2
reg 10   9.2
reg 11   11.2.7.6
Management of Health and Safety
at Work Regulations 1999,
SI 1999/3242   5.5.2, 7.5.2, 8.7.2,
          9.8.2, 10.1, 10.2.9, 11.2.9.1, 14.6
reg 3   10.2.9
reg 3(4)   14.6
reg 4   10.2.9
reg 5   10.2.9
reg 6   10.2.9
reg 13   10.2.9
reg 13(1)   10.2.9
Sch 1   10.2.9, 11.2.10
Manual Handling Operations
Regulations 1992,
SI 1992/2793   7.5.2, 8.6, 8.7.2,
          11.1, 11.2.9, 11.2.9.1
reg 4   11.2.9, 11.2.9.1
reg 5   11.2.9
Sch 1   11.2.9.1

Noise at Work Regulations 1989,
SI 1989/1790   6.7.2, 10.1, 11.1,
          11.2.5, 11.2.6
reg 8   11.2.6
reg 10   11.2.6
Noise Emission in the Environment
by Equipment for use
Outdoors Regulations 2001,
SI 2001/1701   10.1

Offshore Electricity and Noise
Regulations 1997,
SI 1997/1993   11.1

Personal Protective Equipment at
Work Regulations 1992,
SI 1992/2966   8.6, 8.7.2, 11.1
Personal Protective Equipment
Regulations 2002,
SI 2002/1144   7.5.2, 10.2.8,
                               11.2.4
Police (Health and Safety)
Regulations 1999,
SI 1999/860   10.1
Pressure Equipment Regulations
1999, SI 1999/2001   10.1
Protection of Eyes Regulations
1974, SI 1974/1681   10.1

Provision and Use of Work
Equipment Regulations 1992,
SI 1992/2932   7.5.2, 8.6, 8.7.2,
          10.1, 10.2.8, 10.2.11, 11.2.4, 14.6
reg 6(2)   14.6
Provision and Use of Work
Equipment Regulations 1998,
SI 1998/2306   7.5.2, 8.6, 8.7.2,
          10.1, 10.2.8, 10.2.11, 11.2.4, 14.6
reg 4   10.2.11
reg 5(2)   14.6

Quarries Miscellaneous Health and
Safety Provisions Regulations
1995, SI 1995/2036   10.1
Quarries Regulations 1999,
SI 1999/2024   10.1, 11.1

Scotland Act 1998 (Consequential
Modifications) (No 2) Order
1999, SI 1999/1820   11.1
Shipbuilding and Ship-repairing
Regulations 1960,
SI 1960/1932   5.4.1, 10.2.1,
                               10.2.4
regs 49–52   10.2.10
reg 53   5.4.1
reg 53(1)   5.5.2, 10.2.4
reg 76   5.4.1
reg 76(1)   5.5.2, 10.2.4
reg 76(1)(e)   10.2.4
Shipbuilding Regulations 1931,
SI 1931/133   10.2.1
reg 18   5.5.2, 10.1, 10.2.1
Transfer of Undertakings
(Protection of Employment)
Regulations 1981,
SI 1981/1794   12.6
Transfer of Undertakings
(Protection of Employment)
Regulations 2006,
SI 2006/246   12.6

Woodworking Machines
Regulations 1974,
SI 1974/903   6.7.2, 11.1, 11.2.5
reg 44   11.2.5
Working Time Regulations 1998,
SI 1998/1833   9.2, 9.8.2
Workplace (Health, Safety and
Welfare) Regulations 1992,
SI 1992/3004   5.5.2, 7.5.2, 8.7.2,
          10.1, 10.2.10, 11.2.7.1
reg 5   10.2.10
reg 6   10.2.10
regs 6–12   11.2.7.1
reg 9   10.2.10
reg 11   10.2.10
reg 11(1)   10.2.10

GLOSSARY

'A' weighted scale	a scale used by noise meters to give greater significance to sounds within the middle frequencies (500Hz to 8,000Hz), which are the frequencies perceived by the average human ear. An 'A' weighted scale is written as 'dbA' or 'dBA'
amosite	commonly referred to as 'brown asbestos'
anthophyllite	asbestos which is various shades of brown such as yellow-brown, green-brown or brownish-grey, but also green, off-white or grey
asbestos	a fibrous mineral which is heat-resistant to very high temperatures, is a good insulator and is resistant to reaction with chemicals; there are four main types of asbestos, namely chrysotile, crocidolite, amosite and anthophyllite
asbestosis	fibrous tissue damage within the lung; usually a progressive disease, causing breathlessness and cough; life-expectancy can be reduced
bilsom wool	hearing protection, rather like cotton wool, usually dispensed in a long roll
carcinogenic substances	defined by reg 2 of and Sch 8 to the Control of Substances Hazardous to Health Regulations 2002
carpal tunnel syndrome	compression of the median nerve in the carpal tunnel which is in the wrist. Causes pins and needles, numbness and weakness of the hand or fingers
chrysotile	commonly referred to as 'white asbestos'; off-white to grey long flexible fibres
crocidolite	commonly referred to as 'blue asbestos'; bluish short, stiff, strong fibres
date of guilty knowledge	date when the specified risk was known
decibel	a measure of the magnitude of the noise, or sound pressure level; decibels are measured on a logarithmic scale, and thus the doubling of a sound pressure level is represented by an additional 3 decibels

De Quervains
syndrome
Also referred to as De Quervains stenosing tenovaginitis; thickening of the fibrous sheath of the tendons

disease and illness
claims
definition in Pre-Action Protocol for Disease and Illness Claims and covering any illness, physical or psychological, any disorder, ailment, affliction, complaint, malady or derangement other than a physical or psychological injury solely caused by an accident or other similar single event

ear muffs
hearing protection with a hard outer section containing sound insulating material and an outer seal, of foam or fluid filled; fitted with a plastic band to hold them in place on the head and over the ears

epicondylitis
pain and swelling where the muscle joins the bone at the elbow

first action level
daily personal noise exposure of 85dbA (Noise at Work Regulations)

golfer's elbow
medial epicondylitis, with pain and swelling where the muscle joins the bone at the elbow

HAVS
Hand/Arm Vibration Syndrome. Similar to VWF. Causes symptoms in the hand and arm

hearing protection
protection used by the individual worker. Common types of hearing protection are Bilsom Wool, foam ear plugs and ear muffs

hertz
a measure of sound frequency, commonly written as 'Hz' or 'hz'; the basic unit is one cycle per second, or 1Hz; the large number of a hertz in the frequencies audible to humans make it convenient to measure the sound waves in Kilohertz or 'Khz'

kilohertz
see also 'Hertz'; a measure of sound frequency; the basic unit is one cycle per second, 1Hz and thus 1Khz is 1,000hz

Leq
noise dose calculation to take account of the fluctuating noise levels; measured in respect of an 8-hour day

lung cancer
can be caused by asbestos exposure

mesothelioma
in the vast majority of cases it is a malignant tumour of the pleura (outer lining of the lung); can be found in the lining of the abdominal cavity or the lining around the heart; fatal, with a life-expectancy of a few months to about 2 years, although some patients survive for 3 or 4 years

noise
sound which is undesired by the recipient; sound levels are measured in decibels

noise dose	referred to and written as 'Leq' (equivalent sound level); noise dose is a calculation to take account of the fluctuating noise levels and is measured in respect of an 8-hour day
occupational illness	intended to include diseases or medical conditions which arise as a result of exposure at work to substances, forces or environmental factors
peak action level	sound level of 200 pascals; a pascal is a unit of pressure corresponding to a force of 1 newton acting uniformly upon an area of 1 square metre
peri-tendinitis	inflammation of the junction between the muscle and the thumb extensor tendons on the inner side of the wrist
pleural fibrosis	also referred to as 'pleural thickening'. Fibrous damage to the outer lining of the lung (pleura); restricts the function of the lungs, causing breathlessness and disability; can be progressive develop so as to reduce life-expectancy
pleural plaques	scar tissue on the outer lining of the lung; usually symptomless
RMS	root mean squared; vibration measurement for workplace vibration exposures; the average is obtained by summing the squares of the acceleration values measured over time, dividing by the measuring time, and then taking the square root of the resulting value
RSI	repetitive strain injury; discredited term which should not now be used; not a clinical diagnosis
second action level	daily personal noise exposure of 90 dBA (Noise at Work Regulations)
stress	defined as 'an excess of demands upon an individual in excess of their ability to cope' (Stress in the Public Sector (1988)); in 1990 there was a report of the Education Service Advisory Committee of the Health and Safety Commission, A guide for managers and teachers in the schools sector; this adopted a similar definition: 'stress is a process that can occur when there is an unresolved mismatch between the perceived pressures of the work situation and an individual's ability to cope' (Managing Occupational Stress (1990)). 'The reaction people have to excessive pressures or other types of demand placed upon them' (HSE, Stress at Work (1995))

substances
hazardous to health

defined in reg 2 of the Control of Substances Hazardous to Health Regulations 2002. 'substance hazardous to health' means a substance (including any preparation) –

    (a)   which is listed in Part I of the approved supply list as dangerous for supply within the meaning of the Chemicals (Hazard Information and Packaging for Supply) Regulations and for which an indication of danger specified for the substance in Part V of that list is very toxic, toxic, harmful, corrosive or irritant;

    (b)   for which the Health and Safety Commission has approved a maximum exposure limit or an occupational exposure standard;

    (c)   which is a biological agent;

    (d)   which is dust of any kind, except dust which is a substance within paragraph (a) or (b) above when present at a concentration in air equal to or greater than –

        (i)   10 mg/m^3 as a time-weighted average over an 8-hour period. of total inhalable dust, or

        (ii)   4 mg/m^3 as a time-weighted average over an 8-hour period of respirable dust;

    (e)   which, not being a substance falling with sub-paragraphs (a) to (d), because of its chemical or toxicological properties and the way in which it is used or is present at the workplace creates a risk to health.

tendinitis

inflammation of the tendons

tennis elbow

lateral epicondylitis, with pain and swelling where the muscle joins the bone at the elbow

tenosynovitis

inflammation of the synovium (lubricated sheath which surrounds and protects the tendons; used, incorrectly as having a wider meaning; DSS definition: 'traumatic inflammation of the tendons of the hand or forearm or of the associated tendon sheaths'

trigger finger

a form of tendinitis where the inflammed tendons become locked in their sheaths, thus locking the finger

ULD

upper limb disorder; convenient umbrella term; not a clinical diagnosis

vibration white finger	Sometimes referred to as Raynaud's Phenomenon; causes tingling, numbness and episodic whiteness in the fingers and hand
VWF	vibration white finger.
WRULD	work-related upper limb disorder; a convenient umbrella term for examining a number of different medical conditions; used to be called repetitive strain injury (RSI); not a clinical diagnosis

PART 1

GENERAL PRINCIPLES

CHAPTER 1

OCCUPATIONAL ILLNESS

1.1 DEFINITION OF OCCUPATIONAL ILLNESS

The terms 'occupational illness' or 'occupational disease' are not terms of art. The terms themselves have little practical meaning. They are umbrella definitions intended to include diseases or medical conditions which arise as a result of exposure at work to substances, forces or environmental factors. Generally the exposure will have taken place over a long period of time, where each single exposure caused little or no harm. The definition 'occupational illnesses' seeks to distinguish these conditions from workplace injuries where an incident causes an obvious physical injury. In contrast, occupational illnesses usually involve consideration of more technical matters, whether involving ergonomics, engineering or medical evidence.

The Pre-Action Protocol for Disease and Illness Claims ('the Protocol') defines disease as any illness (physical or psychological), any disorder, ailment, affliction, complaint, malady or derangement other than a physical or psychological injury solely caused by an accident or other similar single event.

However, there may be instances where there is a single, damaging exposure, for example where:

- one exposure to asbestos gives rise to the risk of mesothelioma;
- one burst of noise in excess of 120 decibels causes hearing loss;
- the inhalation of extremely toxic fumes causes lung damage or asthma; or
- exposure to chemicals causes dermatitis.

All these examples will give rise to common problems for a litigator, and this book aims to tackle these problems.

The Protocol applies to all personal injury claims where the injury is not the result of an accident but is an illness or disease. Thus, the Protocol does not apply to the single exposure examples given above.

The Protocol is not limited to the workplace but includes diseases occurring in other situations, for example through occupation of premises or the use of products. It is not intended to cover 'group' or 'class' actions. The full text of the Protocol is set out in Appendix 5.

The Protocol applies to disease claims which are likely to be complex and not suitable for fast-track procedures, even though they may fall within fast-track limits. The aim of this book is to help unravel the complexities. It is helpful to group conditions under the heading 'occupational illness' since they share common problems and features which arise during litigation.

1.2   COMMON CONDITIONS

The following conditions may present following a prolonged exposure to substances, forces or environmental factors at work: asbestos disease, asthma, deafness, dermatitis, farmer's lung, sick building syndrome, work-related stress, work-related upper limb disorders and vibration white finger.

1.3   IDENTIFYING THE ISSUES

From their very title, certain conditions clearly point to their cause, and the focus of the claim is then on whether sufficient culpable exposure can be proved in order to establish liability. Asbestos disease is the prime example. The focus of the claim is whether the lung changes seen on x-ray are due to asbestos disease and whether there has been asbestos exposure. In a deafness claim (usually hearing loss, rather than actual deafness) the issues are whether there was exposure to excessive noise over a relevant period and whether the hearing loss is due to damage caused by the excessive noise, or the hearing loss is constitutional or caused by medication or a blow to the head. At the other end of the spectrum are the asthma and dermatitis claims. There is usually no difficulty in establishing the medical diagnosis in such cases, but the problem arises in finding the cause. There may be many substances in the workplace with the potential to sensitise some individuals. The Health and Safety Executive publication *Asthma in the Workplace* lists many different potential sources, ranging from platinum to pig urine (although these two examples are rarely encountered in the same working environment). It may be necessary to consider exposure in the home or in recreational activities. A golfer may be sensitive to chemicals spread on putting greens; a DIY fan may use various glues. Thus it will be appreciated that whilst common problems and common principles must be considered, the approach in these example cases will differ.

Concern about the factual detail or complexities of technical or medical evidence may blur the basic principles. However, these should always be kept in view; they are essential navigation beacons.[1] A good example includes the decision in *Arnold v CEGB*,[2] in which the defendants were provided with a limitation defence in an asbestos case where the exposure had occurred before the Limitation Act 1954. In *Keenan v Miller Insulation and Engineering Ltd*,[3] and *Guidera v NEI Projects (India) Ltd*,[4] the claimants sought to argue around the pleaded limitation defence and the effect of the decision in *Arnold v CEGB* by showing that the damage was caused long after the exposure. These cases will be considered in more detail below.

1.4 BASIC PRINCIPLES

The same basic principles apply to occupational illness claims as to all other types of personal injury claim. The claimant must prove: duty, breach, damage and causation. Each of these principles can then be sub-divided into further issues:

- Was the claimant exposed?
- When was the claimant exposed?
- For how long was the claimant exposed?
- What was the degree of exposure?
- What was the accepted standard at the time of the exposure?
- Were any preventive or protective measures in place?
- Did the claimant use these measures?
- Were instructions and/or warnings apparent?
- Were health checks carried out?
- Did the exposure cause the illness?
- Were there any other potential causes?
- Is apportionment in respect of causes from different sources in issue?

It is important to consider the basic principles, and the issues which each create, in order to apply these principles to occupational illness claims. Thus, an explanation of the issues relating to the five most common occupational illnesses is necessary, not only in dealing with a specific claim, but also to illustrate the working of the principles in the context of the complex and technical matters which arise. That is the subject of Chapter 2.

---

[1]   See Court of Appeal in *Sutherland v Hatton* [2002] 2 All ER 1.
[2]   [1988] AC 228.
[3]   (Unreported) 8 December 1987.
[4]   (Unreported) McCullough J 1988, referred to by CA 30/1/90 transcript.

CHAPTER 2

DUTY AND FORESEEABILITY

A full exposition of the law of negligence is readily available in many definitive texts on the law.[1] The focus here is the principle of negligence, illustrated by some related cases which demonstrate how those principles operate in practice.

2.1 TO WHOM IS THE DUTY OF CARE OWED?

In occupational illness claims, perhaps more than any other personal injury claim, it is easy to lose sight of the foundation on which the claim is to be constructed in an endeavour to come to grips with the evidence. The emphasis should be on finding and developing the evidence in order to establish the requirements of the principles of negligence. The fact that the existence of the duty of care has been tested in a number of occupational illness cases shows that it is an important issue.

Generally, there is no difficulty in establishing that a duty of care was owed to the claimant. An employer has a common law duty to take reasonable care to ensure the safety of his employees. This is not an absolute duty, but a duty is to take reasonable care.[2] There are obligations to provide a competent staff of workers, adequate material, a proper system of work and effective supervision. The duties are often stated as being the duty to provide a safe *place* of work and a safe *system* of work.

Thus it is clear that a duty of care is owed to employees. It is a modest extension of this principle that the duty of care is owed to another employer's workers who are present at the premises, provided the foreseeability test can be satisfied. Therefore, self-employed workers, agency workers and sub-contractors are all owed a duty of care.

The *Donoghue v Stevenson* test was particularly apt in *Margerson and Hancock v JW Roberts Limited*[3] where it was held that persons living in the vicinity of the defendant's asbestos factory satisfied the 'neighbour' test.

---

[1]   See, for example, *Charlesworth and Percy on Negligence* (Sweet & Maxwell, 12th edn).
[2]   *Wilsons and Clyde Coal Company Limited v English* [1938] AC 57.
[3]   [1996] PIQR P154.

Families of workers may fall within the category of persons to whom a duty is owed – foreseebility often being the determining factor.[4] In *Maguire v Harland & Wolff*,[5] it was held not to be reasonably foreseeable to the employer of a boilermaker in the period 1961–1965 that the boilermaker's wife was at risk of serious injury to her health as a result of exposure to asbestos dust carried home each day on her husband's work clothes. In *Pinder v Cape plc*[6] there was no liability which fell on the defendants who had disposed of asbestos waste on a tip where the claimant played as a child in the 1950s. It was not foreseeable at the time that the amount of the exposure or that there might be exposure would create a risk of asbestos disease. These cases would have been decided differently if the exposure had been in the late 1960s or later.

2.2   FORESEEABILITY – EXTENT OF DUTY

In a claim based on common law negligence the extent of the duty of care is governed by the concept of reasonable foreseeability. This is a flexible test which responds over time to the change in knowledge as to the respective dangers. An increase in knowledge almost always requires a lower exposure limit rather than a higher one. It would be interesting to argue that there has been negligence in relation to a level of exposure which was regarded as potentially harmful 20 years ago, but which today is twice as great. Such an argument may also pose interesting questions concerning causation.

In cases where a long period of exposure occurred before damage was sustained, such as asbestos and noise, it is vital to consider the state of knowledge at the date of each exposure, see *Asmussen v Filtrona UK Ltd.*[7] What degree of exposure was considered harmful at the time? To establish common law negligence in respect of an exposure or exposures which occurred some time previously (whether asbestos, noise, fumes, etc) it will have to be determined whether at the date of the exposure the quantity of dust, noise, fumes, etc gave rise to a reasonably foreseeable risk of injury and that the defendant failed to take all reasonably practicable steps to reduce the amount of dust, noise or fumes. This is not always straightforward since standards may have changed over the years.

In *Margereson and Hancock v JW Roberts Limited* (above) (an asbestos case) the Court of Appeal referred to this issue of foreseeability:

> 'We turn now to what we would regard as the only legal issue in the appeal. What was the duty owed to Mr Margereson and to Mrs Hancock? The

---

4   Compare the facts in *Gunn v Wallsend Slipway* (1989) *The Times*, 23 January and *Hewitt v Alf Brown's Transport Limited* [1992] ICR 530, both concerning injury to family members caused by dust brought home on the workers' overalls.

5   [2005] EWCA Civ 01.

6   [2006] EWHC 3630, QB.

7   [2011] EWHC 1734.

answer is to be found almost entirely in the speech of Lord Lloyd in *Page v Smith* [1996] 1 AC at 190 when he said: "The test in every case ought to be whether the defendant can reasonably foresee that his conduct would expose the plaintiff to the risk of personal injury. If so, then he comes under a duty of care to that plaintiff. If a working definition of 'personal injury' is needed, it can be found in s 38(1) of the Limitation Act 1980. 'Personal Injuries' includes any disease and any impairment of a person's physical or mental condition." We add only that in the context of this case we take the view that liability only attaches to these defendants if the evidence demonstrated that they should reasonably have foreseen a risk of some pulmonary injury, not necessarily mesothelioma.'

Thus the occupational disease cases are governed by the same principle of foreseeablity as was expounded in *Hughes v Lord Advocate*[8] and other cases.

A real risk has been defined as 'One which would occur to the mind of a reasonable man in the position of the defendant and which he would not brush aside as far-fetched.' The defendant must be judged in the light of the knowledge and practices of the particular industry at the time of the exposure. In *Thompson v Smiths Ship-Repairers (North Shields) Ltd*,[9] Mustill J adopted and adapted the dictum of Swanwick J in *Stokes v Guest Keen & Nettlefold (Bolts and Nuts) Limited.*[10]

'From these authorities I deduce the principles, that the overall test is still the conduct of the reasonable and prudent employer, taking positive thought for the safety of his workers in the light of what he knows or ought to know; where there is a recognised and general practice which has been followed for a substantial period in similar circumstances without mishap, he is entitled to follow it, unless in the light of common sense or newer knowledge it is clearly bad; but, where there is developing knowledge, he must keep reasonably abreast of it and not be too slow to apply it; and where he has in fact greater than average knowledge of the risk, he may be thereby obliged to take more than the average or standard precaution. He must weigh up the risk in terms of the likelihood of injury occurring and the potential consequences if it does; and he must balance against this the (probable) effectiveness of the precautions that can be taken to meet it and the expense and inconvenience they involve. If he is found to have fallen below the standard to be properly expected of a reasonable and prudent employer in these respects, he is negligent.

I shall direct myself in accordance with this succinct and helpful statement of the law and will make only one additional comment. In the passage just cited Swanwick J drew a distinction between a recognised practice followed without mishap and one which, in the light of common sense or increased knowledge, is clearly bad. The distinction is indeed valid and sufficient for many cases. The two categories are not however exhaustive, as the present actions demonstrate. The practice of leaving employees unprotected against

---

[8] [1963] AC 837.
[9] [1984] 1 All ER 881.
[10] [1968] 1 WLR 1776.

excessive noise had never been followed "without mishap". Yet even the plaintiffs have not suggested that it was "clearly bad", in the sense of creating a potential liability in negligence, at any time before the mid-1930s. Between the two extremes is a type of risk which is regarded at any given time (although not necessarily later) as an inescapable feature of the industry. The employer is not liable for the consequences of such risks, although subsequent changes in social awareness, or improvements in knowledge and technology, may transfer the risk into the category of those against which the employer can and should take care. It is unnecessary, and perhaps impossible, to give a comprehensive formula for identifying the line between the acceptable and the unacceptable. Nevertheless, the line does exist, and was clearly recognised in *Morris v West Hartlepool Steam Navigation Company Limited* [1956] AC 552. The speeches in that case show, not that one employer is exonerated simply by proving that other employers are just as negligent, but that the standard of what is negligent is influenced, although not decisively, by the practice in the industry as a whole. In my judgment, this principle applies not only where the breach of duty is said to consist of a failure to take precautions known to be available as a means of combatting a known danger, but also where the omission involves an absence of initiative in seeking out knowledge of facts which are not in themselves obvious. The employer must keep up-to-date, but the court must be slow to blame him for not ploughing a lone furrow.'

The reasoning in *Walker v Wabco Automotive UK Ltd*[11] can have a wider application to occupational illness claims. The case is considered below under vibration white finger (VWF) claims, but is generally instructive. The claimant alleged that she suffered carpel tunnel syndrome caused by hand-held vibrating power tools. The trial judge was much influenced by the Health and Safety Executive (HSE) publication, *Work-Related Upper Limb Disorders – A Guide to Prevention* (1990), in finding that injury was foreseeable. The Court of Appeal held that in a vibration case too much reliance had been placed on a publication which dealt with mainly twisting and gripping upper limb disorders. The HSE publication should not have carried the day against the evidence that the defendant had been using the same system of work for 20 years without an allegation of VWF. This case should caution against over-confidence in finding a publication that can be said to have some application in theory, but which does not match up to the practical realities of the facts of the particular case.

2.3   FORESEEABILITY IN SPECIFIC OCCUPATIONAL DISEASES

2.3.1   Asbestos

The state of knowledge in respect of the different types of asbestos has developed gradually over the years. Numerous publications set markers on the way. One important factor when considering foreseeability in the

---

[11]   (Unreported) 11 May 1999, CA.

early years is the amount of asbestos exposure. It was only realised at a relatively late date that modest exposure to asbestos could create a risk.

Whilst the annual reports of the Chief Inspector of Factories in the early twentieth century made regular reference to the extremely dusty conditions found in many asbestos works and the injurious nature of the dust, the problem seems to have been seen in general terms without a specific understanding of the diseases which could result from such exposure.

Subsequently, more detailed investigations were made into the health risks in the asbestos textile industry. The 1930 report by Merewether & Price[12] was a landmark. Although the report was limited in its scope it recognised that other categories of workers were likely to be exposed to harmful quantities of asbestos dust. There followed the Asbestos Industry Regulations 1931 which applied to factories and workshops where asbestos textiles and other asbestos articles were manufactured from raw asbestos. It has been held that the Regulations also applied to the production of asbestos paste for sealing plattens of dry cleaning presses to prevent steam escaping.[13]

The Chief Inspector of Factories' report for 1938 stated that:

> 'One of the greatest problems facing industry today is that of dust ... while s 47 of the Factories Act 1937 may be thought somewhat ambiguous in its reference to a substantial quantity of dust of any kind, it is, I consider, an admirable one in that it requires precautions even before it is possible to say specifically that the dust in question is harmful to a recognisable pathological extent. There can be no doubt that dust if inhaled is physiologically undesirable. Moreover, dust that is thought today to be harmless may, following research, be viewed in another light tomorrow. It is not many years ago when the dust of asbestos was regarded as innocuous, while today it is recognised as highly dangerous ... in recent years the suggestion has been made in medical publications that there is some relationship between silicosis or asbestosis and cancer of the lung ...'

In 1955 medical research was published which showed a tenfold excess of bronchial carcinoma in a group of asbestos textile workers. In the same year the Chief Inspector of Factories' annual report reported on deaths attributed to asbestosis where cancer of the lung was also found.

Shell Tankers and Another v Jeromson and Another[14] concerned the years before 1960. At that time a certain knowledge that asbestos dust was dangerous contrasted with an absence of any knowledge or means of knowledge about what constituted a safe level of exposure. The decision

---

[12] 'Report on the effects of asbestos dust on the lungs and dust suppression in the asbestos industry.'
[13] *Shell Tankers and Another v Jeromson and Another* (2001) *The Times*, 2 March.
[14] *Shell Tankers and Another v Jeromson and Another* (2001) *The Times*, 2 March.

in *Shell Tankers* seems to rely upon hindsight; certainly the interpretation of the extent of the warnings in the literature was more favourable than the interpretation of the same literature in earlier cases.

It was not until the 1960s that there was a greater understanding of the affects of asbestos exposure and in particular of more modest exposure. In 1960 a paper produced by Wagner first recognised the risk of mesothelioma from even small amounts of asbestos.[15] A further important paper was published in 1965, and in October 1965 *The Sunday Times* published a front-page article on the dangers of asbestos.

However, there is still scope for argument. In *Smith v P & O Bulk Shipping Ltd*,[16] a docker had been exposed to asbestos in loading and unloading duties for more than two hours at a time in the years before 1977. On the balance of probabilities, it could be shown that the exposure had contributed to his asbestos disease. However, it was held that the reasonable shipowner would not have been aware of the risks from such exposure until receipt of a circular from the Department of Trade in 1977. This decision is regarded as remarkable by many, and just plain wrong by others, the latter consigning it to the category of cases decided on its own facts and evidence and not establishing any precedent. However, the case cannot be dismissed lightly.

Most consulting engineers with experience of asbestos litigation now have a well-researched list of documents which helps to chart the progress of knowledge of the disease, although as can be seen this is not the definitive answer in every case. Account must be taken of specific industries and small firms where detailed technical knowledge is not so readily available.

2.3.2   Noise

It was known as long ago as the nineteenth century that noise levels created in heavy industry could cause deafness. However, noise levels seem to have been accepted as an inevitable part of the job. It was also well known that workers in shipbuilding, ship-repairing, drop forging and similar industries tended to become deaf in later years. For some workers this was described almost as wearing a badge of pride. Despite the existence of a wealth of documentation it was not until the latter half of the twentieth century that the HSE (then the Factory Inspectorate) took any active interest.

In *Kellett v British Rail Engineering Ltd*,[17] the defendants, a large employer with a substantial research department, disclosed documents which showed that they had been actively considering the problem of

---

[15] 'Diffuse pleural mesothelioma and asbestos exposure in the North West Province *Brit J Indust Med* (1960) 17: 260–71.

[16] [1998] 2 Lloyd's Rep 81.

[17] (Unreported) 3 May 1984.

noise-induced deafness from the early 1950s. The employer in *Berry v Stone Manganese Marine*,[18] also knew of the problem in the mid-1950s. There was also awareness of the problem of noise-induced deafness in some shipyards.[19]

In 1963 the publication 'Noise and the Worker' ensured that smaller employers which did not have in-house technical or research departments were made aware of the issue. In *Thompson v Smiths Ship-Repairers (North Shields) Ltd*,[20] it was held on the evidence the employers should have acted from 1963. This was not a decision that before 1963 noise-induced deafness was not a foreseeable risk, so much as that after 1963 a reasonable shipbuilder was under a duty to provide protection against the risk. Put another way, it was known from 1963 that protection could be effective and it was foreseeable that ears could be damaged if unprotected.

However, the evidence in any particular case may point to different dates for 'guilty knowledge' to be attached in different industries. In *Kill v Coastline Buses Ltd*,[21] the date of knowledge for bus drivers was held to be 1972. However, this and other similar cases depended very much on the evidence and it is considered by many that earlier dates could be established.

2.3.3 Work-related upper limb disorders

Many occupations involve repetitive movements and can give rise to a risk of a work-related upper limb disorder. Cases in this area very much turn on the particular facts. Furthermore, the onset of symptoms is likely to be relatively recent. The 1977 HSE Guidance Note MS10, 'Beat Conditions' states:

> 'Tenosynovitis is an important cause of sick absence and is the second commonest prescribed disease in the UK. It occurs in many industries but especially in those where rapid repetitive, twisting and gripping movements are common eg pottery, glaze dipping, brick making, assembly line work and belt conveyor sorting for food canning, press operations and the evisceration and trussing of chickens. The condition is liable to result from trauma, over-use of the wrist and forearm during repetitive operations, unaccustomed work, alteration in work tempo, or from persistent strain. It occurs most often in new employees or on return to work after an absence or on the introduction of a new process or tool which places unusual strain on the muscles.'

---

[18] (1971) 12 KIR 13.
[19] *Baxter v Harland & Wolff* [1990] IRLR 516, CA.
[20] [1984] 1 All ER 881.
[21] *Current Law Digest* (December 2000).

The HSE published further guidance in 1990 with the snappily entitled 'Work-Related Upper Limb Disorders – a Guide to Prevention'. In 2002 the HSE published 'Upper Limb Disorders in the Workplace'.

2.3.4   Vibration white finger (VWF)

The date of 'guilty knowledge' of vibration white finger (VWF) probably began sometime in the mid-1970s. Again, however, cases may turn on their individual facts as established by the evidence called and determined by the court.

In *Mustoe v Saunders Valve Co Ltd*,[22] the judge was satisfied that there was knowledge of the risk of injury in respect of the operators of grinding tools from 1969. In *Armstrong and Others v British Coal*,[23] the date was put at 1973. Other cases have put the date of knowledge at 1975/76.[24] In *Heyes v Pilkington Glass Ltd*,[25] a much later date of post-1985 was set in relation to a crane driver. In *Doherty and Others v Rugby Joinery (UK) Ltd*,[26] the Court of Appeal held that in the woodworking industry the defendant employer was under no duty to assess and monitor its employees for symptoms of VWF before 1991/92, but after that date the employer was in breach of its duty to elicit the existence of symptoms and prevent affected employees from working with vibratory tools at all.

The case of *Walker v Wabco Automotive UK Ltd*[27] is instructive. The claimant alleged that she suffered carpel tunnel syndrome caused by hand-held vibrating power tools. The judge found on the evidence that the cause of the claimant's injury was the work with the tools and went on to hold that the defendant employer had been in breach of its duty of care. The Court of Appeal held that the judge had placed too much reliance on the HSE publication of 1990, 'Work-Related Upper Limb Disorders – A Guide to Prevention', in finding that injury was foreseeable. The HSE guide dealt with upper limb disorders generally and was principally concerned with injuries caused by twisting and gripping. The defendant had been using the same system of work for 20 years without it being alleged that the vibrating tools had caused VWF. There was no other evidence before the judge to support the claim that the defendant should have foreseen that the hand-held power tools could have been the source of the injury. It was held that the defendant had not fallen below the standard expected of a reasonable and prudent employer at the time in question.

---

[22]   (Unreported) 1979.
[23]   [1997] 8 Med LR 259.
[24]   See *Heal v Garringtons Ltd* (unreported) 26 May 1982; and *Shepard and Others v Firth Brown Ltd* (unreported) 17 April 1985.
[25]   [1998] PIQR P303.
[26]   [2004] EWCA Civ 147.
[27]   (Unreported) 11 May 1999.

2.3.5   Work-related stress

Foreseeability is one of the main issues in work-related stress claims. This issue has recently been reviewed by the Court of Appeal and the House of Lords in *Barber v Somerset County Council*.[28] The older cases approached foreseeability by assessing the claimant against a mythical 'person of reasonable fortitude' – an objective test. The recent guidance seems to have moved subtly away from that approach. The test is not radically different but has more components and thus a difference of emphasis, although it can be seen to be firmly rooted on established principle.

The House of Lords left untouched the 16 principles laid out by the Court of Appeal[29] and referred to them as providing 'useful practical guidance, but it must be read as that, and not as having anything like statutory force'. The guiding principles set out by the Court of Appeal were as follows:

(1)   There are no special control mechanisms applying to claims for psychiatric (or physical) illness or injury arising from the stress of doing the work the employee is required to do. The ordinary principles of employer's liability apply.

(2)   The threshold question is whether the kind of harm to the particular employee was reasonably foreseeable: this has two components: (a) an injury to health (as distinct from occupational stress), which (b) is attributable to stress at work (as distinct from other factors).

(3)   Foreseeability depends upon what the employer knows (or ought reasonably to know) about the individual employee. Because of the nature of mental disorder, it is harder to foresee than physical injury, but may be easier to foresee in a known individual than in the population at large. An employer is usually entitled to assume that the employee can withstand the normal pressures of the job unless he knows of some particular problem or vulnerability.

(4)   The test is the same whatever the employment: there are no occupations which should be regarded as intrinsically dangerous to mental health.

(5)   Factors likely to be relevant in answering the threshold question include:

(a)   the nature and extent of the work done by the employee. Is the workload much more than is normal for the particular job? Is the work particularly intellectually or emotionally demanding for the employee? Are demands being made of the employee unreasonable when compared with the demands made of others in the same or comparable jobs? Alternatively, are there signs that others doing the job are suffering harmful levels of

---

[28]   [2004] 2 All ER 385.
[29]   *Sutherland v Hatton* [2002] PIQR P241.

stress? Is there an abnormal level of sickness or absenteeism in the same job or the same department?

(b) signs from the employee of impending harm to health. Does he have a particular problem or vulnerability? Does he already suffer from illness attributable to stress at work? Have there recently been frequent or prolonged absences which are uncharacteristic of him? Is there reason to think that these are attributable to stress at work, for example because of complaints or warnings from him or others?

(6) The employer is generally entitled to take what he is told by his employee at face value, unless he has good reason to think to the contrary. He does not generally have to make searching enquiries of the employee or seek permission to make further enquiries of his medical advisers.

The Court of Appeal approached forseeability by saying that the question is not whether psychiatric injury is foreseeable in a person of 'ordinary fortitude', which amounts to a change of emphasis. In fact the Court of Appeal was concerned to formulate a single test, namely *whether a harmful reaction to the pressures of the workplace was reasonably foreseeable in the individual employee concerned. Such a reaction will have two components: (1) an injury to health, which (2) is attributable to stress at work.* No doubt the court was driven by the problem of determining a standard of reasonable fortitude, but it will be seen that equally difficult questions are raised in determining whether the stresses are foreseeably likely to affect the individual employee.

The Court of Appeal has stated that the answer to the foreseeability question will therefore depend upon the interrelationship between the particular characteristics of the employee concerned and the particular demands which the employer casts upon him. However, it accepts that a number of factors are likely to be relevant. These include the *nature and extent of the work being done by the employee.* Employers should be more alert to picking up signs from an employee who is being over-worked in an intellectually or emotionally demanding job than from an employee whose workload is no more than normal for the job or whose job is not particularly demanding for him. It will be easier to conclude that harm was foreseeable if the employer put pressure upon the individual employee which in all the circumstances of the case was unreasonable. Also relevant is whether there were signs that other employees doing the same work were under harmful levels of stress. It is possible that other employees have already suffered injury to their health arising from their work, or there may be an abnormal level of sickness and absence amongst other employees at the same grade or in the same department. However, if there is no evidence of this, the focus must turn to the individual.

The formulation of a single test is likely to make it easier for an employer to say that it considered that the employee was equal to the stresses of the job. In this way, an employee who appeared to be coping with an excessive workload will have less protection.

The Court of Appeal stated that the most important signs are the *signs from the employee himself*, but qualified this by saying that it is important to distinguish between signs of stress and signs of impending harm to health. Stress is merely the mechanism which may, but usually does not, lead to damage to health. Factors to take into account are frequent or prolonged absences from work for physical or psychological reasons which are uncharacteristic of the person concerned. However, there must also be good reason to think that the underlying cause is occupational stress rather than other factors, ie stress resulting from the nature of the employee's work, complaints made about the work by the employee or from warnings given by the employee or others around him. This puts the onus on the employee.

It is the expressed view of the Court of Appeal that it is not the job but the interaction between the individual and the job which causes the harm. Stress, it has stated, is a subjective concept, namely the individual's perception that the pressures placed upon him are greater than he may be able to meet. Adverse reactions to stress are equally individual, ranging from minor physical symptoms to major mental illness. Thus the question is said to be whether it ought to have been foreseen that the employee was exposed to a risk of mental illness materially higher than that which would ordinarily affect a person in his position with a heavy workload.

In *Murgai v The Home Office*[30] the claimant was unusually vulnerable. However, this fact was unknown to his employer and there was nothing to put a reasonable employer on notice of the need to do anything. In *Barlow v Borough of Broxborne*,[31] the court found that there was no foreseeable risk; the claimant had been in receipt of letters detailing his non-performance and threats of disciplinary action. He also alleged that there had been abusive outbursts directed at him. Whilst that may have been stressful there was no reasonably foreseeable risk of psychiatric illness. In *Foumeny v University of Leeds*,[32] the claimant was an academic who opposed plans to merge his department with another; once again, the claim failed on foreseeability.

What must be foreseen is the risk of personal injury . However, once that threshold test is satisfied, it does not matter that that the psychiatric injury suffered by the claimant was not foreseeable, see *Donachie v Chief Constable of Greater Manchester*.[33]

---

[30] [2003] EWHC 1870, QB.
[31] [2003] EWHC 50, QB.
[32] [2003] EWCA Civ 557.
[33] [2004] EWCA Civ 405.

2.4 CAUSATION

Having established a breach of duty, *it is still necessary to prove that the particular breach of duty caused the harm*. It is not enough to show that occupational stress caused the harm. Where there are several different possible causes (as will often be the case with stress-related illness of any kind), the claimant may have difficulty proving that the employer's breach of duty was one of them.[34] This will be a particular problem if, as in *Garrett v Camden LBC*,[35] the main cause was a vulnerable personality which the employer knew nothing about. However, the employee does not have to show that the breach of duty was the entire cause of his ill-health: it is enough to show that it made a material contribution.[36]

2.5 EXPERT EVIDENCE AND FORESEEABILITY

Expert evidence is usually vital if foreseeability remains an issue. In a number of cases a failure to call appropriate expert evidence has resulted in the claimant failing to establish a necessary ingredient of the claim. Whilst it concerns the foreseeability test in a regulation, the case of *Morrison v Central Electricity Generating Board and Babcock & Wilcox Limited*,[37] is instructive in this respect. The claimant was a fitter working in a power station but engaged by outside contractors. The issue was whether the amount of asbestos to which the claimant was exposed by laggers was 'likely to be injurious' at the date of the exposure. No expert evidence was called on behalf of the claimant and he lost on this point.

---

[34] See *Wilsher v Essex Area Health Authority* [1988] AC 1074.
[35] [2001] EWCA Civ 395.
[36] See *Bonnington Castings v Wardlaw* [1956] AC 613.
[37] (Unreported) 15 March 1986.

CHAPTER 3

CAUSATION, APPORTIONMENT AND CONTRIBUTORY NEGLIGENCE

3.1 DIVISIBLE AND INDIVISIBLE DISEASE

3.1.1 The distinction

If the severity of a disease is affected by how much the victim is exposed to the alleged harmful agent then the disease is said to be divisible or dose-related. Most diseases fall into this category, for example, the noisier the work the deafer the worker becomes.

The following asbestos diseases are currently treated as dose-related and are therefore **divisible**:

*   pleural plaques;[1]
*   pleural thickening; and
*   asbestosis.

Diseases which are not considered to be dose-related (because medical science is imperfect) and are therefore considered **indivisible** are:

*   lung cancer (but see **3.1.2** below); and
*   mesothelioma.

3.1.2 Why the distinction between divisible and indivisible disease matters

Where liability is established against one or more defendants in respect of a divisible injury, damages against each defendant are apportioned in accordance with the dose for which they are responsible. Each defendant's dose is determined by the duration and level of the exposure he caused (*Holtby v Brigham & Cowan (Hull) Ltd*[2]). Moreover, a single defendant is liable only for the dose or contribution to the overall condition irrespective of whether other defendants are also sued or found liable.

---

[1]   Some experts have been known to say that this condition is not dose-related.
[2]   [2000] 3 All ER 421.

So, for example, in an asbestosis case if only one defendant is sued and found liable for, say, half of the victim's lifetime asbestos exposure then the award of damages will be 50 per cent of the total awardable.

In a mesothelioma case where the disease is currently considered indivisible the damages are not apportioned and the claimant is entitled to recover in full against each defendant on a joint and several basis. This is the direct effect of section 3 of the Compensation Act 2006.

Problems arise in lung cancer cases because section 3 of the Compensation Act 2006 applies only to mesothelioma cases. It is currently thought the disease is indivisible but damages arguably must now be apportioned as to the extent of the tortious asbestos exposure caused by a particular defendant. The *obiter dicta* of the majority of the Lords' opinions in *Barker v Corus Plc*[3] indicated that material contribution was a departure from the 'but for' principle in respect of liability and did not determine the extent of a defendant's liability. The Compensation Act 2006 has reversed this aspect of the Lords' opinions in respect of mesothelioma but so far as lung cancer is concerned damages are probably subject to the apportionment exercise described in *Barker* and even though lung cancer is currently considered to be indivisible (see also **3.7** et seq below).

3.2 CAUSATION: THE STANDARD TEST

The standard test for determining whether or not the defendant's breach caused the claimant's loss is the 'but for' test: the claimant's loss would not have occurred but for the defendant's breach of duty. If the claimant's loss would have occurred in any event, irrespective of the breach of duty, the loss does not satisfy the 'but for' test.[4] The Supreme Court in *Sienkiewicz (PR of the estate of Enid Costello v Greif (UK) Ltd)*[5] recently affirmed that departure from the 'but for' principle was only permitted in cases concerning mesothelioma and warned against any future departure from the standard test of causation.

The 'but for' principle has been called into question in the context of mesothelioma and as we shall see in these types of cases the standard test as to causation has been departed from and this has received parliamentary recognition in the Compensation Act 2006 (see further below). Whilst the application of the special rule in mesothelioma cases may well now be without any difficulty (especially following the Supreme Court's decision in *Sienkiewicz*), the test as to causation in lung cancer cases (and indeed in any occupational cancer case) may not be so easy. In

---

[3]   [2006] UKHL 20.
[4]   *Barnett v Chelsea & Kensington Hospital Management Committee* [1969] 1 QB 428.
[5]   [2011] UKSC 10.

order to understand the issues which now face practitioners concerning occupational cancer cases it is necessary to consider in detail the evolution of the special rule.

3.3   MATERIAL CAUSE

In common law negligence cases generally it is not always necessary for the claimant to prove that the defendant's negligence was the sole or principal cause of the loss. Where medical science cannot establish the extent of the contribution of the tortious conduct to the injury, it is enough if it was a 'material' or 'effective' cause.

In *Bonnington Castings Ltd v Wardlaw*,[6] an employee contracted pneumoconiosis after inhaling silica dust from two sources at work. The employer was in breach of duty in respect of only one of those sources and it was likely that the other was the greater source of dust. The medical evidence was that pneumoconiosis is caused by a gradual accumulation of dust inhaled over a period of years, so that if dust came from two sources, the condition could not be wholly attributed to one source or the other. The claimant therefore could not prove that the employer's breach was the sole cause of his injury but the House of Lords held that it was not necessary for him to do so: it was enough that the breach was proved to have materially contributed to his illness. This principle applies only where the disease or condition is 'divisible' so that an increased dose of the harmful agent worsens the disease. The claim succeeded because the tortious exposure to silica dust had materially aggravated (to an unknown degree) the pneumoconiosis which the claimant might well have developed in any event as the result of non-tortious exposure to the same type of dust. The tort did not increase the risk of harm; it increased the actual harm.[7]

Another example of this approach but in a clinical negligence context is found in *Bailey v Ministry of Defence*,[8] where the claimant was admitted to the defendant's hospital for surgery to treat a gallstone. After the surgery she became extremely weak as a result of two cumulative causes: negligent lack of care after the surgery (in particular, failure to resuscitate) and the development of pancreatitis, which was not attributable to the defendant's negligence. The claimant was transferred to another hospital where she vomited after being given a drink and was unable to clear her throat. She aspirated the vomit causing a cardiac arrest which led her to suffer hypoxic brain damage. On her claim against the managers of both hospitals the judge held that the cardiac arrest had been caused by the claimant's weakness, to which the defendant's negligent lack of care had made an unknown but material contribution, and therefore

---

[6]   [1956] AC 613.

[7]   *AB and others v MoD* [2010] EWCA Civ 1317, at para [150].

[8]   [2008] EWCA Civ 883.

held the defendant liable. The Court of Appeal confirmed that the *Bonnington Castings* principle applies in medical negligence cases as it does in other cases and that where medical science cannot establish the probability that 'but for' an act of negligence the injury would not have happened but can establish that the contribution of the negligent cause was more than negligible, the 'but for' test is modified, and the claimant will succeed.

However, the rule in *Bonnington Castings* does not apply where the defendant is responsible for one of several potential causes of the injury but it cannot be proved which of them caused or materially contributed to the injury. In *Wilsher v Essex Health Authority*,[9] the defendant negligently failed to monitor the level of extra oxygen given to a baby born nearly three months prematurely and he developed retrolental fibropassias ('RLF'), resulting in blindness. The Court of Appeal held the defendant liable on the ground that he had created a risk of injury or increased an existing risk of injury to the claimant. The House of Lords held that a number of different factors could have caused RLF, including excessive levels of oxygen, and the defendant's negligence in failing to prevent excess oxygen causing the condition provided no evidence and raised no presumption that it was excess oxygen rather than one of the four other non-tortious factors that caused or contributed to the claimant's condition. There was no evidence either that the each of the risks were cumulative or interacted with each other. They were each as capable as the other to give rise to the condition. The trial judge had not resolved the conflict in the expert evidence as to whether excess oxygen caused or materially contributed to the claimant's condition and that issue had to be remitted for a retrial. The claimant's claim was subsequently settled.

3.4 INCREASING THE RISK – A NEW TORT?

The *Bonnington Castings* principle was applied and extended in *McGhee v National Coal Board*.[10] The employee, who normally worked in pipe kilns, was required to empty brick kilns in hot and dusty conditions for four and a half days and, since no washing facilities were provided, he had to cycle home each day whilst caked in brick dust. He contracted dermatitis, which was attributed to brick dust particles abrading and injuring his skin. The precise cause of the onset of dermatitis could not be medically established but it was accepted that the longer he was exposed to abrasion the greater his chance of developing the condition, and that immediate washing was a proper precaution. The employer was held not to be in breach of duty in respect of the claimant's working conditions but was held to be in breach in failing to provide washing facilities. The House of Lords held by a majority that the lack of washing facilities materially increased the risk of dermatitis and that there was no difference between

---

[9]   [1988] AC 1074.
[10] [1973] 1 WLR 1.

this and 'making a material contribution' to its occurrence. The minority held that there was a difference and that as a matter of policy the law should fill the gap in the medical evidence as to the precise cause of the disease.

What then of the mesothelioma victim who cannot prove what exposure was causative so as to satisfy the 'but for' test? The current state of medical knowledge is that mesothelioma as we have seen[11] is always, or almost always, caused by exposure to asbestos but the precise biological mechanism triggering the condition is not known and that it is not known whether there is even a safe dose. What is known is that the more fibres that are inhaled, the greater the risk of contracting mesothelioma but that, once contracted, further exposure to asbestos has no effect. Mesothelioma is of course an indivisible injury, unlike pneumoconiosis or asbestosis, which are divisible and cumulative or dose-related illnesses. Where an employee is wrongfully exposed to asbestos by more than one employer, or even by only one employer in addition to everyday exposure to asbestos in the atmosphere, there is currently no way of identifying, even on a balance of probabilities, the source of the fibres that initiated the genetic process culminating in the development of the malignant tumour. A claimant who has been exposed to asbestos during different periods of employment with different employers and contracts mesothelioma cannot prove which of his employers exposed him to the relevant fibre and therefore, on the standard tests for causation, cannot establish liability for his loss.

Fairchild v Glenhaven Funeral Services Ltd[12] concerned three such employees. The Court of Appeal dismissed their claims on the ground that they had failed to establish causation against any of the defendants. The House of Lords concluded that where each relevant employer had been in breach of its duty to protect the claimant from the risk of contracting mesothelioma and where that risk had eventuated but, in current medical knowledge, the onset of the disease could not be attributed to any particular or cumulative wrongful exposure, a modified approach to proof of causation was justified, as had happened in *McGhee*. 'The rule in its current form can be stated as follows: when a victim contracts mesothelioma each person who has, in breach of duty, been responsible for exposing the victim to a significant quantity of asbestos dust and thus creating a "material increase in risk" of the victim contracting the disease will be held to be jointly and severally liable for causing the disease.'[13] The House concluded that to hold otherwise would

---

[11] See Chapter 2 above.
[12] [2003] 1 AC 32.
[13] *Sienkiewicz (Administratrix of the Estate of Enid Costello Deceased) v Greif (UK) Ltd* [2011] UKSC 10; per Lord Phillips at [1]. The rule as stated takes account of the effect of s 3(2) of the Compensation Act 2006.

be to make it impossible, with the arbitrary exception of single-employer cases, to enforce the defendants' duty to the claimants, such that the duty effectively did not exist.

Subsequent analysis by the Supreme Court in *Sienkiewicz* suggests that the *Fairchild* case introduced a new tort of negligently increasing the risk of personal injury.[14] As we have seen though, this is currently limited to mesothelioma. Lord Roger said in *Sienkiewicz* that, in cases where the state of medical knowledge makes it impossible for a claimant to prove whether a defendant's breach of duty actually caused his disease, there is no reason why a claimant needs to prove anything more than that the defendant's breach of duty materially increased the risk that he would develop the disease.[15] It is hard though to envisage this special rule applying in principle to any other known disease given that mesothelioma is, to all intents and purposes, a carcinogen-specific cancer compared to other malignancies where there may well be a number of carcinogens involved.

Fairchild concerned claimants whose total exposure to asbestos was caused by the defendants. In *Barker v Corus UK Ltd,*[16] the issues were whether the *Fairchild* exception applied where the defendants were responsible for only part of the claimant's exposure and, where a defendant was held liable he had materially increased the risk of contracting the disease, whether he was jointly liable for the whole of the claimant's loss or only severally liable for a proportion of it. On the second issue the House of Lords held that where more than one person was in breach of duty and might have been responsible, liability should be attributed according to the defendant's relative degree of contribution to the risk, so that the defendant was only severally liable for a share of the damage. That part of the decision has since been reversed by section 3 of the Compensation Act 2006, see **3.6** below. On the first issue, the House held that even if not all the exposures to asbestos which could have caused the claimant's mesothelioma involved breaches of duty by his employers, the *Fairchild* exception would still apply.

In *Sienkiewicz v Greif (UK) Ltd,*[17] only one defendant had exposed the claimant to asbestos dust. The Supreme Court upheld a finding that the defendant was liable for the claimant's mesothelioma even though the total tortious exposure to asbestos was modest compared with the total environmental exposure in the area where she lived and had increased the risk due to the environment by only 18 per cent.

---

[14] [2011] UKSC 10.
[15] At [161]–[162].
[16] [2006] 2 AC 572.
[17] [2010] 1 QB 370.

3.5   EPIDEMIOLOGICAL EVIDENCE AND 'DOUBLING THE RISK'

Where the *Fairchild* exception does not apply, the courts have been prepared to hold that causation is established where the claimant can prove that the risk from the tortious exposure was at least twice as great as the risk from any other exposure.

Evidence of the relevant risk is usually derived from epidemiological evidence, that is, evidence based on data from the study of the occurrence and distribution of events (such as disease) over human populations which seeks to determine if statistical associations between these events and supposed determinants can be demonstrated.

In the Oral Contraceptive Group Litigation,[18] Mackay J accepted the concession by the claimants that it was necessary for them to prove that the risk of suffering cardio-vascular injury from taking one type of oral contraceptive was at least double the risk from taking another type. The logic behind this was that if factor X increases the risk of condition Y by more than two when compared with factor Z, it can then be said, of a group of say 100 with both exposure to factor X and the condition, that as a matter of probability more than 50 would not have suffered condition Y without being exposed to X. If medical science cannot identify the members of the group who would and who would not have suffered Y, it can nevertheless be said of each member that she was more likely than not to have avoided Y had she not been exposed to X.

This approach has been adopted to establish causation. In *Shortell v BICAL Construction Ltd*,[19] the evidence was that the claimant had a 10 per cent risk of lung cancer from smoking and a 5 per cent risk from exposure to asbestos but combined together the total risk was 50 per cent. Mackay J held that that the exposure to asbestos had more than doubled the risk from smoking alone and that, but for that exposure, the claimant would not have developed the disease. In *Cookson v Novartis Grimsby Ltd*,[20] the claimant developed bladder cancer caused by exposure to carcinogenic aromatic amines from dyestuffs in his employer's factory and by amines in cigarette smoke. The expert evidence accepted by the trial judge was that the amines in cigarette smoke act on the body in the same way as the amines in the occupational exposure, that the claimant's cancer had been caused by the additive effects of both the occupational exposure and smoking but that the occupational exposure had accounted for 70 per cent to 75 per cent of the total. The trial judge found for the claimant by applying *Bonnington Castings* but the Court of Appeal held that it had not been necessary to do so: the natural inference to draw from the finding of fact that the occupational exposure was 70 per cent of the

---

[18]   *XYZ and others v Schering Health Care Ltd and others* [2002] EWHC 1420 (QB).
[19]   Unreported, Liverpool District Registry, 16 May 2008.
[20]   [2007] EWCA Civ 1261.

total was that, if it had not been for the occupational exposure, the claimant would not have developed the cancer. In terms of risk, the occupational exposure had more than doubled the risk due to smoking and it must, as a matter of logic, be probable that the disease was caused by the occupational exposure. The 'but for' test had therefore been satisfied.

Sienkiewicz v Greif (UK) Ltd was a mesothelioma case in which the *Fairchild* rule of causation was held to apply even where the contributing causes were confined to a single employer's breach of duty and ordinary atmospheric exposure. In the course of her judgment in the Court of Appeal, however, Smith LJ observed (*obiter*) that, 'in other types of case in which there were multiple potential causes, a claimant can prove causation by showing that the tortious exposure has at least doubled the risk arising from the non-tortious cause or causes'.[21]

On appeal to the Supreme Court, observations were made about this approach, again *obiter*. Lord Philips noted that the Oral Contraceptive Group Litigation had been concerned with a preliminary issue as to the effect of epidemiological evidence and not whether the DVT suffered by the claimants had been caused by the second generation of oral contraceptives that they had taken: therefore the decision was of no direct assistance on the question of whether the 'doubles the risk' test is an appropriate test for determining causation in a case of multiple potential causes. He took the view that the evidence in *Shortell v BICAL Construction Ltd* had been enough to satisfy the *Bonnington Castings* test and questioned the need to establish a doubling of the risk in cases where asbestos and tobacco smoke have combined to cause lung cancer. However, he was prepared to accept that, in terms of risk, if occupational exposure more than doubles the risk due to smoking, it must, as a matter of logic, be probable that the disease was caused by the former.[22]

In short, the Supreme Court considered that it was unnecessary for the claimant to show that the occupational risk was at least double the environmental risk before applying the *Fairchild* principle. So long as the claimant could show exposure in breach of duty, causation flowed by operation of the *Fairchild* principle and recovery was joint and several as provide by the Compensation Act 2006. If and when medical science improved then the issue of causation should be revisited under normal 'but for' principles and nothing in the Act changed the common law in this respect.

The Supreme Court in *Sienkiewicz* also debated the question of whether or not causation can be established solely by epidemiological/statistical evidence. A majority of the House did not think that it could but the issue remains to be decided. Lord Phillips was persuaded by the analogy of the

---

[21] [2010] 1 QB 370, at para [23].
[22] At [78].

town with four cabs, three blue and one yellow. When an RTA occurred and the victim did not know the colour of the cab which hit him statistically the blue cab company were much more probably to blame but the law did not make them liable without some evidence above statistics.

3.6   MESOTHELIOMA AND THE COMPENSATION ACT 2006

Medical science continues to be unable to account for the pathological mechanism by which inhaled asbestos fibres cause mesothelioma. As mentioned earlier, it is possible that one fibre might cause mesothelioma although this possibility is probably as fanciful as suggesting that one lungful of tobacco smoke can cause lung cancer.

The real point is that there is no evidence of a threshold dose below which there is no risk – in other words there is no safe inhaled dose of asbestos (whatever the type of asbestos). Therefore, all asbestos exposure contributes to the risk of mesothelioma, and the risk increases in approximate proportion to the dose of asbestos inhaled over time. These features of the disease together with the imperfection of medical science as to causation as well as the carcinogen-specific nature of the malignancy (asbestos) led to passing of the Compensation Act 2006, which enables claimants to recover in full against any one defendant where breach of duty can be shown and despite being unable to show causation.

As we have seen above, *Barker* refined the material contribution test by holding that each defendant was only responsible for damages limited to the extent to which it caused tortious exposure. The House of Lords decided also by a majority that if a defendant was to come within the *Fairchild* exception, even if there were other non-tortious exposures or where the victim was in part responsible, it was only fair to limit recovery of damages to the extent to which the defendant had contributed to the risk in the first place.

According to *Barker*, in such a case the extent of a defendant's liability should be assessed by the duration and intensity of their exposure just as in other disease cases like asbestosis or noise-induced deafness, see *Holtby*[23] above.

There was discussion in *Barker* of the indivisible nature of mesothelioma and whether this in itself was the answer to the question of apportionment. In the event, the fact that mesothelioma can be caused by only one fibre was considered relevant only to the need for the *Fairchild* exception to establish liability and the issue is not relevant to quantum. Lord Walker said that where a defendant, per *Fairchild*, is liable for wrongfully exposing the victim to a risk of damage, it is the risk he is

---

[23]   See also **3.10.1** below.

liable for and nothing more (para 113): 'The damage was indivisible, but the risk was divisible – a matter of statistics.'

The House of Lords in *Barker* noted that this issue was never raised nor dealt with in *Fairchild* itself. Joint and several liability was assumed to be the natural consequence of the decision. The majority in *Barker* decided that it was important to remember that the basis of liability is **not** that each defendant has contributed to and therefore is actually responsible for the development of the condition but that each defendant has caused a risk of the disease developing so that a defendant should only be held responsible for the extent of its contribution to the overall risk.

Despite the MOD originally indemnifying one of the defendants in the *Barker* appeal to the Lords, the Government swiftly overturned the decision in *Barker* by amending the Compensation Bill which received Royal Assent on 27 July 2006. The position in relation to claims arising out of mesothelioma is now enshrined in section 3 of the Compensation Act 2006 which can be summarised as follows:

(a)   A mesothelioma victim (or his estate and dependants) can recover damages if the defendant tortiously exposed the victim to asbestos irrespective of whether the victim was exposed to asbestos by someone else or exposed himself during, for example, any self-employment.

(b)   Damages are recoverable in full from the defendant(s) on a joint and several basis. The damages are not to be apportioned as between the clamant and the defendant(s) even though, for example, only one defendant has been sued who might only have exposed the victim to a fraction of his overall lifetime dose (being more than a *de minimis* exposure).

(c)   The victim can be found to be guilty of contributory negligence if he exposed himself to asbestos during a period of self-employment, for example.

(d)   Section 3 is deemed always to have been in force save for cases settled or determined before the date of the *Barker* decision published on 3 May 2006.

(e)   The recoverability of damages in the above way depends upon medical science not being able to determine on a balance of probability whether it was the exposure caused by the defendant(s) or another exposure which caused the illness.

(f)   The defendant can recover a contribution from others who also caused tortious exposure and to this extent the contribution will depend on the duration, nature and intensity of the exposure, per *Holtby* above.

(g)   Where insurers of other persons who might have contributed to the total tortious asbestos exposure are insolvent and/or do not exist (usually where the exposure occurred before 1972 before which employer's liability insurance was not compulsory), the defendant can seek an indemnity from the Financial Services Compensation Scheme as where a victim finds that a defendant's insurer is insolvent.[24]

3.7   LUNG CANCER

The connection between asbestos exposure and lung cancer had been suspected from the 1930s, but was clarified in 1955. There is a smaller relative risk of its development with exposure to asbestos than there is for mesothelioma, in other words a greater level of exposure is required for the development of lung cancer than for the development of mesothelioma.

3.7.1   Other causes

Lung cancer, unlike mesothelioma, can be caused by a number of carcinogenic substances, only one of which is asbestos. Lung cancer caused by exposure to asbestos is, currently, medically indistinguishable from lung cancer due to other causes. Therefore, if a claimant has been exposed to more than one such substance, there can be difficulties in establishing which of those substances is more likely to be responsible for the disease. It is necessary to prove on a balance of probabilities at least a doubling of risk as a result of exposure to asbestos to prove attribution.

3.7.2   Lung cancer plus asbestosis

The mechanism leading to the development of lung cancer due to exposure to asbestos is unclear and there has been a debate as to whether lung cancer is the consequence of asbestosis or is independent of that condition. Certainly the presence of asbestosis is thought to increase the risk of the development of lung cancer by about four to five times.

To diagnose asbestosis in a live claimant it is necessary to have clinical and/or radiological evidence of diffuse interstitial fibrosis of the lungs and a history of substantial exposure to asbestos sufficient to have caused fibrosis. In a dead claimant diagnosis of asbestosis is made by identifying diffuse interstitial fibrosis on histological examination of lung tissue in close association with asbestos bodies. The Helsinki Criteria (see **3.7.3** below) require at least two asbestos bodies per five micron thick tissue section of one cm².

3.7.3   Lung cancer without asbestosis

There is evidence that lung cancer also occurs as a result of asbestos exposure in the absence of asbestosis. An international meeting of experts

---

[24]   See also Chapter 6. Sections 3 and 16 of the Act are set out in Appendix 5.

who met in Helsinki in January 1977 produced a consensus document on diagnosis and attribution, known as the 'Helsinki Criteria'. This stated that for the attribution of lung cancer to asbestos inhalation, one or more of six factors were required:

(i)   the presence of asbestosis;
(ii)   an estimated cumulative exposure to asbestos of 25 fibre years or more;
(iii)   an occupational history of one year's heavy exposure or five to ten years' moderate exposure and a ten year time lag at least between the exposure and the onset of cancer;
(iv)   a count of 5,000–15,000 asbestos bodies per gram of dry lung tissue;
(v)   uncoated fibre burden of two million amphibole fibres more than 0.005 mm in length;
(vi)   one million amphibole asbestos fibres more than 0.001 mm in length.

Therefore the Helsinki Criteria do not require the presence of asbestosis for attribution of lung cancer to asbestos exposure.

The risk of lung cancer appears to vary between different industries where there are similar levels of exposure to asbestos, perhaps as a result of the different asbestos fibre types present. As a result different risk formulae have been used by some experts suggesting a doubling of the risk of lung cancer at up to 100 fibre years rather than 25 fibre years.

3.7.4   Smoking and other causes

In the general population smoking is a major risk factor for lung cancer. However, in those who have been heavily exposed to asbestos the risk for lung cancer is more than doubled in both smokers and non-smokers. A person's risk of contracting lung cancer increases by a factor of around ten by smoking, and by a factor of around five by asbestos exposure. The effect of both smoking and asbestos exposure then has a cumulative effect so that such a person's risk of lung cancer is increased by a factor of 50. Asbestos exposure is said then to have a multiplicative effect.

Developing evidence as to genetic factors for lung cancer risks may raise further issues as to the proof of causation.

In his speech in *Barker* Lord Hoffmann said, referring to the exception to the 'but for' test in *Fairchild* set out above:

> 'I do not think the exception applies when the claimant suffers lung cancer which may have been caused by exposure to asbestos or some other carcinogenic matter but may also have been caused by smoking and it cannot be proved which is more likely to have been the causative agent.'

None of the other speeches contain references to lung cancer and it is not apparent that this point was raised in argument before their Lordships. However, although this *obiter dicta* might provide encouragement to defendants, arguably it states little more than has always been the accepted position, that to prove attribution of lung cancer to exposure to asbestos it is necessary to prove at least a doubling of risk as a result of such exposure over all the other risk factors.

It is therefore necessary to be able to prove that although there may be potential causes other than asbestos exposure for the lung cancer, of those possible causes asbestos is the more likely cause, and therefore that the exposure to asbestos experienced by the claimant has at least doubled that risk.

On this basis, it may well be possible to establish attribution of lung cancer to asbestos exposure in the presence of asbestosis or where exposure is substantial, even when the claimant has been a smoker. It will be necessary in any disputed claim to have evidence from both medical and engineering experts, and depending on the nature of the dispute also epidemiological experts, to address causation, and to establish whether the exposure to asbestos at least doubled the risk and so was more likely to have been the causative agent.

Causation and lung cancer in the absence of asbestosis was considered at length in a first instance decision in West Australia by Heenan J In *Ellis v The State of South Australia*,[25] the claimant sought damages for the death of her husband from lung cancer. He was a chronic smoker and was also exposed to asbestos at work. He did not develop pleural thickening or asbestosis. The possible causes of his lung cancer were: [1] the smoking; [2] the asbestos exposure; [3] the background risk of lung cancer. In a very long judgment, Heenan J awarded damages to the claimant and ruled that lung cancer was a divisible disease (paragraph 679) because on the medical evidence the cancer was caused and advanced or aggravated by smoking and/or asbestos. He also ruled that the question to ask was:

> '(687) Whether on the probabilities Mr Cotton's two sequential periods of occupational exposure to asbestos acting in combination with his habit of smoking, contributed to the development and/or progress of his fatal tumour ... a not insignificant contribution to the combined causative effect was due to this asbestos exposure.'

The issue of lung cancer was touched on in obiter comments by Lord Philips in *Sienkiewicz*. The application of the 'doubling the risk' test where two causes operate cumulatively and simultaneously was rejected by Lord Phillips who suggested in a lung cancer case where the victim also

---

[25]   [2006] WASC 270.

had a smoking history similar to that in *Shortell* that it was not necessary to prove that the asbestos exposure alone doubles the risk of lung cancer. He said at paragraph 75:

> 'The expert evidence given by both medical and epidemiological experts but based in the case of each I suspect on epidemiological data was that asbestos and cigarette smoke not merely combined cumulatively to cause lung cancer but that they had a synergistic effect in doing so. This evidence was as enough, as I see it, to satisfy the *Bonningon* test of causation, as the victim had been exposed to both significant quantities of asbestos and to significant cigarette smoke.'

This analysis though ignores the indivisible nature of lung cancer unlike the silicosis in *Bonnington* which was dose-related. It ignores *Wilsher* and Lord Hoffmann's view about lung cancer in the presence of both smoking and cigarette smoke in *Barker*. In *Shortell* the court found that the claimant's 5 per cent risk of lung cancer form smoking had been increased to 25 per cent as a result of the asbestos exposure which acted synergistically with the cigarette smoke. Thus 20 per cent of the total 25 per cent increased risk was in whole or in part due to asbestos so that causation could be made out in the normal way, ie on the balance of probability the lung cancer is unlikely to have occurred but for the asbestos exposure. What though of the case concerning lighter asbestos exposure and heavier smoking where it cannot be shown that the risk is increased by more than two fold as result of asbestos? On Lord Philips' analysis causation is still made out (albeit, presumably, subject to apportionment). It is suggested that these obiter comments may not bear closer scrutiny.

3.8   DE MINIMIS EXPOSURE

Clearly for causation to be made out the breach of duty must be in relation to more than trivial amounts of asbestos exposure or, more than *de minimis*. There is though no legal or other formula to apply so as to define what is and what is not trivial or de minimis. Each case must turn on its own facts. Expert evidence is crucial in this respect.

However, in the context of mesothelioma claims very slight exposure indeed can found causation. In *Sienkiewicz* the allied case of *Willmore v Knowsley MBC* was also determined in favour of the claimant. In that case exposure was very slight. The deceased was a pupil at the defendant's school and exposure occurred when some asbestos ceiling tiles were removed and stored in the corridors and in the girl's toilets. There was only limited evidence of asbestos disturbance. The first instance judge's (Nicol J) findings on exposure were described as 'truly heroic' by Lady Hale in the Supreme Court. First instance judges were exhorted in future cases to be wary of being too ready to find material exposure.

Yet given the current state of medical knowledge it will be very difficult for a defendant to challenge the materiality of any proven exposure unless there is a real attempt at comparing this with other sources of exposure. In *Sienkiewicz* the increase in the environmental risk was 18 per cent. The environmental risk was itself very low. Lord Phillips put it this way (at paragraph 111):

> 'The reality is that, in the current state of knowledge about the disease, the only circumstances in which a court will be able to conclude that wrongful exposure of a mesothelioma victim to asbestos did not materially increase the victim's risk of contracting the disease will be where that exposure was insignificant compared to the exposure from other sources.'

Where then in a multiple exposure case it can be said that the defendant's exposure was less than 1 per cent of the total asbestos burden it may well be said by the defendant that its contribution to the risk of mesothelioma was immaterial or trivial so as not to be in breach of duty.

3.9   ASYMPTOMATIC ASBESTOS CONDITIONS

3.9.1   Pleural plaques

Pleural plaques are the most common type of benign pleural disease. There are a large number of, mainly, men who have asbestos-induced pleural plaques which are symptomless. Occasionally plaques do give rise to a restrictive defect in association with very extensive plaques but plaques are usually not responsible for any physical symptoms but of course the knowledge of their presence causes many claimants anxiety about the future risks of malignancy.

3.9.2   The decision in *Johnston*

In *Johnston v NEI International Combustion*[26] the House of Lords reversed nearly 50 years of legal practice by deciding that asymptomatic pleural plaques give rise to no cause of action even where there was an associated psychiatric condition and an increased risk of some other asbestos-related condition. For a cause of action to be complete there must be actionable damage as a result of the breach of duty. What amounts to actionable damage is a fact-sensitive question and the threshold before which a sufficient level of damage has been suffered is not high. However, Lord Hoffmann said in *Johnston* that the law ought not to concern itself with trivial injuries before going on to say:

> '... Damage in this sense is an abstract concept of being worse off, physically or economically, so that compensation is an appropriate remedy. It does not mean simply a physical change, which is consistent with making one better,

---

[26]   [2006] EWCA Civ 27.

as in the case of a successful operation, or with being neutral, having no perceptible effect upon one's health or capability.

8. How much worse off must one be? An action for compensation should not be set in motion on account of a trivial injury. *De minimis non curat lex.* But whether an injury is sufficiently serious to found a claim for compensation or too trivial to justify a remedy is a question of degree. Because people do not often go to the trouble of bringing actions to recover damages for trivial injuries, the question of how trivial is trivial has seldom arisen directly. It has however arisen in connection with the Limitation Act, under which the primary rule is that time runs from the date on which the cause of action accrues. In an action for negligence, that means the date upon which the claimant suffered damage which cannot be characterised as trivial. To identify that moment was the vital question in *Cartledge v E Jopling & Sons Ltd* [1963] AC 758, in which the employees had suffered death or serious injury from damage to their lungs caused by exposure to fragmented silica. At a date earlier than the commencement of the limitation period their lungs had suffered damage which would have been visible upon an X−ray examination, reduced their lung capacity in a way which would show itself in cases of unusual exertion, might advance without further inhalation, made them more vulnerable to tuberculosis or bronchitis and reduced their expectation of life. But in normal life the damage produced no symptoms and they were unaware of it. The House of Lords affirmed the view of the trial judge and the Court of Appeal that a cause of action had arisen and the claims (as the law then stood) were statute-barred.

9. The members of the Court of Appeal and the House of Lords used slightly different words to express the degree of injury which must have been suffered. In the Court of Appeal ([1962] 1 QB 189) Harman LJ spoke (at p 199) of loss or damage "not being insignificant" and Pearson LJ said (at p 208) that the cause of action accrues when "the plaintiff concerned has suffered serious harm". In the House of Lords ([1963] AC 758) Lord Reid said (at pp 771–772) that the cause of action accrues when the wrongful act has caused personal injury "beyond what can be regarded as negligible". Lord Evershed (at p 774) spoke of "real damage as distinct from purely minimal damage". Lord Pearce (with whom all the rest of their Lordships agreed) said (at p 779): "It is for a judge or jury to decide whether a man has suffered any actionable harm and in borderline cases it is a question of degree. It is a question of fact in each case whether a man has suffered material damage by any physical changes in his body. Evidence that those changes are not felt by him and may never be felt tells in favour of the damage coming within the principle of *de minimis non curat lex.* On the other hand, evidence that in unusual exertion or at the onset of disease he may suffer from his hidden impairment tells in favour of the damage being substantial.'

What about the associated anxiety and psychiatric reaction? In respect of a free-standing psychiatric condition, the Lords in *Johnston* considered that a claimant could not recover damages where no physical injury was caused, unlike the claimant in *Page v Smith.*[27] It could not be said that a

---

[27] [1996] 1 AC 155 HL.

pleural plaques sufferer came within the 'zone of danger' test implicit within *Page*. The asbestos exposure occurred many years before and it is the knowledge of the onset of the *disease* which gives rise to the anxiety/psychiatric condition, not the *circumstances which led to the breach of duty*. Mr Page thought he was going to be hit by the defendant's car although in fact there was no collision. Mr Page, however, suffered a recrudescence of his quiescent chronic fatigue syndrome because of the shock of the near miss. It follows that mere anxiety short of a psychiatric reaction cannot elevate the asymptomatic pleural plaques into a cause of action.

There might be scope for argument in respect of asymptomatic asbestosis or pleural thickening which conditions often result in a reduction in lung function because of the restriction imposed on lung expansion which in turn inhibits respiration. In many cases the restrictive component may be so mild as not to be measurable on formal lung function testing even though the possibility of restriction is shown on imaging. In the absence of any evidence that symptoms will ever be suffered in the future then actionable damage will be difficult to make out. There can be no claim where there is less than a 50 per cent risk that the condition will progress to cause symptoms.[28]

In *Owen v Esso Exploration and Production UK Ltd and 1 other*,[29] (which was decided before the House of Lords decision in *Johnston* but after the Court of Appeal decision which was subsequently upheld), the claimant suffered from asbestosis, pleural thickening and pleural plaques. None of these conditions produced symptoms. Even though he accepted that the claimant's condition was worse than those claimants in *Johnston*, HHJ Stewart, QC considered himself bound by *Johnston* in the absence of the claimant showing that the injured condition of his lungs had advanced, that the scarring was extensive or that the damage was such that it was sufficient to diminish appreciably the elasticity of the lungs and deprive them of much (or indeed any) of their reserve capacity. Furthermore, there was no evidence that the claimant was at more than just a low risk of the condition progressing. Had there been such expert medical evidence there may well have been an award in the claimant's favour despite the absence of symptoms.

In a number of cases concerning mild asbestosis in which the argument arose as to whether actionable damage had been suffered in accordance with the decision in *Johnston*, HHJ Walton gave judgment in *Beddoes and others v Vintners Defence Systems Ltd and Others.*[30] In finding for some but not all of the claimants he said as follows.

---

[28]   *Gregg v Scott* [2005] 2 AC 176.
[29]   Liverpool CC, unreported, 16 November 2006.
[30]   (2009) Newcastle County Court, unreported.

'129. It follows that if by perceptible he means symptomatic, I reject ... (the) ... suggested rule that lung fibrosis would have to be found to have had some perceptible effect before it could be regarded as damage. That formulation would as I understand it, also exclude from consideration the extent of lung tissue affected, which for myself I would think ought to go into the equation. The evidence tended to suggest that the greater the area affected, the greater the probability of adverse affect.

130. But I also reject ... (the) ... suggestion that it is sufficient if there is a disease process which is abnormal and irreversible. That errs in the opposite direction: on that test the first appearance of fibrosis would be actionable, without there being any discernible effect at all on the claimants' functioning, and without regard to the area affected, and that seems to me to go too far. While Keenen proceeded on the basis that fibrotic change was itself damage, the evidence in that case appears to have referred to what was visible on chest radiograph, not CT or HRCT scan. The judge was not being asked to identify what level of fibrotic change would be enough for the cause of action to accrue: the choice given to him was between the time when asbestos fibres first entered the body or the later time when fibrotic change was apparent on X-ray.

131. In short, it seems to me that if medical science can identify an effect upon the claimant before he is aware of a symptom, that can amount to damage, provided it is more than minimal.

132. Mr Beddoes. ... has fibrosis at several levels and bilateral crepitations at the bases of both lungs. ... the fibrosis affects between 5 and 10 per cent of his lungs. ... That extent of fibrosis is in no sense trivial and seems to me significant.

133. ... Mr Beddoes currently does not have respiratory symptoms .... Having said that Professor Britton made it clear that in agreeing that proposition he was not surrendering his point that asbestosis was producing a minor restriction on Mr Beddoes' lung function when he engaged in vigorous activity. That restriction was present notwithstanding reserve lung capacity.

134. ... by the time Professor Britton examined Mr Beddoes' crepitations were present in the bases of both lungs. Professor Hendrick accepted in Mr Beddoes' case "a hint of ventilatory restriction", and accepted that he fell four square within Group 2 of the Staples research. Some effect of breathlessness as a result of asbestosis identified on CT scan would at least be consistent with that research. In the result, given particularly the 5–10% estimate of affected lung, I do accept there is in his case what might be characterised as a subtle but real, contribution to breathlessness on activity as a result of asbestosis. The disease will make Mr Beddoes more breathless than he would otherwise have been, to a small but identifiable extent. I accept Professor Britton's estimate of a total respiratory disability of 5 per cent. That has to be apportioned between three conditions, asbestosis, emphysema and obesity, giving a contribution from asbestosis of 1.6 per cent.

135. In my judgment the combination of a significant area of lung fibrosis and an identifiable, if subtle, contribution to breathlessness is an injury which should be regarded as more than minimal. It follows that I consider there is damage in his case sufficient to complete a cause of action.

136. It is sufficient to note that for quantum purposes there being a compensatable injury, account can also be taken of the risk of progression and anxiety. I have already accepted that asbestosis is at least a potentially progressive condition. Dr Rudd thought there was a 5 per cent risk of progression. I think myself that is as good an estimate as any of the risk that Mr Beddoes will come to a position in his lifetime when he will suffer more extensive symptoms.'

As HHJ Walton's judgment shows, recoverability in these types of case is entirely dependent on the medical evidence. Whilst recoverability may be possible where the court is satisfied that there is an effect on the claimant's lung function even though he is unaware of it, clearly the argument is much stronger where there is both objective evidence of appreciable damage on imaging as well subjective evidence of breathlessness even if this is restricted to impairment at the limit of exertion or where lung function would be impaired in the presence of some other unrelated condition.

In *England v Foster Wheeler*,[31] HHJ Bullimore dismissed a claim on the basis that the claimant could not show that he had symptomatic pleural thickening and there was an issue about the importance of the costophrenic angle being blunted before pleural thickening could be said to be capable of giving rise to symptoms.

In contrast, Recorder Baker QC found in favour of the claimant in *Hirst v William Procter*[32] in a case which concerned only a 1 per cent respiratory disability caused by asbestosis.

3.10   APPORTIONMENT OF DAMAGES IN DIVISIBLE DISEASE CASES

3.10.1   The basis

In *Holtby* the claimant suffered from asbestosis, which is a divisible or dose-related condition. He had had multiple asbestos exposures during the course of his various employments over 20 years. He sued the defendant who had exposed him for only about half of this time. The judge deducted only 25 per cent from the damages to reflect the exposure by the other employers. The Court of Appeal upheld the deduction. Why, if the defendant was responsible for only half of the total exposure?

---

[31]   Unreported, LTL 2.10.09.
[32]   Unreported, LTL 21.1.08.

Firstly, the Court of Appeal made it clear that apportioning damages was essentially a jury question and that the exercise ought usually to be carried out in the claimant's favour. It affirmed the words of Stuart-Smith LJ in *Thompson v Smiths Shiprepairers (North Shields) Ltd*[33] (a case concerning noise-induced deafness):

> 'What justice does demand, to my mind, is that the court should make the best estimate which it can, in the light of the evidence, making the fullest allowances in favour of the plaintiffs for the uncertainties known to be involved in the apportionment. In the end, notwithstanding all the care lavished on it by the scientists and by counsel I believe that this has to be regarded as a jury question and I propose to approach it as such.'

Secondly, there was no express expert evidence at the trial that had he not been exposed by the defendant his condition would have been half as serious in any event.

Thirdly, the trial judge found that the disease was an insidious condition which progressively disabled the lungs but where for a considerable period the victim will not notice any symptoms. In this way the condition appears to have been treated not simply as a linear one but one where the symptoms are threshold based and rise in an upward curve rather than in a straight line.

3.10.2   Apportionment in practice

In *Holtby* there may have been a degree of judicial reluctance to reduce the award which would have been the result had the Court of Appeal agreed to apportion on a time exposed basis. However, in respect of other similar cases, Stuart-Smith LJ agreed that apportioning damages on a time exposure basis was the correct approach in law unless there was some unusual feature such as exposure to blue asbestos in some periods but not others.

In *Barker*, Lord Hoffmann indicated that where an apportionment exercise had to be carried out then reference to the duration, the type of asbestos and the intensity of exposure might all be relevant issues.

In practice, because exposure will have taken place a long time ago it is usually very difficult to attempt any real analysis of the degree of any particular exposure in comparison to other exposures so that a time exposed basis is the only realistic method of apportioning.

In *Matthews v Associated Portland Cement and one other*[34] Mitting J apportioned liability equally between the two defendants because it was impossible to do otherwise. Both had materially contributed to the risk of

---

[33]   [1984] QB 405.
[34]   Unreported, LTL 19.10.01.

the claimant's mesothelioma and although there was expert evidence this was based on speculation as to the degree of exposure suffered including the type of asbestos in question.

3.10.3 Expert evidence

In certain cases where the evidence from the victim is detailed, expert analysis of the exposure can usefully be attempted but such cases are probably uncommon and in any event will still involve a considerable degree of speculation on the expert's part. In any event, in a disputed case expert evidence will still be vital where there is uncertainty about the presence of asbestos in the claimant's old workplace. Certainly experts are helpful and often crucial in the investigative process.

3.10.4 Does the defendant have to plead and prove apportionment?

By a majority in *Holtby*, the Court of Appeal held that as a matter of principle it was 'desirable and preferable' that a defendant plead that the disease for which damages are sought has been partly caused by others and that there must be evidence to enable the court to consider the degree of apportionment if any. The claimant shoulders the onus of proof.

3.10.5 Death from asbestosis – is an apportionment exercise necessary?

There seems to be little doubt that a living victim of asbestosis is liable to have his damages reduced where he suffered asbestos exposure from sources other than the defendants.

What about cases where the asbestosis victim dies? Some commentators have suggested that in this scenario damages should be recoverable in principle from each defendant jointly and severally given that death cannot be partially caused.

This commentary must now be doubted. The House of Lords' decision in *Barker* restricted material contribution as an appropriate departure from the 'but for' rule because of the imperfection of medical science and the relative injustice that this causes victims as opposed to employers and their insurers. In so far as this relates to mesothelioma this has been overtaken by the Compensation Act 2006 as above but the *dicta* concerning the test for causation remains, it is suggested, powerful. In an asbestosis case, all exposure increases both the risk and the severity of the condition. It is not necessary and therefore not possible to depart from the 'but for' test so as to rely on only whether a particular defendant materially contributed to the risk that the victim might get asbestosis. The various tortious exposures are consecutive. Damages arising from death are no less capable of being apportioned between tortfeasors. A deceased and his dependants will have their claims reduced in the event of contributory negligence on the part of the deceased where the cause of action arises from the contraction of a disease for which the defendant may only be responsible in part.

If the medical evidence is that but for the defendant's exposure the asbestosis would not have developed either at all or not to the extent that it later killed the victim, then damages would arguably be recoverable in full against the defendant.

3.11 CONTRIBUTORY NEGLIGENCE

The issue of contributory negligence and the extent to which it will serve to reduce the damages has some overlap with the issue of apportionment above – hence some insurers might argue that the victim should have his damages for an asbestos-induced condition reduced on a time exposure basis. This approach ignores the need for the court to look at the totality of tortious conduct in this case, in other words to compare the blameworthiness of the victim with that of the defendant (see Lord Ackner's speech in *Fitzgerald v Lane*).[35]

Contributory negligence was an issue at first instance in *Barker*. The claimant's deceased husband had three periods of tortious exposure:

(i)   six weeks in 1958 for an insolvent and uninsured firm called Graessers;
(ii)   six months for the defendant in 1960;
(iii) three separate short-lived periods during self-employment as a plasterer in 1974/75.

Moses J found the deceased 20 per cent to blame. The extent of contributory negligence was not questioned in the Court of Appeal or House of Lords. Moses J referred to *Fitzgerald* and said:

> 'It is not just a question of length, but also of blameworthiness. A large organisation is better equipped to acquaint themselves with their statutory obligations and necessary precautions, and far better placed to take such precautions. Moreover the exposure, I find, for which the defendants were responsible, was far greater than that which occurred whilst the deceased was self-employed.'

No one knew what the deceased in *Barker* knew about asbestos when he exposed himself in breach of duty whilst self-employed. That the information about the risks involved in working with asbestos was available to the deceased at the time was in evidence. Mr Barker's occupational and exposure history is by no means uncommon. The judgment of Moses J is probably a good yardstick to measure the extent

---

[35]   [1989] AC 328, p 345.

of any contributory negligence in an asbestos-induced illness case irrespective of the condition for which damages are sought.

In *Badger v MOD*,[36] the deceased was found 20 per cent to blame for his continued smoking. He died of lung cancer at the age of 63 as a result of asbestos exposure when employed by the MOD as a boiler-maker. He had received numerous warnings about the damage that his continued smoking was causing to his health and the government had issued the first health warnings about smoking in the 1970s. Despite the warnings he never did stop smoking.

Burnton J ruled that even though the deceased had been specifically advised about the damaging effects of smoking on his health and had been advised to stop smoking on numerous occasions he could not criticise the deceased for starting to smoke because when he began smoking the connection between smoking and serious ill-health was not widely accepted. His real fault was in failing to give up smoking even though he was not so addicted that he could not have given up. The reduction in damages that was just and equitable had to take account of the relative blameworthiness of the parties' conduct. The contribution to his combined risk made by his continued smoking (when he should have stopped) was in the region of a half of his ultimate risk but that did not ultimately determine the level of contributory negligence which was primarily based on overall blameworthiness.

---

[36] [2005] EWHC 2941 (QB); neither breach of duty nor causation were in issue.

CHAPTER 4

LIMITATION

In the field of occupational illness limitation is a creature of statute governed by the Limitation Act 1980 as amended. Unless otherwise stated, references in this chapter to section numbers are to that Act.

4.1   WHY HAVE LIMITATION OF ACTIONS?

Limitations on the time in which claims can be brought exist to ensure that claims are not too stale when they reach court and to give certainty to the parties – particularly the defendant and its insurers who will wish to be able to close their books on potential claims.

In *Robinson v St Helens Metropolitan BC*[1] Sir Murray Stuart-Smith said: 'The Limitation Acts are designed to protect defendants from the injustice of having to fight stale claims especially when any witnesses the defendants might have been able to rely on are not available or have no recollection and there are no documents to assist the court in deciding what was done or not done and why.' He went on to say, in the context of a dyslexia claim against an education authority but potentially of relevance in a claim against a health authority: 'These cases are very time consuming to prepare and try and they inevitably divert resources from the education authority to defending the claim rather than teach.'

4.2   PERSONAL INJURY CLAIMS

A claim founded on tort where the damages do not consist of or include damages in respect of personal injuries must be brought within six years from the date on which the cause of action accrued – section 2.

However, the period is both shortened and potentially lengthened in the case of 'any action for damages for negligence, nuisance or breach of duty (whether the duty exists by virtue of a contract or of provision made by or under a statute or independently of [either]) where the damages claimed by the claimant … consist of or include damages in respect of personal injuries …' – section 11(1).

---

[1]   [2003] PIQR P128.

In this case the claim 'shall not be brought after the expiration of ...'[2]

> 'three years from the date on which the cause of action accrued or the date of knowledge (if later) of the person injured'.[3]

Personal injuries are defined in section 38 as including 'any disease and any impairment of a person's physical or mental condition'.

4.3   INTENTIONAL TORT OR BREACH OF DUTY?

In *Stubbings v Webb*[4] the House of Lords held that section 11 did not apply in the case of deliberate assault as intentional trespass to the person is not an action for 'negligence, nuisance or breach of duty'. This decision was overruled in *A v Hoare*[5] on the basis that it was wrongly decided, putting all claims in tort in which damages for personal injuries are claimed on the same footing, and subject to section 11 and not section 2.

4.4   DOES EXPIRY OF THE LIMITATION PERIOD PREVENT A CLAIM BEING BROUGHT?

The Limitation Act provides the defendant with a defence which it may claim if it wishes to but if it does not then the claimant can pursue his claim. If not pleaded by the defendant, it is not a matter with which the court will be concerned. The Act does not mean that the bringing of an action after the time provided is prohibited.

A claimant can therefore start a valid action even if on the face of it the action is out of time. It used to be a common practice not to refer to limitation in the Particulars of Claim. If the limitation defence was raised in the defendant's statement of case, then the claimant could draft a Reply as necessary to raise all relevant issues.

The situation has changed under the Civil Procedure Rules. The use of the Pre-Action Protocols, with the Letter of Claim and the defendant's considered reply to the claim, should have identified whether or not limitation is to be seriously in issue. Thus it will often be necessary for a claimant to address limitation in the Particulars of Claim setting out matters relevant to sections 11 and 14 and section 33 (see below). If the issue of limitation is first raised in the Defence then the claimant will need to serve a Reply to raise those further matters.

---

[2]   Section 11(3).
[3]   Section 11(4).
[4]   [1993] AC 498.
[5]   [2008] UKHL 6.

4.5 WHEN TIME BEGINS TO RUN

By section 11 a claim for personal injuries shall not be brought after the expiration of three years from:

(a) the date on which the cause of action accrued; or
(b) the date of knowledge (if later) of the person injured.

4.6 ACCRUAL OF A CAUSE OF ACTION

A cause of action for damages for personal injury for breach of duty accrues when damage occurs, that is when there is injury or disease. Until damage is caused, the cause of action is not complete.

There must be 'actionable injury', and 'while such damage need not be substantial it must be more than minimal'.[6] In *Rothwell v Chemical & Insulating Co Ltd*[7] the House of Lords found that developing pleural plaques as a result of having been negligently exposed to asbestos in the course of employment did not constitute damage as it was symptomless and did not cause other asbestos-related diseases.

> '[A]n injury without any symptoms at all because it cannot be seen or felt and which will not lead to some other event that is harmful has no consequences that will attract an award of damages.'[8]

> 'The fact that negligence has produced a physiological change that is neither visible nor symptomatic and which in no way impairs the bodily functions should not attract legal liability.'[9]

Knowing when damage has occurred can be particularly difficult in occupational illness claims. The further query that frequently arises is not when did injury occur, but when did the claimant first have knowledge that damage had been sustained.

4.7 KNOWLEDGE UNDER SECTION 14

The date of knowledge is defined by section 14(1) as:

> 'the date on which the person concerned first had knowledge of the following facts:
> (a) that the injury in question was significant; and
> (b) that it was attributable in whole or in part to the act or omission which is alleged to constitute negligence, nuisance or breach of duty; and

---

[6] *Rothwell v Chemical & Insulating Co Ltd* CA [2006] EWCA Civ 27 at 19.
[7] *Rothwell v Chemical & Insulating Co Ltd* CA [2006] EWCA Civ 27.
[8] Lord Hope in *Johnston v NEI International Combustion Ltd (the Rothwell case)* [2007] UKHL 39 at 47.
[9] Lord Phillips CJ in *Rothwell* CA at 61.

(c)   the identity of the defendant; and

(d)   if it is alleged that the act or omission was that of a person other than the defendant, the identity of the person and the additional facts supporting the bringing of an action against the defendant;

and knowledge that any acts or omissions did or did not, as a matter of law, involve negligence, nuisance or breach of duty is irrelevant.'

4.8   ONUS OF PROOF

Where a claim is issued more than three years after the cause of action accrued the onus of proving knowledge is on the claimant.[10]

4.9   'KNOWLEDGE'

In occupational illness claims the date of knowledge is hugely important and careful consideration needs to be given to what amounts to knowledge. In *Nash & Ors v Eli Lilly & Co & Ors*,[11] the Court of Appeal declined to lay down a definition but said that:

'knowledge is a condition of mind which imports a degree of certainty and that degree of certainty which is appropriate for this purpose is that which, for the particular claimant, may reasonably be regarded as sufficient to justify embarking upon the preliminaries to the making of a claim for compensation, such as taking legal advice.'

Where a claimant held a firm belief which was of sufficient certainty to justify the taking of preliminary steps for proceedings, by obtaining advice about making a claim for compensation, such a belief is knowledge within the meaning of section 14 and the limitation period begins to run. Appropriate knowledge has also been described as knowledge of the facts constituting the *essence of the complaint of negligence*.[12] Suspicion alone therefore is not normally enough.[13]

4.10   CONSTRUCTIVE KNOWLEDGE

In deciding whether the claimant had knowledge of the matters set out under section 14(1), it is necessary to take into account not only the claimant's actual knowledge but also imputed or constructive knowledge. Section 14(3) provides:

'a person's knowledge includes knowledge which he might reasonably have been expected to acquire:

---

[10]   *Nash & Others v Eli Lily & Co* [1993] 1 WLR 782 at 796H.
[11]   [1993] 1 WLR 782.
[12]   *Haward v Fawcetts* [2006] UKHL 9.
[13]   *Albonetti v Wirral MBC* LTL 11/8/2006.

(a) from facts observable or ascertainable by him; or

(b) from facts ascertainable by him with the medical or other appropriate help of expert advice which it is reasonable for him to seek;

but a person shall not be fixed with knowledge of a fact ascertainable only with the help of expert advice so long as he has taken all reasonable steps to obtain (and where appropriate to act on) that advice.'

The test has been said to be that of the reasonable man of moderate intelligence.[14] The test is objective. In a dyslexia claim, *Adams v Bracknell Forest Borough Council*,[15] Lord Hoffmann said:

'I do not see how [a particular claimant's] character or intelligence can be relevant. In my opinion Section 14(3) requires one to assume that a person who is aware that he has suffered a personal injury, serious enough to be something about which he would go and see a solicitor if he knew he had a claim, will be sufficiently curious about the causes of the injury to seek whatever expert advice is appropriate.'

The knowledge test does not allow for consideration of a particular claimant's readiness to resort to litigation, but is an objective test. In *Forbes v Wandsworth HA*[16] it was recognised that a patient who is not cured when he hoped to be might respond by saying 'Oh well, it is just one of those things. I expect the doctors did their best' or he might decide to take a second opinion as lack of success might be because of want of care.

'I do not think that the person who adopts the first alternative can necessarily be said to be acting unreasonably. But he is in effect making a choice either consciously … or unconsciously. Can a person who has effectively made this choice many years later, and without any alteration of circumstances, change his mind and then seek advice which reveals that all along he had a claim? I think not. It seems to me that where, as here, the plaintiff expected or at least hoped that the operation would be successful and it manifestly was not, with the result that he sustained a major injury, a reasonable man of moderate intelligence, if he thought about the matter, would say that the lack of success was "either just one of those things … or something may have gone wrong and there may have been a want of care. I do not know which but if I am ever to make a claim, I must find out".'

Forbes was applied in *Whiston v London Strategic Health Authority*,[17] in which the claimant developed cerebral palsy as a result of brain damage during his birth in 1974. Proceedings were not issued until 2006. At first instance it was accepted that, despite the claimant's mother being a nurse and trained midwife, the circumstances of the claimant's birth were not discussed with him until 2005. It was found that the claimant had neither actual nor constructive knowledge. In considering the defendant's appeal

---

[14] *Nash & Ors v Eli Lilly & Co. & Ors* (see **4.9** above).

[15] [2005] 1 AC 76.

[16] [1997] QB 402 at 412D.

[17] [2010] EWCA 195.

the Court of Appeal noted that the House of Lords had 'tightened up' the requirements of constructive knowledge and accepted that 'the decision in Adams requires the court to expect a heightened degree of curiosity of the reasonable claimant than it would do absent section 33'.[18] The Court of Appeal held that a reasonable person in the claimant's position would have wanted to know about the circumstances which had given rise to his medical difficulties. Constructive knowledge was attributed from when the claimant was in his early twenties. One of the reasons why the court felt able to take a strict, or objective, view of constructive knowledge was because of the room for subjective factors in the exercise of discretion pursuant to section 33, and on the facts of that case section 11 was disapplied by the exercise of that discretion.

4.11   'KNOWLEDGE THAT THE INJURY IN QUESTION WAS SIGNIFICANT' (SECTION 14(1)(A))

The claimant must have knowledge that the injury in question was significant. Section 14(2) provides that:

> 'an injury is significant if the person whose date of knowledge is in question would reasonably have considered it sufficiently serious to justify his instituting proceedings for damages against a defendant who did not dispute liability and was able to satisfy a judgment.'

There was uncertainty as to whether there was scope for some subjective element in applying this test so that the personal characteristics of the claimant, whether pre-existing or consequent on the injury suffered, could be taken into account. That has been resolved by the House of Lords in *A v Hoare*.[19]

> 'The material to which [the test under Section 14(2)] applies is generally "subjective" in the sense that it is applied to what the claimant knows of his injury rather than the injury as it actually was. Even then, knowledge may have to be supplemented with imputed "objective" knowledge under Section 14(3). But the test itself is an entirely impersonal standard; not whether the claimant himself would have considered the injury sufficiently serious to justify proceedings but whether he would "reasonably" have done so. You ask what the claimant knew about the injury he had suffered, you add any knowledge about the injury which may be imputed to him under Sections 14(3) and you then ask whether a reasonable person with that knowledge would have considered the injury sufficiently serious to justify his instituting proceedings for damages against a defendant who did not dispute liability and was able to satisfy a judgment.'[20]

As Lord Hoffmann pointed out:

---

[18]   [2010] EWCA 195 at para 59.
[19]   [2008] UKHL 6 at para 34.
[20]   Lord Hoffmann at para 34.

'Judges should not have to grapple with the notion of the reasonable unintelligent person. Once you have ascertained what the claimant knew and what he should be treated as having known, the actual claimant drops out of the picture.'[21]

Therefore there is a three stage test:

(1) What did the claimant actually know about the injury?
(2) What should the claimant have known (under section 14(3))?
(3) Would a reasonable person with all of that knowledge have considered the injury significant, ie sufficiently serious to justify instituting proceedings against a defendant who did not dispute liability and was able to satisfy a judgment?

Hoare was following in *Sir Robert Lloyd & Co Ltd & Ors v Bernard Hoey*[22] where the defendant employers appealed the decision at first instance that the claim had been brought within three years of the date of knowledge. The claimant had been exposed to asbestos in the course of his employment with the five defendant companies between 1947 and 1992 and brought a claim in relation to a 2008 diagnosis of calcified pleural plaque and bilateral diffuse pleural thickening which was issued on 13 August 2010. The claimant had first developed chest pain in 1984 and 1985. However, he was unaware that this was symptomatic of an underlying injury. Pleural thickening (while noted in x-rays) was not suspected as a cause of the chest pain. There was no failure by the claimant to seek professional help and so no additional knowledge could be attributed to the claimant. The claimant had suffered transient bouts of chest pain in the 1980's but he did not know that he had suffered a 'significant injury' until 2008.

Whether an exacerbation of an injury could be considered separately from the injury itself for the purposes of limitation was considered in *McManus v Mannings Marine Limited*.[23] The claimant in *McManus* suffered from vibration white finger but did not consider the original injury was sufficiently serious to institute proceedings. The claim was brought after the subsequent exacerbation of this injury. The Court of Appeal rejected the defendant's argument that it was not possible to separate the injury and its subsequent exacerbation.

The case of *McManus* has been contrasted to the earlier decision of *Miller v London Electrical Manufacturing Co Limited*.[24] In *Miller* the plaintiff contracted dermatitis as a result of the defendant employer's negligence in 1967 but no proceedings were issued. In May 1971 the claimant's dermatitis became constitutional, incapable of relief and

---

[21] At para 35.
[22] *Spargo v North Essex DHA* [1997] PIQR P235.
[23] [2001] EWCA Civ 1668, CA.
[24] [1976] 2 Lloyd's Law Reports 284.

virtually incurable. The Court of Appeal found that the claim was time-barred. Lord Denning MR found:

> 'In cases of a trivial injury, in which it is not worth bringing an action at the beginning, in that case, if it turns out to be much more serious afterwards, he should be given leave; and it is a serious injury for which he ought to have brought an action within three years, leave should not be given because it becomes more serious afterwards.'[25]

4.12 'KNOWLEDGE THAT THE INJURY WAS ATTRIBUTABLE IN WHOLE OR IN PART TO THE ACT OR OMISSION WHICH IS ALLEGED TO CONSTITUTE NEGLIGENCE, NUISANCE OR BREACH OF DUTY' (SECTION 14(1)(B))

'Knowledge that any acts or omissions did or did not as a matter of law involve negligence, nuisance or breach of duty is irrelevant' – section 14(1). It is knowledge of the injury being attributable to the act or omission complained of, and the legal consequences of such act or omission, that is relevant.

The test is one of attributability not causation and 'attributable' means 'capable of being attributed to' in the sense of a real possibility.[26]

What is needed is knowledge of the essence of the act or omission to which the injury is attributable rather than knowledge of the details of how the case may subsequently be pleaded.

In *Wilkinson v Ancliff (BLT) Ltd*[27] the claimant suffered asthma in 1981 which he believed was caused by inhaling toxic fumes at work. Hospital tests that year confirmed that this was probably the cause but it was not until 1984 that the claimant discovered from the report of an expert chemist that his defendant employer's system of work was faulty which had resulted in the exposure. However, the court found that the claimant had sufficient knowledge in 1981 at the time of the hospital test and therefore the claimant was out of time.

In *Bentley v Bristol & Western HA*,[28] the first instance judge had held that the claimant did not have knowledge of attributability when, following a hip replacement operation, her sciatic nerve was damaged to her knowledge; she only had the requisite knowledge when she knew the operation had not been carried out properly and that there had probably been excessive traction on the nerve. The Court of Appeal in the

---

[25] [1976] 2 Lloyd's Law Reports at 287.
[26] [2011] EWCA Civ 1060.
[27] [1986] 1 WLR 1352, CA.
[28] [1991] 2 Med LR 359.

subsequent case of *Broadley v Guy Clapham & Co*[29] held that *Bentley* had been wrongly decided and that the knowledge needed for the purposes of section 14 was 'that her injury had been caused by damage to the nerve resulting from something which (the treating surgeon) had done or not done in the course of the operation'.

In *Jones v Liverpool HA*,[30] the claimant had suffered injury following surgery in 1974 and knew, in 1997, that his condition was caused by damage to his femoral artery in 1974, that further operations had not cured his problems and that until after the third operation he had not been treated with anti-coagulants. However, until 1991, he did not know that his problems could have been prevented by immediate corrective surgery after the first operation and the administration of anti-coagulants. Nonetheless, he was held to have known the facts which constituted the essence of the complaint in 1977, and consequently at that time had knowledge for the purposes of section 14(1).

In *Whiston v London Strategic Health Authority*[31] the claimant, who suffered from cerebral palsy as a result of oxygen deprivation during his childbirth, had known that he had been delivered by forceps. He had not, however, known that a junior doctor had used the wrong forceps and persisted with them for more than half an hour before seeking assistance from a more experienced registrar who delivered the claimant in less than five minutes with different forceps. The claimant did not have actual knowledge of the facts which constituted the essence of the complaint, though he was found to have had constructive knowledge.

Godfrey v Gloucestershire Royal Infirmary NHS Trust[32] concerned the birth of a severely disabled baby following pre-natal scans which should have revealed the abnormalities. Knowledge that 'the injury was attributable ... to the [defendant's] act or omission' was held to have been present from the birth, at which point it was known that there had been scans, that no indication had been given to the claimant of any abnormalities and that the child when born was very severely disabled. It was not necessary to await the results of a medico-legal investigation to have the requisite knowledge.

While attribution is established as soon as the act or omission complained of is capable of being attributed to the defendant in broad terms, it is necessary that the actual act or omission which causes the injury is known. In *Rowbottom v Royal Masonic Hospital*[33] the claimant's case was that the amputation of his leg was the result of failure to administer antibiotics following a hip replacement operation. It was held, by a

---

[29]   [1994] 4 All ER 439.
[30]   [1996] PIQR P251.
[31]   [2010] EWCA Civ 195.
[32]   [2003] EWHC 549 (QB).
[33]   [2002] EWCA Civ 87.

majority and accepting that it was a borderline case, that prior to the addendum to the medical report to that effect the claimant was under the erroneous belief that the cause of the infection was a failure to install a drain, and not the absence of antibiotics. The claimant did not know that his injuries were capable of being attributed to the omission, the failure to administer antibiotics, until the later date.

In *Martin v Kaisary*[34] the claimant suffered a cardiac arrest and brain damage following an operation for prostate cancer as a result of internal bleeding. He believed that the cause of the bleeding had been the administration of the drug heparin and his subsequent monitoring. Subsequently he was informed that the bleeding was from the operation site itself and not because of the administration of the drug. It was held that the claimant had not been reasonably able to discover the cause of his ongoing conditions until that subsequent information was provided to him.

In *Spargo v North Essex DHA*[35] the principles were summarised as follows:

(a)   The knowledge required is a broad knowledge of the essence of the causally relevant act or omission to which the injury is attributable.

(b)   Attributable in this context means 'capable of being attributed to' in the sense of being a real possibility.

(c)   The claimant has the requisite knowledge when he knows enough to make it reasonable for him to begin to investigate whether or not he has a case against the defendant, or the claimant will have such knowledge when he firmly believes that his condition is capable of being attributed to an act or omission which he can identify (in broad terms).

(d)   But the claimant will not have the requisite knowledge if he thinks he knows the acts and omissions he should investigate but in fact is wrong – or if his knowledge of what the defendant did or did not do is so vague or general that he cannot fairly be expected to know what he should investigate – or if his state of mind is such that he thinks his condition is capable of being attributed to the act or omission alleged but is not sure about this and would need to check with an expert before he could be properly said to know that it was.

---

[34]   [2005] EWHC 531 (QB).
[35]   See **4.11** above.

4.13 'KNOWLEDGE OF THE IDENTITY OF THE DEFENDANT' (SECTION14(1)(C))

As there are often long delays in bringing occupational health claims it can be difficult to establish the identity of the defendant. Over time the defendant company may have changed its name, merged or been taken over by a different company.

The claimant will generally be fixed with constructive knowledge if the identity of the defendant, although not known to the defendant, should have been ascertained by his or her solicitors. In *Henderson v Temple Pier Co Limited*[36] the claimant was injured in January 1993 when she fell while walking down a metal gangway to a restaurant on board a ship. The claimant's solicitors were unable to identify the defendant ship owners until July 1994 due to their misspelling of the name of the ship. The Court of Appeal found that a solicitor collecting facts was not an expert under section 14(3). The name of the ship's owner was something that the claimant could have reasonably discovered without any legal expertise.

However, the date of knowledge could be postponed for as long as it reasonably took to make and complete the appropriate enquiries where the identity of the defendant was uncertain or wrongly stated to the claimant. In *Cressey v Timm*[37] the claimant had been injured at work and brought the claim against the company stated on his payslips. That company was in fact an associate company of the claimant's employer but its insurers admitted liability. The defendant employer's application to strike out a second claim brought against them on the grounds that it was statute barred was rejected as the date of knowledge ran from when the identity of the defendant was known.

4.14 'ACT OR OMISSION … BY A PERSON OTHER THAN THE DEFENDANT' (SECTION 14(1)(D))

Limitation will not begin to run against a second defendant until their identity became reasonably ascertainable. In *Copeland v Smith*[38] the claimant had a road traffic accident in 1993 and issued proceedings against the first defendant within the limitation period. After the limitation period expired the claimant obtained police evidence that a third party (the second defendant) could have been responsible. The second defendant was added five years after the accident and appealed arguing that the claimant should be fixed with the constructive knowledge of facts that his solicitors should reasonably have ascertained within the limitation period. The Court of Appeal found that while the claimant would be fixed with knowledge ascertainable by his solicitors (*Henderson*

---

[36] [1998] 1 WLR 1540; [1998] 3 All ER 324; [1999] PIQR P61.
[37] *Cressey v Timm* [2006] PIQR P9.
[38] [2000] 1 WLR 1371; [2000] 1 All ER 457.

applying) on the facts the claimant's solicitors could not have ascertained the identity of the second defendant until a late stage.

4.15   WHEN DOES THE LIMITATION PERIOD EXPIRE?

Time starts to run the day after the cause of action accrues, and presumably also the day after the day of knowledge. Issuing proceedings stops the clock running. If an incident causing immediate injury occurs at some time on 16 April 2005, or that day is the date of knowledge, then the last day on which to issue is 16 April 2008.[39]

If the last day falls on a weekend or court holiday, then the limitation period does not expire until the end of the next day when the court offices are open.[40]

If although received by the court on 16 April 2008 the court delays issue, then the date of receipt is deemed to be the date of issue – CPR 7PD para 5.1 – and the court stamp on the claim form held on the court file or on the letter which accompanied the claim form should record that date (para 5.2).[41] Wisely perhaps para 5.4 states:

> 'Parties proposing to start a claim which is approaching the expiry of the limitation period should recognise the potential importance of establishing the date the claim form was received by the court and should themselves make arrangements to record the date.'

4.16   CAN THE PERIOD BE EXTENDED BY AGREEMENT ETC?

A defendant can agree not to rely on or otherwise to waive his right to protection bestowed by a limitation period. An agreement should be clear and ideally in writing.

Conduct might be enough to act as a waiver, so that an estoppel was established in *Lubovsky v Snelling*[42] where an insurance company's representative agreed that negotiation should proceed 'on the basis of an admission of liability', and in *Hare v PRs of Malik*[43] where the defendant agreed to conduct negotiations with the claimant on the basis that both parties agreed that the case should proceed and neither should take a technical point against the other.

---

[39]   See for example *Marren v Dawson Bentley* [1961] 2 QB 135.
[40]   *Pritam Kaur v Russell & Sons* [1973] QB 336.
[41]   *St Helens MBC v Barnes* [2007] PIQR P118.
[42]   [1944] 1 KB 44.
[43]   (1980) 124 SJ 328.

However, making a voluntary interim payment where liability was not in question is not sufficient to act as a waiver,[44] and the defendant's failure to respond to the claimant's written request for an extension of time is not sufficient, even though the claimant genuinely understood that the defendant's silence amounted to consent.[45]

4.17 THE COURT'S DISCRETION UNDER SECTION 33

The three year time limit under sections 11 and 14 of the 1980 Act is subject to the discretion of the court under section 33, to disapply them:

> 'if it appears to the court that it would be equitable to allow an action to proceed having regard to the degree to which:
> (a)   the provisions of section 11 prejudice the claimant or any person whom he represents; and
> (b)   any decision of the court under this sub-section would prejudice the defendant or any person whom he represents.'

The Law Reform Committee report resulting in the introduction of the discretion now to be found in section 33 rejected the proposal that the court should have a general discretion to extend time in meritorious cases, but recommended that 'in a residual class of cases' regarded as '*exceptional*' the court should have a discretion to weigh the hardship to the parties and allow the claim to proceed if it would be equitable to do so. However, in *Firman v Ellis*[46] the Court of Appeal rejected an interpretation of the resulting legislation on this basis.

It is clear that the court has a wide discretion to allow the claim to proceed in spite of it having been commenced outside the three year time limit.

It is under section 33 that the subjective matters now excluded from consideration under the objective interpretation of section 14 are relevant and may be decisive, normally as one of the matters to be taken into account in the exercise of the discretion under sub-section (3)(a) as 'the reasons for … the delay on the part of the claimant'.

The discretion applies only to claims which are time-barred by reason of the provisions of section 11 or 11A – Consumer Protection Act claims – or section 12 – Fatal Accident Act claims.

---

[44]   *Deerness v John R Keeble* [1983] 2 Lloyds LR 260.
[45]   *K Lokumal & Sons (London) Limited v Lotte Shipping Co Pte Ltd* [1985] 2 Lloyds LR 28.
[46]   [1978] QB 886.

4.18 PREVIOUS PROCEEDINGS

The House of Lords in *Horton v Sadler*[47] overruled its previous decision
in *Walkley v Precision Forgings Ltd*[48] and as a result section 33 can be
invoked even where the initial cause of action was commenced within the
limitation period and it is now sought to pursue a second set of
proceedings.

Attempts to argue that resurrecting personal injury claims struck out for
procedural failures was an abuse of process have failed. Discretion under
section 33 can still be relied upon (see *Aktas v Adepta: Dixie v British
Polythene Industries Plc*[49]).

4.19 CONSIDERATIONS IN EXERCISING THE DISCRETION

In applying the provisions of section 33 the court has to weigh the
prejudice to the claimant of being unable to pursue his claim against the
defendant, against the prejudice to the defendant of having to defend the
claim after the primary limitation period has expired.

Section 33 requires the court to have regard to all the circumstances of the
case and to pay particular regard to the matters set out in section 33(3).

> 'In acting under this section the court shall have regard to all the
> circumstances of the case and in particular to:
> (a) the length of, and the reason for, the delay on the part of the claimant;
> (b) the extent to which having regard to the delay, the evidence adduced or
> likely to be adduced by the claimant or the defendant is or is likely to
> be less cogent than if the action had been brought within the time
> allowed by section 11, by section 11A or (as the case may be) by
> section 12;
> (c) the conduct of the defendant after the cause of action arose, including
> the extent (if any) to which he responded to requests reasonably made
> by the claimant for information or inspection for the purpose of
> ascertaining the facts which were or might be relevant to the claimant's
> cause of action against the defendant;
> (d) the duration of any disability of the claimant arising after the date of
> the accrual of the cause of action;
> (e) the extent to which the claimant acted promptly and reasonably once
> he knew whether or not the act or omission of the defendant, to which
> the injury was attributable, might be capable at that time of giving rise
> to an action for damages;
> (f) the steps, if any, taken by the claimant to obtain medical, legal or
> other expert advice and the nature of any such advice he may have
> received.'

---

[47] [2006] 2 WLR 1346.
[48] [1979] 1 WLR 606.
[49] [2010] EWCA Civ 1170.

The matters set out in section 33(3) are exemplary and are not definitive. The court's discretion is unfettered.

The issue of limitation should be determined prior to deciding the issue of liability. To rely on findings on liability to assess the cogency of evidence for the purpose of determining limitation would 'put the cart before the horse'.[50] It was argued by defendant appellants in *Raggett v Society of Jesus Trust 1929 for Roman Catholic Purposes and Preston Catholic College Governors*[51] that it was inappropriate for the first instance judge to have determined substantive findings of fact in relation to historical sexual abuse taking place prior to considering whether to exercise the section 33 discretion. The Court of Appeal held that it was a matter for the judge to decide in which order to deal with issues in a judgment. It was found that when considering section 33, the Judge had not directed her attention to her findings as to the happening of the abuse but to the cogency of the evidence. There was no error of law.

Whilst there is a judicial reluctance to provide any guidelines which might unduly restrict the operation of the discretion within the statutory framework, some general principles can be ascertained. In many cases the prejudice to the claimant and the prejudice to the defendant will be equal and opposite. The stronger the claimant's case the greater the prejudice to him in the application of the limitation defence and the greater the prejudice to the defendant in its disapplication. Accordingly, the prejudice to the defendant resulting from the loss of the limitation defence will almost always be balanced by the prejudice to the claimant from the operation of the provision. On the other hand, if it is shown that the claim is a weak case which will involve the defendants in substantial costs in defending it against an impecunious claimant there may be significant relevant prejudice to the defendants if the limitation provisions are disapplied. *Ministry of Defence v AB & Others*[52] involved claims for personal injury said to have been caused be nuclear testing. It was found to be inequitable to exercise discretion under section 33, primarily because the claims were so weak on causation.

Legally aided claimants pose a particular costs risk to defendants, as also may the litigant in person or the claimant on a conditional fee with no or insufficient insurance cover. There may also be arguments that had the claim been brought earlier and before the introduction of conditional fee agreements the defendant would not have been liable to pay the additional liabilities under a CFA.[53]

---

[50] *KR v Bryn Alyn Community* [2003] EWCA Civ 85 at para 74(vii).
[51] [2010] EWCA Civ 1002.
[52] [2010] EWCA Civ 1317.
[53] See for example *Smith v MOD* [2005] EWHC 682.

Under section 33 what is of paramount importance is the effect of delay on the defendant's ability to defend.[54] But with the CPR, an added factor is proportionality. 'The question of proportionality is now important in the exercise of any discretion, none more so than under section 33' – *Robinson v St Helens Metropolitan BC*, approved in *Adams v Bracknell*.[55]

4.20   ONUS UNDER SECTION 33

The burden of showing that it would be equitable to disapply the limitation period rests on the claimant. It is an 'exceptional indulgence' to a claimant to be granted only where equity between the parties demands it.[56] However, according to Leveson LJ in *Kew v Bettamix Ltd*[57] 'exceptional indulgence' means:

> 'no more than an indulgence that represents an exception to the general rule that a claim should be brought within the primary limitation period. Inevitably that casts a burden on the claimant to demonstrate good reason to justify the exception. ... The discretion remains unfettered but its exercise requires justification the reasons for which are articulated by the judge's judgment.'

4.21   SECTION 33(3)(A): THE LENGTH OF AND REASONS FOR THE DELAY

It is only the delay after the expiry of the limitation period that is relevant here. However, when considering 'all the circumstances of the case' the court can include prejudice accruing within the limitation period.[58]

Where the delay is short, a claimant may well be allowed to proceed. So where proceedings were issued one day late, the solicitors having been instructed six weeks after the accident, the discretion was exercised in the claimant's (and her solicitors') favour[59] as also where the delay was nine days[60] and where the delay was five and a half months.[61] In *Hartley*[62] it was said that:

> 'if there was a short delay, which was in no way due to the plaintiff, but to a slip on the part of her solicitors which did not affect in the smallest degree the ability of the Defendant to defend the case because there had been early

---

[54]   *Hartley v Birmingham City District Council* [1992] 1 WLR 968 at 980C, *KR v Bryn Alyn* [2003] QB 1441 at para 81.

[55]   See **4.10** above.

[56]   *KR v Bryn Alyn Community (Holdings) Ltd* [2003] QB 1441 at para 74(ii).

[57]   [2009] PIQR P210 at para 28.

[58]   *Donovan v Gwentoys Ltd* [1990] 1 WLR 472; *Price v United Engineering Steels Ltd* (CA 12.12.97).

[59]   *Hartley v Birmingham City District Council* [1992] 1 WLR 968.

[60]   *Hendy v Milton Keynes HA* [1992] 3 Med LR 114.

[61]   *Corbin v Penfold Metallising Co Ltd* [2000] Lloyds Rep Med 247.

[62]   See above.

notification of the claim, the exercise of the discretion in favour of the plaintiff would be justified even if the plaintiff, if not allowed to proceed, would have a cast-iron action against her solicitors.'

The test with regard to establishing the reasons for delay is subjective, but having established what the reasons were, the court goes on to consider whether in fact the reason was a good one, or whether the claimant is culpable or not.[63]

Not thinking it worthwhile to bring proceedings is unlikely to suffice as a good reason for delay. In *Buckler v Sheffield City Council*[64] the injury was pleural plaques but it predated the case of *Rothwell* (see **4.6** above). When the claimant was informed of his right to sue by his doctor in 1991 the injury had been described to him as slight scarring. The claimant only brought a claim after it was described to him as 'pleural plaques' in 1999 and he mistakenly believed that this meant that his condition had worsened. It was found that the claimant had knowledge of his injury and his right to sue but took a conscious decision not to take action on the basis. Although objectively a 'significant injury' the claimant had thought it too mild a condition to justify action. The Court of Appeal found that there was no equitable reason to justify disapplying the period of limitation.

While poor legal advice may be very relevant as an explanation for delay, failing to take legal advice as to whether a claim in law existed may result in the discretion not being exercised.[65] But the claimant who had done his best to obtain appropriate medical and legal advice, and for example having initially obtained adverse expert medical opinion only subsequently obtains supportive medical evidence, would suffer an injustice if deprived of the opportunity to bring proceedings where there was no significant prejudice to the defendants.[66]

In *AB & ORS v The Nugent Care Society*[67] the Court of Appeal considered the impact of *A v Hoare*[68] in exercising the section 33 discretion in claims for negligence in historic sexual abuse cases. At first instance the Judge found that the claimants had been sexually abused but that the claims were brought out of time as proceedings had been brought long after the expiry of the three year limitation period which ran from claimants' date of knowledge. The claimants appealed against the Judge's refusal to exercise his discretion pursuant to section 33. The Court of Appeal referred to *A v Hoare* which found that:

---

[63] *Coad v Cornwall HA* [1997] 1 WLR 189.
[64] *Buckler v Sheffield City Council* [2004] EWCA Civ 920 (a pleural plaque case prior to the HL decision in *Johnston v NEI International* (see above)).
[65] *Skerratt v Linfax Ltd* [2003] EWCA Civ 695.
[66] *Sniezek v Bundy (Letchworth) Ltd* [2000] PIQR 213.
[67] [2009] EWCA Civ 827.
[68] [2008] UKHL 6.

'the right place to consider the question whether the claimant, taking into account his psychological state in consequence of the injury, could reasonably have been expected to institute proceedings, is under section 33. This consideration was previously treated as relevant to knowledge and not to the exercise of the discretion: see *Bryn Alyn*[69] at [76]. At [49] Lord Hoffmann expressly treated this part of the reasoning in *Bryn Alyn* as wrong. As he put it, sub-section 3(a) requires the judge to give due weight to evidence that the claimant was for practical purposes disabled from commencing proceedings by the psychological injuries he had suffered.'[70]

The Court of Appeal found that the first instance decision failed to consider the psychological factors on the claimants' knowledge of injury or their ability to issue proceedings in determining whether or not section 33 should be exercised. The impact of delay on the evidence was also considered (see **4.22** below). The case was remitted to the lower court for reconsideration of section 33.

It is not possible to lay down clear guidelines as to what are acceptable reasons for delay and acceptable periods of delay. It is a matter of fact and degree in each individual case. Each case will depend on its own facts.

The reasons for the delay and its length have to be balanced against the effect the delay has on the cogency of the evidence (see **4.22** below). In cases where the evidence is largely to be found in copious records, long delays are less likely to persuade the court not to exercise its discretion.

4.22   SECTION 33(3)(B): THE EXTENT TO WHICH THE EVIDENCE IS LIKELY TO BE LESS COGENT

Where a defendant can establish a significant loss of evidential cogency, the action is seldom allowed to proceed. The loss of important witnesses, or a witness' loss of memory of relevant facts, or the loss of relevant documents during the period of delay will be highly relevant to establishing the defendant's prejudice.

A long delay may raise a presumption of prejudice.[71] However, the burden of proving such prejudice rests with the defendant[72] and therefore something more than vague or general assertions of prejudice will be required.

In *AB & ORS v The Nugent Care Society*[73] the Court of Appeal considered appeals against a first instance decision to refuse to exercise the section 33 discretion in claims for negligence in historic sexual abuse

---

[69]   *KR v Bryn Alyn Community (Holdings) Ltd* [2003] QB 1441.
[70]   *AB & Others v Nugent Care Society* [2009] EWCA Civ 827 at para 16.
[71]   *Buck v English Electric Co Ltd* [1977] 1 WLR 806.
[72]   *Burgin v Sheffield City Council* [2005] EWCA Civ 482.
[73]   [2009] EWCA Civ 827.

cases. At first instance the Judge declined to exercise his discretion primarily because the claims dealt with systematic negligence taking place many years before and he considered that the defendant would be unduly prevented from having a fair trial. The Court of Appeal noted that it was no longer necessary for evidence to cover the whole system being operated in the relevant home over the period as the defendant could be vicariously responsible for the abuse rather than just liable for systematic negligence.

> 'In our opinion the difficulties of establishing those matters can be overstated. On the claimant's side the fact of the abuse depends largely, if not entirely upon the evidence of the claimant and must be set against any evidence available to the defendant.'

The case was remitted for reconsideration of section 33.[74] In relation to the second claimant Irwin J exercised discretion pursuant to section 33 finding that the delay was principally because of a strong desire to suppress or avoid the abuse suffered. The cogency of the evidence was not diminished to any great degree by the death of the alleged abuser. However, in relation to the fourth claimant there were discrepancies and conflicts in his account and a significant number of key witnesses for the defence had died. There was a real risk of injustice if the fourth claimant's claim were allowed to proceed.

In *Whiston v London Strategic Health Authority*[75] the claim was brought 32 years after the cause of action accrued. Some evidence had been destroyed, namely the CTG record, which may have exonerated the doctor alleged to have caused the brain injury by negligent delay. However, this was found to be only a small part of the evidence and it could not be said whether it would have assisted the defence case or not. Their Lordships found that it was equitable to allow the claim to proceed as a fair trial was still possible and the decision of the claimant's parents not to pursue a claim earlier should not be held against the claimant.

4.23 SECTION 33(3)(C): THE CONDUCT OF THE DEFENDANT AFTER THE CAUSE OF ACTION AROSE

The conduct of the defendant or his insurers or legal representatives has no effect on the running of time but it is a very relevant factor which may influence the court in the exercise of its discretion. A defendant who is perceived to have impeded the claimant in obtaining evidence such as relevant documents, or to have made it difficult for him to interview potential witnesses, runs the real risk of losing the sympathy of the court. It is not just deliberate conduct which may be relevant; unintentional

---

[74] [2010] EWHC 1005 (QB).
[75] [2010] EWCA Civ 195.

conduct having the same effect can be held against the defendant in the exercise of the court's discretion. It is a matter of degree in each case.

4.24   SECTION 33(3)(D): THE DURATION OF ANY DISABILITY OF THE CLAIMANT

This refers to a disability which arises after the date of the accrual of the cause of action. In *Thomas v. Plaistow*[76] the debate as to whether the disability under this sub-section which might have resulted in the claimant delaying is a legal disability arising from mental incapacity, or whether it can also refer to physical disability was resolved by the Court of Appeal.

'Disability' for the purposes of section 33(3)(d) refers only to the concept of a person under a disability by reason of mental disorder so as to be a patient within the meaning of the Mental Health Act 1983, or now a protected party under the Mental Capacity Act 2005. A disability not amounting to mental disorder or lack of capacity may still be relevant, although not under this sub-section, in explaining the claimant's delay or generally as part of all the circumstances of the case.

4.25   SECTION 33(3)(E): THE EXTENT TO WHICH THE CLAIMANT ACTED PROMPTLY AND REASONABLY ONCE HE HAD 'KNOWLEDGE'

Where the claimant had 'knowledge' within the meaning of section 14 but was ignorant of his legal rights he will not have been able to stop the limitation clock running, but his subsequent conduct may be relevant to the exercise of the discretion. Once he has personal knowledge the court will consider whether there was further delay, and if so, whether it was reasonable. The court is looking to the conduct of the claimant himself, rather than that of his solicitors.

4.26   SECTION 33(3)(F): THE STEPS TAKEN BY THE CLAIMANT TO OBTAIN MEDICAL, LEGAL OR OTHER EXPERT ADVICE

It is the claimant's conduct that is relevant, rather than that of his solicitors. The court has regard to the steps taken by the claimant to obtain medical, legal or other expert advice and the nature of the advice received. A failure to seek advice will lead the court to consider whether or not that failure was reasonable in the particular circumstances. The court is likely to be understanding where the claimant has sought advice

---

[76]   [1997] PIQR P540.

and obtained negative advice, be it from his solicitor, barrister or other expert, provided the claimant has provided them with a full history and all relevant detail.[77]

Where the nature of the advice received is relevant, the defendant is entitled to know whether that advice was negative or not, although the claimant cannot be forced to waive privilege. However, that does not remove other elements of professional privilege. As a matter of practical reality, professional privilege is often waived and the full text of the advice disclosed.

4.27   SETTING ASIDE THE DISCRETION

There are circumstances in which the court might, at a later stage in the proceedings, set aside the exercise of the discretion. This might occur, for example, if on the hearing of the damages assessment documents came to light which indicated that facts were not as had been found in the preliminary issue on limitation.[78]

4.28   COSTS

If a claimant succeeds on a section 33 application, but loses on issues as to date of knowledge, then he will not necessarily be entitled to all of his costs if the hearing is largely concerned with the issues on which the claimant loses.[79]

4.29   CLAIMS FOLLOWING DEATH

4.29.1   Law Reform (Miscellaneous Provisions) Act 1934 claim

'If the person injured dies before the expiration of the period mentioned in subsection 4 above, the period applicable as respects the cause of action surviving for the benefit of his estate by virtue of section 1 of the Law Reform (Miscellaneous Provisions) Act 1934 shall be three years from –
(a)   the date of death; or
(b)   the date of the personal representative's knowledge;

whichever is the later.' Section 11(5).

Therefore a claim by the deceased's estate for a fatal injury must be brought within three years of the date of death or the date of knowledge of the personal representatives, and can only be brought if the deceased's own claim was not statute barred at the time of his death.

---

[77]   See for example *Smith v Ministry of Defence* [2005] EWHC 682 (QB).
[78]   *Long v Tolchard & Sons Ltd* [1999] EWCA Civ 987.
[79]   *Kew v Bettamix* [2009] PIQR P210.

4.29.2   Fatal Accident Act 1976 claim

Similar provisions apply to those in relation to an estate's claim. Section 12(1) provides that:

> 'An action under the Fatal Accidents Act 1976 shall not be brought if the death occurred when the person injured could no longer maintain an action and recover damages in respect of the injury (whether because of the time limit in this Act or in any other Act of for any other reason).'

If the claim would have been barred at death by the provisions of section 11, then no account is to be taken of the possibility of that time limit being disapplied under section 33.

The time limit is set out under section 12(2) where it is provided that:

> 'No such action shall be brought after the expiration of three years from:
> (a)   the date of death; or
> (b)   the date of knowledge of the person for whose benefit the action is brought;
>
> whichever is the later.'

Where there are several dependants, then the date of knowledge provision is to be provided separately to each one of them. If that results in one or more but not all of the dependants being outside the time limit, then the court shall direct that any person outside that limit shall be excluded from those for whose benefit the action is brought – section 13.

Section 28 applies and therefore time does not run against a dependant under a disability.

4.30   SECTION 33 AND CLAIMS FOLLOWING DEATH

Section 33(1) applies the discretion to disapply the limitation period to claims barred by section 11 (Law Reform Act claims) and section 12 (Fatal Accident Act claims). Section 33(4) provides that where the deceased died after expiry of his limitation period 'the court shall have regard in particular to the length of and the reasons for the delay on the part of the deceased' and section 33(5) provides that where the relevant date of knowledge is that of someone other than the deceased, then the considerations under section 33(3) will be modified so that references to the claimant include references to any other person whose date of knowledge is relevant, such as the personal representatives.

4.31 DISABILITY

4.31.1 Who is under a disability?

A person is under a disability 'while he is an infant or lacks capacity to conduct legal proceedings' – section 38(2).

A person lacks capacity in relation to a matter 'if at the material time he is unable to make a decision for himself in relation to the matter because of an impairment of, or a disturbance in the functioning of, the mind or brain' – section 2(1) of the Mental Capacity Act 2005.

4.31.2 The effect of disability

Section 28 provides, by application of subsection (1) and (6), in relation to claims affected by section 11 (live claims and estate claims) or section 12(2) (Fatal Accident Act claims), that:

> 'If on the date when any right of action accrued for which a period of limitation is prescribed by this Act, the person to whom it accrued was under a disability, the action may be brought at any time before the expiration of 3 years from the date when he ceased to be under a disability or died (whichever first occurred) notwithstanding that the period of limitation has expired.'

Therefore a child who suffers personal injuries has a three year period in which to bring a claim expiring when they reach the age of 21.

In relation to a person lacking mental capacity when they suffer personal injuries, the limitation period does not start to run until they cease to lack such capacity. If they never gain capacity, limitation never starts to run.

There is no long stop and no equivalent to section 33 discretion during a period of disability. So in *Headford v Bristol and District HA*[80] the Court of Appeal allowed an appeal against an order striking out a claim because of prejudice to the defendant when brought 28 years after the events complained of by a person under a disability.

If, however, the claimant has capacity at the time of injury, but loses capacity later then that does not suspend limitation. Similarly, if a claimant without capacity at the outset regains capacity for a period then the limitation period is not suspended again when they lose capacity again. The subsequent mental capacity will, however, be relevant to an application under section 33 by subsection 3(d) ('the duration of any disability of the claimant arising after the date of the accrual of the cause of action').

---

[80] [1995] 6 Med LR 1.

PART 2

TYPES OF OCCUPATIONAL ILLNESSES

CHAPTER 5

ASBESTOS-RELATED ILLNESSES

5.1 TYPES OF ASBESTOS AND ITS USES

Asbestos is a term for a group of fibrous minerals known for their thermal resistance, tensile strength and acoustic insulation. It is believed that it was first used around 6,000 years ago by the ancient Egyptians.

There are two mineral groups within asbestos: Amphibole and Serpentine within which there are four primary types that have been used commercially.

Four main types of asbestos were used extensively.

(1) *Chrysotile* is called white asbestos. It was the most commonly used form of asbestos and the most abundant, easiest to mine and considered the least harmful. Its fibres have less strength and less resistance to corrosion that blue asbestos. It is used in fire resistant materials and has had extensive commercial use. There has been debate about whether Chrysotile asbestos causes lung cancer or mesothelioma. Contamination with tremolite (otherwise known as commercial chrystotile) is reported to have increased the risk of using white asbestos.
(2) *Crocidolite* is often referred to as blue 'asbestos'. Its fibres provided better heat and chemical resistance. It has shorter, stiffer fibres and was thus less useful for some applications such as making asbestos cloth or rope. Its fibres are stronger than those of Chrysotile. It has the unenviable reputation of being the form of asbestos most likely to cause serious asbestos-related disease.
(3) *Amosite* is often referred to as brown asbestos. It was mainly used as an insulator or in pottery. It is regarded as more dangerous to health than Chrysotile, but less dangerous than Crocidolite.
(4) *Anthophyllite* was mined in Finland and reported as giving rise to lung cancer and mesothelioma.

Asbestos has been used in the manufacture of plain and corrugated paper, yarn, cloth, tape, cement, mastics and sealants, fire resistant blankets, pipe and boiler insulating material, corrugated roofing, cement wall tiles, wall insulation, asphalt floor tiles, furnace cement, rail and mill boarding, brake linings and brake blocks.

One of the most significant uses of asbestos was as insulating material in the construction and shipbuilding industries for hot boilers, pipes and exhausts.

The importation of blue asbestos stopped in 1972 and brown asbestos importation finished in 1980. The Asbestos (Prohibitions) Regulations 1985 prohibited importation of blue and brown asbestos from January 1986 onwards.

5.2   EXPOSURE TO ASBESTOS

Exposure to asbestos occurred in a variety of ways. Workers who milled and mined rock for asbestos have had high rates of death from lung cancer and mesothelioma.

Asbestos was shipped to the United Kingdom from Canada and South Africa. Loose powdered asbestos was merely put into hessian sacks. These were manhandled by dock workers and fibres were released through the hessian sacking, or sacks were ripped, perhaps with a dockers' hook. In later years asbestos was imported in paper sacks which contained the asbestos more successfully but tended to rip or burst when dropped. Dock workers, merchant seamen and customs officers were all at risk.

Workers involved in the manufacture of asbestos products were at risk of exposure to asbestos fibres. Originally, raw asbestos was tipped by hand into hoppers and mixed with other compounds in open vessels. Finished products such as cloth and rope were cut, releasing fibres. Asbestos board and other asbestos products were finished by sawing, cutting, drilling, grinding, turning, and abrading, all of which liberated clouds of asbestos fibres.

Asbestos contained in a cement sheet is safe, but fibres may be released by abrasion, sawing, cutting and drilling and contact with asbestos cement leads to a high rate of mesothelioma.[1]

Asbestos was used to insulate pipes, valves and boilers in power stations, factories, hospitals, schools, blocks of flats, railway locomotives and ships. Railway carriages were sprayed with asbestos. When old asbestos lagging was removed during the course of maintenance works, the debris fell to the floor and was dispersed by workers and vehicles. Asbestos debris was often dry swept and placed in containers for recycling or for disposal.

---

[1]   GK Suis-Cremer *et al*, 'The Mortality of Amphibole Miners in South Africa 1946–1980', Br.J. Ind. Med. (1992), vol 49, 566–575.

Many asbestos products were used in building and engineering construction to clad structural steel, as cladding for walls, in the formation of partitions, on ceilings (particularly in kitchens) in tiles, as soffit boards, and as gutters and downpipes. Asbestos was used as insulation around pipework, valves, boilers and tanks, and as packing in cable runs. Tradesmen such as carpenters and painters who worked alongside asbestos laggers were also vulnerable to exposure.

Asbestos sheet was installed in ovens, commercial chip fryers, electric fires and other appliances. In the manufacture of these products asbestos sheet had to be cut, sawn, drilled and abraded. Asbestos blankets and pads were used by tradesman such as welders.

Secondary exposure to asbestos dust has been known to occur to workers in the same room or area as those who are primarily exposed. Asbestos dust has often been described as creating a dust cloud that lingers in the atmosphere.

Occupying buildings made with walls or floorboards containing asbestos or in which pipes and boilers are lagged with asbestos creates a low risk of asbestos-related disease. In 1986 the Department of the Environment published the guidance 'Asbestos Materials in Buildings'. This showed that occupying buildings in which materials were made of white asbestos only created a risk of 1 in 100,000 over a lifetime. This risk was 6–10 times higher if the asbestos was blue or brown.

Relatives of workers who were exposed to asbestos are susceptible to secondary exposure. This has occurred when they have washed clothes/overalls covered in asbestos dust.

5.3 ASBESTOS DISEASES

There are a number of diseases causes by inhaling asbestos dust/fibres.

5.3.1 Pleural plaques

Pleural plaques are a benign disease of the pleura (the lining around the lung). Plaques are small areas of thickening of the pleura. They are usually bilateral and are seen on x-rays when they have become calcified. The latency period is usually around 20 years or more following exposure. Pleural plaques are no longer capable of being compensated following the decision of the House of Lords in *Johnston v NEI Combustion*.[2] In this case the House of Lords decided that asymptomatic pleural plaques gave rise to no cause of action even where there was an associated psychiatric condition and an increased risk of some other asbestos-related condition.

---

[2]   [2006] EWCA Civ 27.

However, pleural plaques are evidence of asbestos exposure, and thus relevant to some issues in a claim.

5.3.2   Pleural thickening

This connotes thickening of the pleural surfaces. It can be caused by lower doses of asbestos than are required to cause asbestosis. It is best discovered by a CT scan. The latency period is around 20 years or more. In respect of symptoms, pleural thickening can be associated with breathlessness and can give rise to pleuritic chest pain. Once pleural thickening has formed it may remain static but it may also progress to cause increasing respiratory disability over around 8–10 years in 10–25 per cent of cases.

The presence of asbestos-related pleural thickening is evidence of previous significant asbestos exposure and the risk of developing other forms of asbestos induced illness.

Pleural thickening can occur as a result of conditions other than exposure to asbestos. It can occur as a result of tuberculosis, bleeding in the pleural space and sometimes after drug use.

5.3.3   Pleural effusion

Asbestos may cause the formation of a benign asbestos-related effusion. These usually occur within an average of 13–20 years of exposure and are related to a higher intensity of exposure. They may also occur after longer lower exposure and up to 50 years after exposure. Effusion can be a marker for the development of malignancy and especially mesothelioma. Benign effusions can asymptomatic or can cause pain. They may last for 3–4 months and can progress to pleural thickening.

5.3.4   Asbestosis

Asbestosis, or fibrosis of the lungs, develops as a result of scar tissue in or around the alveoli of the lung. The scar tissue contracts gradually and gradually produces a strangulation effect. In respect of causation, common difficulties involve the differential diagnosis of fibrosis of unknown cause. Other causes of lung fibrosis include silicosis, sarcoidosis, and hypersensitivity pneumonitis.

Asbestosis can be asymptomatic and may not be visible on an x-ray or CT scan.

When asbestosis is symptomatic, problems can include shortness of breath and coughing and chest pain.

The typical latency period is around 20 years. Asbestosis is considered to be a dose-related disease. In 1930 a study of asbestosis in textile workers who worked with asbestos materials correlated fibrosis with the amount of exposure.[3] The severity of the asbestosis depends on the amount of dust inhaled and the greater the period of time over which exposure occurs the greater the extent of the asbestosis.

Asbestosis is typically a progressive illness. It is a marker of significant asbestos exposure. Life expectancy may be reduced if symptoms increase thereby increasing the chance of malignancy.

5.3.5 Lung cancer

Exposure to significant amounts of asbestos creates a risk of developing lung cancer. This develops when lung tissue cells become abnormal and grow out of control thereby forming a mass of cells constituting a tumour. The tumour is commonly picked out from a chest X-ray. A CT scan is typically required to establish the staging of the lung cancer. Symptoms include a persistent or changing cough, breathlessness, blood in the sputum, pain, weight loss and wheezing from the affected side of the chest.

Cancers caused by asbestos are not distinguishable from those caused by smoking. The risk increases with dose or the length of time of exposure.

The Helsinki Group 1997 agreed that a minimum lag time of ten years from the first asbestos exposure is required to attribute the lung cancer to asbestos.

A smoker is at a greater risk of suffering lung cancer than a non-smoker. Selikoff found an increase in the risk by eight times (800 per cent) when smoking and asbestos dust exposure were combined.[4] This study concluded that a smoker is much more vulnerable to the risks created by inhaling asbestos dust than a non-smoker. A smoker has a 10.9 risk of developing lung cancer compared to a non-smoker (1.0). However, negligent exposure to dust increases the risk to a smoker to 53.9 and to the non-smoker to 10.9.

Needless to say the absence of the ability to differentiate between asbestos-related lung cancer and smoking-related lung cancer has led to difficulties when it comes to causation. Some experts look for evidence of asbestosis on the basis that lung tissue is irritated by asbestos fibres and this irritation causes cancer. Other experts do not agreed that this process in necessary. There have been a number of cases decided either way. In

---

[3] Merewether and Price, 'Report on the Effects of Asbestos Dust in the Lungs', HMSO 1930.

[4] IJ Selikoff *et al*, 'The occurrence of Asbestosis among Insulation Workers in the United States', Annals of the N.Y. Academy of Sciences (1965), Vol. 132, 139–155.

McAnerney v Scott[5] the claimant failed to establish that asbestos caused lung cancer where there was no asbestos. In *Parkes v PLA*[6] and *Shortell v BICAL*[7] the claimants succeeded without such proof. In *Shortell*, the claimant's husband had worked for the defendant at a number of power stations. He died from lung cancer. He had been a smoker for a number of years but had given up smoking 20 years before his death. There was no evidence of asbestosis although the deceased did have signs of bilateral pleural plaques together with pleural thickening. The trial judge held that the deceased had more than doubled his risk of contracting lung cancer over his lifetime due to asbestos exposure. His smoking constituted contributory negligence for failing to take care of his health and a 15 per cent reduction in damages was appropriate.

5.3.6   Mesothelioma

Mesothelioma is a malignant tumour of the pleura (lining of the lung) but can also be found less commonly in the lining of the abdominal cavity or the lining around the heart. The name comes from the tumour growing in the mesothelial cells of the pleura which begin to surround the lung. The aggressiveness of the disease is such that the tumour can double in size four times per year. Symptoms include chest pain which becomes persistent and severe, laboured breathing on exertion, coughing, weight loss, fever and fatigue. The mean survival period following diagnosis is only 9–12 months.

Latency periods have been identified as as short as 15 years from initial exposure to as long as 60–70 years. The typical period is around 30 years but often 40–50 years.

Mesothelioma can be contracted from very light exposure to asbestos (theoretically one fibre will suffice). However, the risk of developing mesothelioma increases in proportion with the quantity of asbestos inhaled. Studies have suggested that the length of the asbestos fibres may be relevant to the carcinogenic qualities.

Statistical research suggests that mesothelioma deaths will continue to increase and peaking at around 2011 and 2015 with annual figures of between 1,950 and 2,450.

5.4   BREACH OF DUTY

In all asbestos induced illness cases the claimant must prove on the balance of probabilities the following elements:

---

[5]   21 December 1990, unreported.
[6]   [1983] Davies J, 3 December 1983.
[7]   [2008] Lawtel, Mackay J, QBD Liverpool, 16 May 2008.

(a)   the defendant owed him a duty;[8]
(b)   the duty has been breached; and
(c)   as a result of the breach the claimant suffered some form of injury.

In mesothelioma cases, the claimant does not have to prove that the injury was caused by exposure by the particular defendant he is suing. It is sufficient to prove that the risk of injury was increased by the defendant upon which each potential defendant was joint and severally liable: *Fairchild v Glenhaven Funeral Services Ltd.*[9] The House of Lords introduced the concept of proportionate liability in *Barker v Corus PLC.*[10] This produced an untenable situation of a claimant having to sue all employers who exposed him to asbestos in order to recover full damages. In asbestos litigation, it is all but inevitable that one or more historical employers will be insolvent or uninsured or there may be difficulty in tracking down insurance. Following political backlash, the effect of this decision on asbestos litigation was reversed by section 3 of the Compensation Act 2006.

5.4.1   Date of knowledge

Almost all asbestos cases involve very historic employment. The fact that it is now known that asbestos is hazardous to health is irrelevant in such cases. It is necessary to establish what the employer knew or ought to have known of the danger arising from the exposure to asbestos dust complained of.[11] The employer is required to weigh up the risk in terms of the likelihood of injury occurring and the potential consequences and balance that against the effectiveness, expense and inconvenience of the precautions. Several points arise from the *Stokes* case which are summarised below:

(a)   An employer will not be found to have fallen below the standard expected of a reasonable and prudent employer if he followed a recognised practice, unless it was clearly bad practice.
(b)   An employer must keep reasonably abreast of developing knowledge and not be too slow to apply it.
(c)   It is not a defence for a defendant to say that he was not aware that a risk of pulmonary injury might arise from his actions.
(d)   It is no defence for an employer to rely upon the fact that his industry was generally not aware of the risk without further information about the general state of knowledge being available.

---

[8]   *Caparo v Dickman* [1990] 2 AC 605: the claimant must prove sufficient foreseeability of damage of the type he suffered; sufficient proximity between the claimant and the defendant to impose a duty; and it must be fair, just and reasonable to impose a duty. The defendant does not have to foresee the particular disease or illness but instead the risk of some pulmonary injury: *Page v Smith* [1996] 1 AC 155, HL.
[9]   [2002] UKHL 22.
[10]   [2006] UKHL 20.
[11]   *Stokes v Guest, Keen and Nettlefold (Bolts and Nuts) Ltd* [1968] 1 WLR 1776.

There are varying dates of knowledge emanating from a number of sources such as reports, Regulations and governmental papers. Here is a summary of the date of knowledge in respect of establishing a common law duty of care:[12]

YEAR	KNOWLEDGE
From the mid 1920s	Certain factory occupiers and employers could be found to have knowledge of the risk to their employees from prolonged and heavy exposure to asbestos. Those outside the factory exposed at the same level as those inside the factory would also be owed a duty.
1932	Asbestos Industry Regulations impose duties on factories that might previously not have had a common law duty. By this time, substantial and prolonged exposure to asbestos was clearly dangerous.
1945	Shipbuilding and ship repairing industry receive a letter from Chief Inspector– put on notice of problems and given suggestions.
1949	The reasonable employer should know that care is needed to be taken with asbestos.
1955	Employers should know that there is no safe level of asbestos exposure and that substantial exposure should be lowered to lowest level reasonably practicable. Lower exposures continue to be the subject of emerging knowledge.
1960	Should be possible to fix knowledge of the dangers of asbestos dust on all employers and occupiers, even of those working outside factories.
1965	Employers should be aware of harm of small amounts of asbestos, not only to workers but to their family. Uncertain hazard and clear that reduction of level of exposure imperative.
1967	Employers should know that the only safe course is to eliminate the escape of asbestos dust into the air.

Statutory duty has slowly evolved through the 20th century. A summary of the statutory duties is tabled below:[13]

---

[12]   *Asbestos Claims: Law, Practice and Procedure*, 2nd edn (9 Gough Square).
[13]   *Asbestos Claims: Law, Practice and Procedure*, 2nd edn (9 Gough Square).

STATUTE/REGS	DATES IN FORCE	RELEVANT PROVISIONS	FACTORIES	SHIPBUILDING/ SHIP REPAIRING	CONSTRUCTION
Asbestos Industry Regulations 1931	1 March 1932-14 May 1970	All	Applies	Applies	Applies only in very limited circumstances
Factories Act 1937	1 July 1938–1 April 1962	Sections 4 and 47	Applies	Applies	Applies in limited circumstances
Building (Safety, Health and Welfare Regulations) 1948	1 October 1948–1 March 1962	Regulation 82	Does not apply	Does not apply	Applies to certain circumstances
Shipbuilding and Ship Repairing Regulations 1960	31 March 1961–1 October 1989	Regulations 53 and 76	Does not apply	Applies to operations on vessels in shipyards, not in shipyards alone	Does not apply
Factories Act 1961	1 April 1962–1 January 1993	Sections 4 and 63	Applies	Applies	Applies in limited circumstances
Constructions (General Provisions) Regulations 1961	1 March 1962–14 May 1988	Regulation 20	Does not apply	Does not apply	Applies in certain circumstances

STATUTE/REGS	DATES IN FORCE	RELEVANT PROVISIONS	FACTORIES	SHIPBUILDING/ SHIP REPAIRING	CONSTRUCTION
Construction (Working Places) Regulations 1966	1 August 1966–2 September 1996	Regulation 6(2)	Does not apply	Does not apply	Applies in certain circumstances
Asbestos Regulations 1969	14 May 1970–1 March 1988	All	Applies	Applies	Applies
Control of Asbestos at Work Regulations 1987	1 March 1988	All	Applies	Applies	Applies

5.4.2   Causation

Dose-related (or known as divisible diseases) are distinct from indivisible diseases. Pleural plaques, pleural thickening and asbestosis are examples of the former. Lung cancer and mesothelioma are examples of the latter.

In dose-related litigation, where liability is established against one or more defendants in respect of a divisible injury, damages against each defendant are apportioned in accordance with the dose for which they are responsible. The dose is determined by the duration and level of the exposure he caused.

As mentioned above, section 3 of the Compensation Act 2006 had the effect of removing the injustice arising from the House of Lords decision in *Barker v Corus PLC*. A mesothelioma victim or his estate can recover damages if the defendant tortuously exposed the victim to asbestos irrespective of whether the victim was exposed to asbestos by someone else (or even if he exposed himself to asbestos in self employment). There is no apportionment between potential tortfeasors. Defendants can recover a contribution from others who exposed the victim to asbestos. However, the Act only applies to mesothelioma cases. The problem of proportionate liability still exists with regards to lung cancer.

Although the common test of causation is the well known 'but for' test, the Supreme Court in *Sienkiewicz (PR of the estate of Enid Costello v Grief (UK) Ltd)*[14] suggests that the departure from this test was only permitted in cases concerning mesothelioma and warned against any future departure from the standard test of causation. This alternative test considered in *Sienkiewicz* is the 'Increasing the Risk' test. In *Fairchild v Glenhaven Funeral Services*[15] the Court of Appeal dismissed the claims of three employees on the ground that they had failed to establish causation against any of the defendants. The House of Lords concluded that where each relevant employer had been in breach of its duty to protect the claimant from the risk of contracting mesothelioma and where the risk had eventuated but the onset of the disease could not be attributed to any particular or cumulative wrongful exposure, a modified approach to causation was justified because the state of medical knowledge made it impossible for a claimant to prove which breach of duty caused the disease. The claimant simply needed to prove an increased risk that he would develop the disease. In *Sienkiewicz*, the Supreme Court decided that it was unnecessary for the claimant to show that the occupational risk as at least double the environmental risk before applying the *Fairchild* principle. If the clamant could show exposure in breach of duty, then causation flowed by operation of the *Fairchild* principle and recovery was joint and several as provided by the Compensation Act 2006.

---

[14]   [2011] UKSC 10.
[15]   [2011] UKSC 10.

5.4.3   Apportionment of damages

In *Holtby v Brigham & Cowan (Hull) Ltd*[16] the claimant suffered from asbestosis which is a divisible or dose-related condition. He had experienced multiple asbestos exposures during the course of his various employments over 20 years. He sued the defendant who had exposed him for only about half of this time. The judge deducted 25 per cent from the damages to reflect the exposure by the other employers. The Court of Appeal upheld the deduction. The exercise of apportioning should usually be carried out in the claimant's favour. Furthermore there had been no expert evidence at the trial going to the issue of exposure and its attribution to the condition. In addition the disease was insidious which progressively disabled the lungs after a considerable period in which the victim would not notice any symptoms.

5.4.4   Contributory negligence

A victim's damages can be reduced smoking and by for example, self employed periods of exposure to asbestos. In *Badger v MOD*[17] the deceased was found 20 per cent to blame for his continued smoking. He died of lung cancer at the age of 63 as a result of asbestos exposure when employed by the MOD as a boiler-maker. He had received warnings about the damage that his smoking was causing to his health. Burnton J concluded that the deceased could not be criticised for starting smoking because at that time there was no widely accepted link between smoking and serious ill-health. He had, however, failed to give up smoking despite persistence advice. The reduction in damages had to take into account the relative blameworthiness of the parties' conduct. Although the contribution to the combined risk by smoking was around half, that did not determine the level of contributory negligence which was based overall on blameworthiness.

5.5   SPECIFIC CONSIDERATIONS FOR ASBESTOS-RELATED CLAIMS

5.5.1   Medical diagnosis

Type of asbestos-related disease:

- pleural plaques;
- pleural fibrosis/thickening;
- asbestosis;
- lung cancer;
- mesothelioma.

---

[16]   [2000] 3 All ER 421.
[17]   [2005] EWHC 2941 (QB).

Is there an non-asbestos alternative diagnosis for the symptoms?

5.5.2   Applicable law

- Common law negligence.
- Asbestos Industry Regulations 1931.
- Regulation 18 of the Shipbuilding Regulations 1931.
- Section 4(1) of the Factories Act 1937.
- Section 47(1) of the Factories Act 1937.
- Regulation 82 of the Building (Safety Health and Welfare) Regulations 1948.
- Regulation 53(1) of the Ship and Ship-Repairing Regulations 1960.
- Regulation 76(1) of the Ship and Ship-Repairing Regulations 1960.
- Section 29(1) of the Factories Act 1961.
- Section 41(1) of the Factories Act 1961.
- Section 63 of the Factories Act 1961.
- Regulation 20 of the Construction (General Provisions) Regulations 1961.
- Asbestos Regulations 1969.
- Control of Asbestos at Work Regulations 1987.
- Management of Health and Safety at Work Regulations 1992.
- Workplace (Health, Safety and Welfare) Regulations 1992.
- Management of Health and Safety at Work Regulations 1999.
- Control of Asbestos at Work Regulations 2002.

5.5.3   Exposure

When:

- differing states of knowledge of the risks from asbestos exposure;
- long latency period for development of asbestos disease, certainly 10 years and probably 15–40 years or more.

Where:

- detailed circumstances of the workplace.

Type of work:

- removing lagging, mixing dry asbestos, applying lagging, drilling, cutting, sawing.

Degree of exposure:

- ventilation;
- protective equipment

  (a)   masks
      (i)   type

(ii)   effectiveness – glasses – beard
(b)   overalls.

5.5.4   Causation
- Did that degree of exposure create at the time a foreseeable risk of injury; and/or was there a breach of statutory duty at that time?

5.5.5   Apportionment of damages

If disease not dose-related (lung cancer and mesothelioma) will there be apportionment in respect of non-actionable 'innocent' exposure and 'guilty' exposure?

5.5.6   Limitation
- When was the tort completed; and/or
- When was any breach of statutory duty actionable?
- Limitation Act 1980, ss 11 and 14.
- Discretion to waive the time-limit under s 33 of the Limitation Act 1980.

5.5.7   Medical prognosis
- How is the diagnosed condition likely to progress?
- What are the chances of contracting other asbestos-related conditions?
- Provisional damages.

5.5.8   Damages
- General damages.
- Handicap on the labour market.
- Loss of earnings.
- Cost of treatment, care and aids.

CHAPTER 6

NOISE-RELATED CONDITIONS

6.1   INTRODUCTION

Noise may cause nuisance and disturbance, but at levels commonly experienced in everyday living it does not cause damage to hearing. Hearing may be damaged by a single noise of great intensity, such as an explosion or the noise from a high-revving jet engine, but we are concerned here with exposure to high levels of noise which tend to cause damage over a long period of time.

The human ear is designed to intercept sound pressure waves which are created by noise, and to transmit the noise to the brain for interpretation. Without attempting to explain the workings of the ear, it is enough for the purposes of this book to understand that sound waves stimulate acoustic receptor cells, and it is damage to these receptor cells by excessive noise which causes hearing loss and/or tinnitus.

The ear receives and interprets sound waves of different intensity. The intensity of the noise, or sound pressure level, is measured in decibels (db). Put in simple terms the higher the decibel reading, the louder the noise. Decibels are measured on a logarithmic scale, so that doubling a sound pressure level is represented by an additional three decibels. Thus, 93db is twice as loud as 90db.

The use of a logarithmic scale of measurement means that it is not possible to take the decibel readings from two or more machines and add them together to obtain the total sound level produced when the machines are operating together.

Sound waves occur in different frequencies and/or wavelengths. The different frequencies are measured in hertz (hz) and kilohertz (Khz), so that 3000hz is equivalent to 3Khz. The basic unit of frequency is one cycle per second (1hz). Human speech uses the range of frequencies between 0.25Khz and 8Khz, although most speech is contained between the frequencies of 1Khz and 4Khz. The ear receives a mixture of sounds across this range of frequencies. Frequencies will differ according to the noise being created; thus a flute and drum produce noise of different frequencies but both sounds are heard at the same time. Damage to hearing occurs across the frequencies but is not evenly distributed. More damage from excessive noise is sustained as frequencies increase from 0.25Khz, usually peaking at 4Khz and then declining slightly.

The ear is more vulnerable to injury from noise in the range at 4Khz to 6Khz. Leaving aside the single extreme noise of, for example, an explosion, injury to the ear occurs only gradually. Prolonged exposure to noise in the vulnerable frequencies at a noise intensity of 90db or more is liable to result in hearing loss. At lower frequencies, for example 1Khz, and at higher frequencies, for example 8Khz, the ear is not so vulnerable. Noise in these low and high frequencies is subjectively less 'loud', even though the noise may exceed 90db. It is for this reason that these frequencies are adopted as the 'anchor points' to establish the age associated hearing loss percentiles for ISO 7029 (1984). Higher noise levels are required before damage is sustained in those high and low frequencies. To take account of these features, noise meters give different weight to the sound levels measured. Noise meters measure sound intensity across all frequencies and then give greater significance to sounds within the middle frequencies, so as to take these factors into account. An adjusted measurement is referred to as being 'A weighted'. Thus the notation used is 'dbA' or 'dBA'.

Generally, damage to hearing occurs from prolonged exposure to noise levels in excess of 90db. Thus the concept of the 'noise-dose' received by a worker is important. Some people's hearing is more vulnerable, which may cause problems of foreseeability in cases concerning noise-related illness. As a basic approach, for damage to occur exposure must have been in excess of 90db for 8 hours a day for 5 days a week for a number of years, commonly 5 years or more. Since noise levels are not constant and work routines may differ a total noise-dose must be calculated. The lower the noise-dose the less risk there is to the worker. The noise-dose is referred to as the 'Leq' – a slightly curious abbreviation of 'equivalent sound level'.

Taking as the base line 90db for 8 hours a day for 5 days a week, exposure to 90db for less than 40 hours a week will put the worker in a lower risk category. Unless the employer knows that his employee is particularly susceptible to noise, liability will not be established. Since noise levels frequently exceed 90db the length of the exposure to noise at that higher level is important. It will be recalled that a doubling of the sound intensity from 90db gives a measurement of 93db. If the noise intensity has doubled the same noise-dose will be received in half the time. Thus exposure at 93db for 4 hours a day is the same as exposure to 90db for 8 hours a day.

The following table may be helpful:

90db for 8 hours
93db for 4 hours

96db for 2 hours
99db for 1 hour
102db for 30 minutes
105db for 15 minutes
108db for 7 minutes 30 seconds
111db for 3minutes 45 seconds

The following examples may also be of assistance:

rivetting – 130dbA
unmuffled road drill – 115dbA
power tools – 100dbA

6.2   THE AUDIOGRAM

An audiogram is a graph showing the results of measurements taken of the claimant's hearing ability. The points on the graph represent the threshold between hearing and deafness. Noise frequencies are marked along the bottom horizontal axis and the hearing level is marked on the vertical axis. The points are obtained by a relatively simple test. The patient/claimant is fitted with earphones and a tone is played. The patient is asked to say when he can discern the tone. That point is recorded. A random selection of tones is played at different frequencies and at different noise intensity levels. The results obtained are then averaged over the main frequencies 1Khz, 2Khz, 3Khz and 4Khz and often at lower and higher frequencies to give a more complete picture.

The results of an audiogram test can be affected by whether the patient/claimant has recently been exposed to loud noise. The test can also be affected by different machines or tests on different days, usually because of the calibration of the machine or technique of the operator. Thus variations of 5db are not regarded as significant when comparing audiograms from different dates.

A typical audiogram of a person who has suffered damage to his hearing by prolonged exposure to high levels of noise shows a worsening of hearing ability at about 4Khz. This 'spike' on the graph is often referred to as 'the notch at 4Khz'.

Here is a sample audiogram

The results for the right ear are shown by an 'O' and the results for the left ear are shown by an 'X'.

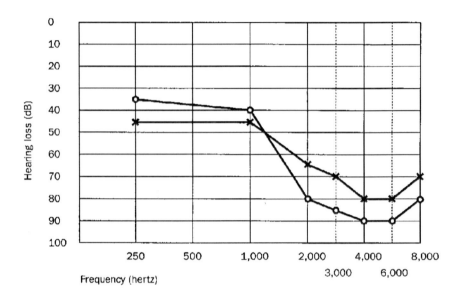

Frequency (hertz)

6.3   INTERPRETATION

It must be borne in mind that the audiogram is only part of the process of diagnosis. A person with perfect hearing would produce a graph which runs horizontally along the top line, showing a nil decibel loss. The reading will usually be around the 5db level. With increasing age this background level of hearing loss will increase. In the example audiogram graph there is good hearing in the lower frequencies but a much more marked hearing loss for sound at the frequency of 4Khz.

The graph illustrates that the hearing loss is not uniform. Nor is it correct to say that the patient/claimant is deaf, although the term 'deaf' is commonly used for people who have reduced hearing ability. Musical low notes and very high notes might be reasonably clear, but the middle and high notes cause difficulties. Some sounds can be heard clearly, but others cannot be picked out from the background of sounds. Speech discrimination takes place at frequencies around 4Khz. Where the loss of hearing is higher at around this frequency, speech becomes distorted to the listener, and particularly affects sibilant sounds. A person may be aware of sound when someone is talking, but may be unable to make out what is being said. People with normal hearing experience this distortion if the background noise in a pub or club, for example, is very loud.

Damage suffered at different frequencies means that hearing loss cannot be overcome merely by turning up the volume of the television, for example. Modern, more expensive hearing aids are now available which amplify some frequencies more than others. Such hearing aids may be an item of special damage in legal proceedings.

An audiogram is only one of the diagnostic tools, albeit a very important one. The claimant's medical history is also important – head injuries and certain medications can cause hearing loss. A claimant's working history is also important, as are his hobbies. For example, the claimant may be a guitarist in an amateur rock band; alternatively, service in the armed forces or shooting game and rabbits may explain some or all of the hearing loss.

An audiogram is usually carried out using air conduction. Tones are played directly into the ear and conveyed to the ear drum. However, audiograms may also be performed using bone conduction. Here the sound is conveyed to the ear drum along the bony structures in the skull. In normal cases the results will be similar. However, if there is damage to the ear canal or other part of the outer ear caused by something other than prolonged noise exposure, a bone conduction audiogram will show better results. The bone conduction method is used particularly where a person's history or medical records suggest a cause of hearing loss other than exposure to noise. This method can also help to identify a malingerer. If malingering is suspected, other more objective tests may be used, such as invoked response audiometry. The medical expert will advise on whether such testing is needed.

6.4   CALCULATING THE HEARING LOSS

A short-cut method of comparing different cases has been developed which averages hearing loss in both ears over either 1Khz, 2Khz and 3Khz or over 1Khz, 2Khz and 4Khz. The first set of ranges is used in assessing industrial disablement benefit. Given the importance of loss of hearing at 4Khz, it might be thought that the second set of ranges is better, but this would ignore loss of hearing at 3Khz, which is usually more than loss at 2Khz but less than loss at 4Khz. The system has been called arbitrary and unsophisticated. It is suggested that where it is possible, comparison is best made by looking at the readings for 1Khz, 2Khz, 3Khz and 4Khz for each ear. Where this is not possible it is necessary to understand how the averaging systems work.

An average hearing loss for each ear is calculated by taking readings from the audiogram for the frequencies used for the right ear, adding them together and dividing by three. This process is repeated for the readings for the left ear.

The calculation of the loss for both ears (the bilateral loss), involves making an allowance for the ear which has less hearing damage since this ear helps with overall hearing ability. The allowance is made by multiplying the result for the better ear by 4, adding that to the average for the worst ear and then dividing that sum by 5 to produce an average for both ears.

Example

If the hearing losses for the right ear at 1Khz, 2Khz and 4Khz are 15db, 20db and 55db, the average for the right ear is 30db.

If the hearing losses for the left ear at 1Khz, 2Khz and 4Khz are 10db, 15db and 35db, the average for the left ear is 20db.

Thus the bilateral average is:

$$30 + (20 \times 4) \div 5 = 30 + 80 \div 5 = 110 \div 5 = 22db$$

Arguments may be raised by the defendant about the degree to which a claimant would have suffered hearing loss by reason of advancing age even without exposure to noise at work. Such loss can usually be calculated as an average figure. A defendant may then argue that compensation should be reduced to take account of this natural hearing loss. However, two things must be borne in mind. First, hearing loss due to age would have been relatively moderate on its own. The hearing loss caused by the defendant's negligence is in addition to this normal age-related loss and causes the extra handicap. The defendant must take the claimant as he finds him.[1] Secondly, most claimants are of middle age or more and would have suffered age-related loss in any case. A younger claimant would have developed age-related loss inevitably as he got older and thus he should be compensated for his total handicap.

6.5   AWARENESS OF DATA-COLLECTION METHODS

Measurements of sound levels should be taken using the weighted scale of dbA (dBA) as discussed above. Measurements in some early cases were unweighted.

It may be significant to know when the sound meter was calibrated, so as to keep it accurate. It is also necessary to consider for how long sampling of sound levels was taken and whether this gave representative readings of the sound levels experienced throughout the working period.

The positioning of the sound meter can be important in obtaining an accurate measurement of the noise created and received by the worker. Noise surveys undertaken in earlier years tended to measure noise levels at the machine. It was then a matter of evidence as to where the claimant worked in relation to the machine or a particular part of the machine. Subsequently, measurements were made by positioning the meter microphone near to the worker's ear in order to give a more accurate reading of the noise levels experienced by the individual.

---

[1]   *Smith v Leech Brain* [1962] 2 QB 405.

Consideration must be given to whether the measurements taken many years previously continue to be representative of noise levels experienced in later years. Were new machines installed, old machines scrapped, more machines put to work, or baffles and screens introduced?

6.6   HEARING PROTECTION

It will be a matter of evidence in each case as to what type of ear protection was provided at the relevant time. Although provision of ear protection may have been suitable for that time, the way in which it was used may not have been appropriate. There is significant information in the public domain that the 'real world' attenuation of hearing protectors is substantially less than claimed by manufacturers. This is typically because of poor fit, and overuse.

The first type of hearing protection provided was generally bilsom wool. This was usually dispensed in a long roll, and pieces were pulled off and pushed into the ear, like cotton wool. The degree of protection offered by bilsom wool was around 10db.

Subsequently, foam ear-plugs were provided. These were rolled and squeezed so that they could be inserted completely in the ear, where they would expand to fill the ear canal. If they were not properly fitted they would not provide the claimed maximum protection of between 20db and 28db depending on the product. Some training was required to obtain an effective fit, and training was required to prevent workers falling into careless habits. Ear-plugs needed to be replaced from time to time.

Ear muffs have a hard outer section containing sound insulating material and an outer seal of foam or fluid-filled. A pair of ear muffs were provided with a plastic band to hold them on the head and over the ears. If the seal was not effective, sound attenuation was not effective. The seal could be damaged if the muffs were worn over a hard-hat or other protective equipment. Spectacle arms also reduced the effectiveness of the seal. The seal itself needed replacing from time to time.

In the last few years custom fitted ear-plugs designed to deal with specific frequencies have been available.

6.7   SPECIFIC CONSIDERATIONS FOR NOISE-RELATED CLAIMS

6.7.1   Medical diagnosis

6.7.1.1   Typical audiogram pattern with 'notch' at 3–4, or 6Khz, Symmetrical shape to both ears, history of noise damage.

Alternative cause of damage:

- constitutional condition;
- sensitive hearing;
- head injury;
- certain types of medication;
- noisy hobbies;
- shooting;
- night clubs/discos/concerts, etc.

6.7.2   Applicable law
- Common law negligence.
- Woodworking Machines Regulations 1974.
- Noise at Work Regulations 1989.
- Control of Noise at Work Regulations 2005.

6.7.3   Exposure

Time of exposure:

- pre-1963 unlikely to establish liability except for very large employers;
- long period for development of significant symptoms, usually 10 years or more.

Where did exposure occur?

- detailed circumstances of the workplace.

6.7.3.1   Type of noise source

Length of exposure:

- need to build up history of 'noise-dose' in order to calculate a Noise Immission Level (NIL).Note that Noise Immission Levels of above 90 dB(A)NIL are required.

Noise reduction:

- enclosure;
- baffles;
- screens.

Protective equipment:

- bilsom wool;
- foam ear-plugs;
- ear muffs;
- custom-made ear-plugs.

6.7.4   Causation

Did that degree of exposure create at the time a foreseeable risk of injury; and/or was there a breach of statutory duty at that time?

6.7.5   Apportionment of damages

With different exposures and with different employers, without specific evidence there will be apportionment of damages on a straight line basis

6.7.6   Limitation

When was the tort completed – awareness of symptoms; and/or when was any breach of statutory duty actionable?

Limitation Act 1980:

- s 11 (limitation period);
- s 14 (date of knowledge); and
- s 33 (discretion to waive time-limits).

6.7.7   Medical prognosis

How is the diagnosed condition likely to progress? In cases of noise damage, any deterioration in hearing after the last period of noise exposure must be as a result of other non-noise factors such as age or constitutional problems.

6.7.8   Damages
- General damages.
- Handicap on the labour market.
- Loss of earnings.
- Cost of hearing aids, special telephone, headphones.
- Tinnitus Management Devices;
- Cognitive Behavioural Therapy.

CHAPTER 7

WORK-RELATED UPPER LIMB DISORDER

7.1 INTRODUCTION

The term 'work-related upper limb disorder' (WRULD) serves as a convenient umbrella term for examining a number of different medical conditions. The term 'repetitive strain injury' (RSI) was much criticised because it tended to pre-judge the issues of whether the work was repetitive and whether it was that particular work which caused the injury. WRULDs is more commonly used although it is subject to a similar criticism, that of pre-judging an issue. In any case once the particular medical condition has been identified it is better to use the specific medical term.

Repetitive stressful work may cause injury or aggravate a condition to certain parts of the body, particularly the shoulder and back, but the focus here is on the more commonly encountered conditions affecting the hands and arms, although the same principles usually apply.

Condition	Symptoms
Carpal tunnel syndrome	Compression of the median nerve in the carpal tunnel which is in the wrist. Causes pins and needles, numbness and weakness of the hand or fingers
De Quervains syndrome	Also referred to as De Quervains stenosing tenovaginitis. Thickening of the fibrous sheath of the tendons
Epicondylitis	Pain and swelling where the muscle joins the bone at the elbow

Golfer's elbow	Medial epicondylitis, with pain and swelling where the muscle joins the bone at the elbow
Peri-tendinitis	Inflammation of the junction between the muscle and the thumb extensor tendons on the inner side of the wrist
Tendinitis	Inflammation of the tendons
Tennis elbow	Inflammation of the synovium (lubricated sheath which surrounds and protects the tendons). Used incorrectly as having a wider meaning; DSS definition 'traumatic inflammation of the tendons of the hand or forearm or of the associated tendon sheaths'
Trigger finger	A form of tendinitis where the inflamed tendons become locked in their sheaths, thus locking the finger

WRULDs is used as a term to cover injuries as various and varied as tenosynovitis, tendinitis, De Quervains syndrome, carpal tunnel syndrome, trigger finger, epicondylitis and cramp of the hand or forearm. The list is not exhaustive. These conditions occur as a result of different underlying pathologies. The first problem is to determine whether the claimant suffers or has suffered from a recognised condition. Conditions of generalised fatigue or indeterminate aching will not form the basis for a successful claim. However, the rather unspecific 'cramp of the hand or forearm' may be enough (see **7.4** below).

7.2   FORESEEABILITY AND BREACH

The essential elements in WRULD cases are the same as in other occupational illness claims and ordinary negligence claims:

(a)   was there a reasonably foreseeable risk of injury from the work thus creating a duty of care?;

(b)   was there a breach of the duty of care?; and

(c)   was the breach causative of the injury?

The nature of the work giving rise to upper limb disorders varies enormously and the assessment of foreseeability of the risk of injury is different in every case. One has to look at the work process in every case with the statutory and common law requirements in mind. An employer must have had actual or constructive knowledge that the work carried an inherent risk of not insignificant injury. In *Allison v London Underground Ltd* Smith LJ provided guidance on the issue of what an employer ought to have known and how. A suitable and sufficient risk assessment was identified as critical. What the employer ought to have known about the risks in the workplace is all that an employer would have known had it carried out a suitable and sufficient risk assessment.[1] In WRULD cases, more often than not, a suitable and sufficient risk assessment would require some expert input.

The claimant has to establish that the injury caused relates to the breach alleged, as opposed to work in general. To take a simple example, it is difficult to see a failure to provide a foot rest causing hand injury or if the absence of a warning is to be relied upon as a breach, then the claimant must be able to say that the warning would have made a difference.

In determining foreseeability and breach of statutory or common law duty the work process needs to be looked at including the force used, frequency and duration, posture, warning, rotation, job design, supervision and advice, training. All these aspects of the task needs careful examination to decide what preventative steps could or should have been taken to minimise the risk of injury.

7.3   CAUSATION

Medical causation is likely to be the most significant issue in WRULD cases. All the conditions mentioned above occur irrespective of the type of work carried out. Some conditions are constitutional, often occurring with advancing age; some may be as a result of trauma; and some may be caused by recreations such as playing a musical instrument or hobbies such as knitting or excessive DIY.

The fact that symptoms are experienced when at work does not prove that the work is the cause of the condition. The work may bring a constitutional condition to light. It may aggravate a very mild condition so as to precipitate troubling symptoms. The claimant may have been vulnerable to injury in certain circumstances and this vulnerability was not known to the defendants so that there is no breach of duty unless the activity gave rise to a foreseeable risk of injury in a 'normal' or non-vulnerable person.

---

[1]   [2008] EWCA Civ 71.

7.4   A DEFINED MEDICAL CONDITION

It is generally considered that a claim for WRULDs will not succeed unless there is proved to exist a recognised medical condition. This school of thought was given support by the case of *Mughal v Reuters*,[2] a case concerning a journalist which attracted the attention of a large number of journalists. Although the headlines proclaimed that the judge had decided that 'RSI' did not exist, a reading of the judgment reveals a different story. The judge did find on the evidence that the claimant did not have a recognised pathological condition which was known to medical science. The claimant suffered a diffuse condition and complained of pain caused by his work at a keyboard. He had no recognisable clinical signs, no inflammation, and no swelling and no crepitus. The nerve conduction studies were normal. Thus there was no medical evidence to support the claimant's claims for injury. The success of the claim was thus dependant on whether the judge accepted the claimant's evidence about his condition. It is apparent from the judgment that the judge found the claimant to be a most unreliable witness. In finding against the claimant the judge did make comment about the term 'RSI' but the case is not authority for a wider proposition.

The situation has been made more complicated by the definitions of the prescribed conditions defining entitlement to industrial injury benefit. These conditions are set out under the general heading of 'tenosynovitis' which is hardly an aid to clarity. The conditions are concerned with injuries arising out of any occupation involving manual labour or frequent or repeated movements of the hand or wrist, and include cramp of the hand or forearm. No further medical definition or elucidation is given. To qualify for benefit the claimant must show that his work involved 'prolonged periods of handwriting, typing or other repetitive movements for the fingers, hands or arms; for example, typists, clerks and routine assemblers'. It is said that the condition is probably due to a combination of physical fatigue of muscles and an underlying neurosis. On examination there are no abnormal physical findings. Symptoms can be spasms, tremor and pain in the hand or forearm 'brought about by attempts to perform a familiar act involving a frequently repeated muscular action'. Thus if his account of symptoms had been accepted, Mr Mughal would have qualified for state benefits under these provisions. It is difficult to see how logically this condition should not be accepted as forming the basis for a civil claim.

The advantage of having a defined medical condition diagnosed is that it assists with establishing the claimant's credibility and with establishing whether work task was the cause. The disadvantage of not having a diagnosis of a recognised medical condition is that it weakens the case on

---

[2]   [1993] IRLR 571.

causation and may weaken the case on foreseeability. If the medical pathology is unknown, how can the employer be said to be at fault for not guarding against the consequences?

The work task should be examined carefully, and a detailed written description of the task compiled. In some cases a video of the work task may be of great assistance. The full nature of the repetitive tasks must be considered. The amount of force used is relevant, as is the degree to which movements are undertaken by the fingers, hand and wrist, as opposed to the arm. A worker who trims plants in pots will use both arms to perform the task properly. The precise method of work may not be realised by the claimant, and trying to recall it without handling the tools and components can be misleading. The work should be simulated or actually undertaken to reveal the real nature of the movements. This is good practice even for tasks as seemingly obvious as using a keyboard. The position of the hands, the vertical and horizontal angles of the wrist and the use or over-use of a particular finger or thumb are all likely to be more important than the number of key strokes made. The set-up of the workstation may also be important, whether this is a desk and chair or a conveyor and workbench. Focusing merely on the number of items handled or worked upon can be misleading since the repetitive task itself may not give rise to the relevant strain or stress of the muscles or tendons.

Medical experts must explain the mechanical basis for any injury they diagnose. A diagnosis of epicondylitis (which can arise independently of the work) is of no use if the task does not involve relatively heavy work which places a strain on the muscle connection at the elbow. It helps to concentrate the mind of the medical expert if he has to explain in layman's terms, perhaps demonstrating with his own hands and arms, how the work action causes distress to the relevant anatomical structure. This can be very important when looking at causation.

There may be issues about the onset of the symptoms. If a claimant has been performing the same task year-in year-out without problem then the reason for the onset of the symptoms at a particular time needs to be explained. There may have been a change, sometimes small, in the pattern of work.

7.5   SPECIFIC CONSIDERATIONS FOR WRULD CLAIMS

7.5.1   Medical diagnosis

Type of medical condition:

- Carpal tunnel syndrome
- Epicondylitis

(a) Lateral epicondylitis – tennis elbow
(b) Medial epicondylitis – golfer's elbow.

- Peri-tendinitis
- Tendinitis
- Tenosynovitis
- Trigger finger

Is there an alternative diagnosis for the symptoms?

- Constitutional
- Advancing age
- Hobbies

7.5.2 Applicable law
- Common law negligence
- Management of Health and Safety at Work Regulations 1992
- Management of Health and Safety at Work Regulations 1999
- Workplace (Health, Safety & Welfare) Regulations 1992
- Manual Handling Operations Regulations 1992
- Provision and Use of Work Equipment Regulations 1992
- Provision and Use of Work Equipment Regulations 1998
- Personal Protective Equipment at Work Regulations 1992
- Health and Safety (Display Screen Equipment) Regulations 1992

7.5.3 Exposure

When:

- Short period for development of condition.
- Symptoms often arise after an increase in work, or change in working pattern.
- Can arise after an absence from work.

Where:

- Not usually critical.

Type of work:

- Important to describe and understand the mechanism of the work.
- Consider whether need to video the work.

Length of exposure:

- Continuous work.
- Rotation work.
- Regular breaks.

Work equipment used – foreseeability:

- Was there a risk assessment?
- Did the hand-arm movement create a foreseeable risk of injury?

7.5.4 Causation
- Did the work cause the condition?
- Was there another cause of the condition?

7.5.5 Apportionment of damages

If there is more than one factor creating symptoms there is likely to be apportionment.

7.5.6 Limitation
- When was the tort completed – onset of symptoms; and/or
- When was any breach of statutory duty actionable?
- Limitation Act 1980, sections 11 and 14.
- Discretion to waive the time-limit under section 33 of the Limitation Act 1980.

7.5.7 Medical prognosis
- How is the diagnosed condition likely to progress?
- What are the chances of recurrence?

7.5.8 Damages
- General damages.
- Handicap on the labour market.
- Loss of earnings.
- Cost of treatment and supportive splints.

CHAPTER 8

VIBRATION WHITE FINGER

8.1   INTRODUCTION

Hand held vibratory tools are very widely used, across of range of occupations, industries and also in the home. In 2003 the HSE referred to a report which estimated that about 5 million people are exposed to hand-arm vibration at work and of those as many as two million might be exposed to levels of vibration that risked injury.[1]

For many years the awareness of the effects of hand-arm vibration was limited and the consequences of exposure were not regarded as particularly serious. However, the potentially serious effects of prolonged exposure to vibrating machinery were recognised by the Court of Appeal in the multi-party litigation of *Armstrong v British Coal Corpn*,[2] which is recommended reading for practitioners undertaking this type of litigation. It was followed by two other judgments that further raised the profile of VWF and the dangers of hand-arm vibration.[3]

As the names suggest there is a difference between vibration white finger (VWF) and hand-arm vibration syndrome (HAVS). In practice a litigator need not be concerned with any subtlety of difference. The terms are used to refer to the same broad range of symptoms, namely tingling, numbness and episodic whiteness in the fingers and hand, which have been caused by long-term exposure to vibration transmitted to the hands from tools and machinery. The term 'Raynaud's Phenomenon' should, strictly speaking, be confined to cold-induced episodic whiteness of the fingers irrespective of cause. Raynaud's Phenomenon may have causes other than exposure to vibration and may be constitutional in origin. The terms are sometimes used interchangeably as though they are the same, but that is not correct: VWF is a form of Raynaud's Phenomenon which has a specific cause, namely exposure to vibration.

---

[1]   HSE Consultation Document on Proposals for Control of Vibration at Work Regulations, November 2003, Preface to Annex 2.
[2]   [1997] 8 Med LR 259, CA.
[3]   *Hall v British Gas* (7 April 1998, unreported), *Allen v British Rail Engineering Ltd* (7 October 1998, unreported).

The syndrome is summarised in the HSE booklet *Hand-Arm Vibration HSG88* as follows:

'66. The term HAVS has been used to describe the effects of hand-transmitted vibration on the upper limb but is not clearly defined. In the United Kingdom, HAVS is considered to exist if, after prolonged exposure to hand-transmitted vibration, involvement of the vascular and/or peripheral nervous system occurs, with or without musculoskeletal involvement.

67. The symptoms result from pathological effects on the peripheral vascular system, peripheral nervous system, muscles, bones, tendons and soft tissues. Episodic finger blanching is the most widely known of these effects, but sensory changes are now being given greater importance. A particular worker who has signs or symptoms of one or more of the possible effects of hand-transmitted vibration on the upper limb may be considered as suffering from HAVS.'

Whilst acute exposure to high levels of vibration may cause symptoms of tingling and aching, this is generally temporary. It is long-term exposure that causes VWF, producing long-term symptoms for which there is no treatment, although the condition may improve if exposure to vibration is avoided. The severity of the symptoms is generally related to the total vibration dose to which the claimant has been exposed. Symptoms consist of finger tingling, numbness and episodes of whitening of the fingers precipitated by exposure to cold temperatures or cold objects. The whitening at first affects the tips of some of the fingers but then extends to the base of the fingers and involves all the fingers. A person's grip may become affected. Between episodes of finger whitening the fingers appear normal. Symptoms interfere with activities at work and home, as well as affecting recreations particularly where there is exposure to cold.

Diagnosis is not always easy, because there is no objective test to support the existence of VWF. In the region of 4 per cent to 6 per cent of men suffer from constitutional white finger, or Primary Reynaud's Disease (and the figure is higher for women). For that reason factual evidence is essential, because a diagnosis of VWF can only properly be made when other possible medical causes for the complaints have been excluded, there is good evidence of exposure to hand-arm vibration and the claimant has given a description of symptoms that is consistent with the diagnosis.

The need for good evidence of symptoms consistent with the condition has recently been affirmed by the Court of Appeal in the case of *Whalley v Montracon Ltd*.[4] At the trial the claimant's expert changed his opinion of the diagnosis having heard the claimant's witness evidence describing his symptoms. He agreed with the defendant's expert that the claimant was not suffering from VWF. However, the judge at first instance accepted the claimant's evidence and concluded that he was suffering from VWF, in

---

4   [2005] EWCA Civ 1383, [2005] All Er (D) 269 (Nov).

the face of the expert medical opinion. The Court of Appeal dismissed the defendant's appeal, on the basis that the judge was entitled to accept the totality of the claimant's evidence. This case is of course of general application to the Court's ability to reject expert opinion, but in this context underlines the vital importance of obtaining a clear and consistent description of symptoms from a claimant.

VWF can develop at any time between about 6 months and 20 years after exposure to hand-arm vibration. The development of symptoms is often related to the extent of the dose and so it is essential to have a good history from the claimant about the machinery used and over what periods the exposure occurred, broken down into hours per day or week if possible ('anger time').

Carpal tunnel syndrome can also be caused by exposure to vibration and occurs when the median nerve becomes compressed in the carpal tunnel in the wrist. Symptoms are pins and needles, numbness and weakness of the hand and fingers. Other conditions that have been held to be actionable include Palmer Arch Disease (damage to the artery in the palm of the hand that supplies blood to the fingers)[5] and Hypothenar Hammer Syndrome (damage to the artery at the base of the thumb).

8.2   CAUSES OF VWF

VWF is caused by exposure of the hands to severe vibration transmitted from a hand-held tool or piece of equipment. The vibration causes neurological and vascular symptoms, which appears are caused by repeated pressure on the nerves and arteries of the hands. There is a latency period (see **8.1** above, between 6 months and 20 years), which varies according to the individual and is inversely proportional to the severity of the vibration. The first symptoms usually appear after exposure to vibration for some considerable time.

Following the appearance of the first symptoms, progression of the condition varies. In severely advanced cases, tissue necrosis of the finger may occur, and in extreme cases chainsaw operators who ignored the rapidly developing condition have been known to lose fingers through the onset of gangrene.

Any expert medical opinion must consider the issue of causation and in particular whether there is a non-work-related explanation for the symptoms, especially in light of the fact that the condition can develop constitutionally. Again, a clear and consistent description of the symptoms from the claimant is essential.

---

[5]   See for example *Griggs v Transco plc* [2003] EWCA Civ 564.

Nowadays the preferred classification is the Stockholm Workshop scale, that was developed in 1986 and has taken over from the Taylor/Pelmear Scale. The Stockholm scale is preferred because it assesses neurological and vascular symptoms separately, which allows for a more precise appreciation of the severity of symptoms. That is useful because VWF causes symptoms that affect sensitivity (tingling etc) and hence neurological, as well as finger blanching which is a vascular phenomenon. The Stockholm Workshop scales are recommended by the HSE and are set out in its guidance booklet *Hand-arm Vibration.*[6]

Disability is now measured by using one or both of two scales: the Taylor-Pelmear scale and the Stockholm Workshop Scale, although the latter is now preferred. The condition of each hand is then made the subject of a notation of the scale indicating the number of affected fingers. For example, 2L(1)/2R(1) indicates two left fingers at stage 2 (moderate) and two right fingers at stage 1 (mild). These scales are considered further in Chapter 14 on damages.

8.3   PRESCRIBED DISEASE

Prescription for industrial disease benefits for VWF did not occur until 1985. The prescribed condition is confined to the following occupations:

(a)   the use of hand-held chainsaws in forestry;
(b)   the use of hand-held rotary tools in grinding or in the sanding or polishing of metal or the holding of materials being ground or metal being sanded or polished by rotary tools;
(c)   the use of hand-held percussive metal-working tools or the holding of metal being worked upon by percussive tools in rivetting, caulking, chipping, hammering, fettling or swaging;
(d)   the use of hand-held powered percussive drills or hand-held powered percussive hammers used in mining, quarrying, demolition or on roads or footpaths including road construction;
(e)   the holding of material being worked upon by pounding machines in shoe manufacture.

Thus the fact that the claimant may not have been accepted as having a prescribed disease should not be a discouragement to bringing a civil claim for damages.

8.4   VIBRATION DOSE

Once it has been established that exposure has occurred after the relevant date of knowledge applicable to a particular industry[7] and the condition has been properly diagnosed, it is necessary to establish the vibration dose

---

[6]   HS(G)88, Table 5.
[7]   See **2.3.4** above.

in order to consider potential breaches of the employers common law and/or statutory duties. It is only once the dose has been determined that the claimant can consider whether he or she has been exposed to a foreseeable risk of injury. In order to determine the vibration dose it will be almost essential to obtain expert engineering evidence, but it is useful to understand the basic principles behind the relevant calculations.

There is no clear 'safe' or 'unsafe' dose of vibration as some people are more susceptible than others. In order to prove a breach of duty it is necessary for the claimant to prove that he was exposed to a quantity of vibration that was known at the relevant time to create a risk of injury in most of the population. That quantity of vibration is the 'vibration dose'. The magnitude of the vibration is measured as the acceleration of the frequency measured in metres per second – referred to as the unit 'ms^2'. To obtain a value that represents the level of the acceleration measured over the time period (T), the average vibration signal over the time period is taken to obtain the RMS value, an acceleration that is related to the energy content of the vibration.

This RMS value is often referred to as the equivalent acceleration value Aeq. It is important to understand that the acceleration (vibration) generated by a machine such as a grinding tool or chipping hammer is made up of many components, which occur at different vibrational frequencies. For instance, the vibration from an angle grinder contains a component that is generated by the rotation of the motor and a component that is generated by the rotation of the grinding wheel. All of these components are combined when the RMS value is calculated.

In order to take account of the sensitivity of the body to vibration the International Standards Organisation has developed a series of frequency weighting curves which includes a hand–arm frequency weighting curve. The frequency weighting curve has the effect of cutting down very high and very low frequencies when measurements are taken.

In 1975 a British Standards Institution draft development publication (DD43) referred to vibration magnitudes of below 1.0 ms^2 as 'acceptable vibration magnitudes' and magnitudes above 10 ms^2 as 'unacceptable vibration magnitudes'. The lower guideline figure applied to exposure lasting 400 minutes per day (6 hours 40 minutes a day). The 10ms^2 guideline applied to exposure lasting 150 minutes (2 hours 30 minutes) in a day. Vibration magnitudes falling between the lower and upper guideline figures were assessed according to the duration of the exposure.

In 1987 British Standard BS6842 was produced, which set out the conditions that were expected to result in 10 per cent of the population developing blanching after 8 years of exposure. In 1994 the Health and Safety Executive Guidance Document HS(G)88 referred to a standard based on an 'action level' of 'A8 of 2.8ms^2'. The A8 is based on an 8-hour energy equivalent value and 2.8ms^2 is the vibration magnitude. The 2.8ms^2 is the average vibration level over the course of an 8-hour working day. At that level 10 per cent of persons exposed for 8 hours a day over 8 years would experience symptoms of finger blanching. If the number of years of exposure altered or the length of the working day is changed, or if the vibration levels are changed, the total energy equivalent value has been changed. However, the alteration of the factors does not take place in the same proportion. There is a useful table in the booklet that allows for an initial assessment of the possible exposure levels and hence an initial view of the strength of a potential claim.[8]

Work with vibrating tools is rarely continuous and as such the time of exposure ('anger time') must be considered. An alteration in the hours of exposure is significant. If the time of exposure is halved from 8 hours to 4 hours then the magnitude of the vibration can be adjusted to 4ms^2. If the time were reduced to 2 hours then the magnitude would be 5.6ms^2. Two hours of exposure allows for 5.6ms^2 and 1 hour of exposure allows for 8ms^2. If the number of years were reduced to 4 years the equivalent vibration dose would be 5.6ms^2. Over 16 years this figure would be 1.4ms^2. In practice it is easier to consider these figures in a table form.

Frequency weighted vibration acceleration magnitudes (m/s^2 rms) which may be expected to produce finger blanching in 10% of persons

Daily expo-sure	Period of exposure					
	6 months	1 year	2 years	4 years	8 years	16 years
8 hrs	44.8	22.4	11.2	5.6	2.8	1.4
4 hrs	64	32	16	8	4	2
2 hrs	89.6	44.8	22.4	11.2	5.6	2.8
1 hr	128	64	32	16	8	4
30 mins	179.2	89.6	44.8	22.4	11.2	5.6
15 mins	256	128	63	32	16	8

It is useful to have some idea of the vibration magnitudes created by some common vibratory tools. A common disc sander produces around 5ms^2 of vibration; a road breaker produces some 10ms^2. Used for 2 hours a day for 4 years would take the worker over the guideline figure of A8 of 2.8ms^2. Over 8 years the daily exposure needs only to be 40 minutes to create a risk of developing VWF.

---

[8]   HS(G)88, figure 10, page 43.

Jack-hammers, rock drills and scaling chisels produce around 20ms^2 of vibration. Used 4 hours a day for 18 months produces an equivalent to an A8 of 2.8ms^2. Over 8 years the daily exposure needs only to be 10 minutes to create a risk of developing VWF.

If exposure levels are an issue it is difficult to see how a claim can be contested without expert engineering evidence, either from a joint or single experts.

8.5 COMMON LAW DUTY

If the claimant can establish exposure to a vibration dose in excess of A8 of 2.8ms^2 after the relevant date of knowledge applicable to the particular industry and symptoms consistent with a diagnosis of VWF, common law liability will follow. It is useful to consider the comments of Swanwick J in *Stokes v Guest, Keen and Nettlefield (Bolts and Nuts) Ltd*:[9]

> '... the overall test is still the conduct of the reasonable and prudent employer, taking positive thought for the safety of his workers in the light of what he knows or ought to know; where there is a recognised and general practice which has been followed for a substantial period in similar circumstances without mishap, he is entitled to follow it, unless in light of common sense or newer knowledge it is clearly bad; but, where there is developing knowledge, he must keep reasonably abreast of it and not be too slow to apply it; and where he has in fact greater than average knowledge of the risks, he may be thereby obliged to take more than the average or standard precautions. He must weight up the risks in terms of the likelihood of injury occurring and the potential consequences if it does; and he must balance against this the probable effectiveness of the precautions that can be taken to meet it and the expense and inconvenience they involve. If he is found to have fallen below the standard to be properly expected of a reasonable and prudent employer in these respects, he is negligent.'

The simplest method of reducing the risk is to reduce the time spent using the tools. However, where the work has been performed over many years the risk will arise even with only short daily exposure. Many men have worked with vibrating tools for 10 or 20 years and their daily dose might have been very limited. The problem can be tackled at source by providing special gloves and mitts that reduce the levels of vibration experienced by the operator. Similarly, handles and controls of the tools can be designed to reduce the vibration. After the relevant date of knowledge the employer is under a duty to reduce the risk to the lowest level reasonably practicable, usually by reducing exposure time (eg by rotation), limiting the effects of vibration (by provision of protective equipment and measures) and by operating a system of health surveillance. Those various measures were set out by the HSE in the 1994 Guidance (HS(G)88). The

---

[9]   [1968] 1 WLR 1776, at 1783.

Court of Appeal considered a series of steps that the prudent employer should take if the action level is exceeded in *Brown v Corus (UK) Ltd.*[10]

Once it has been established that the claimant was exposed to excessive levels of vibration the burden shifts to the defendant to justify why it failed to take steps to reduce the exposure.[11] However, if the claimant was unusually sensitive and there was no evidence to suggest that any realistic reduction in the vibration levels could have been achieved or would have prevented the claimant developing the condition, there will be no breach of duty.[12]

8.6   STATUTORY DUTY

The following 'six pack' regulations apply to work involving hand-arm vibration: The Provision and Use of Work Equipment Regulations 1992 (from 1 January 1993 to 4 December 1998), The Provision and Use of Work Equipment Regulations 1998 (in force from 5 December 1988), the Personal Protective Equipment at Work Regulations 1992 (from 1 January 1993) and the Manual Handling Operations Regulations 1992 (from 1 January 1993). There is no authority as to the application of these regulations to the use of vibratory tools in particular.

The Control of Vibration at Work Regulations 2005 (CVWR) came into force on 6 July 2005 and are accompanied by HSE Guidance that replaces HS(G)88. The CVWR set a daily exposure limit of $5m/s^2$ and a daily exposure action value of $2.5m/s^2$, which is of course a lower level than the $2.8m/s^2$ common law level. There is a transitional period for compliance with the exposure limit value in the case of work equipment provided before 6 July 2007; for such equipment compliance commences on 6 July 2010. However, the transitional period does not apply to the daily exposure limit of $2.5m/s^2$.

The duties imposed by the CVWR are similar in ambit to those imposed by the other six pack regulations. There is a duty to carry out suitable and sufficient assessment of the risks of using vibratory machinery and to identify measures needed to meet the requirements of the Regulations (reg 5); elimination or, where not reasonably practicable, reduction to as low a level as is reasonably practicable of exposure to vibration (reg 6(1)); health surveillance (reg 7); provision of suitable and sufficient information and training (reg 8).

---

[10]   [2004] EWCA Civ 374, per Scott Baker LJ at paras 51–55.
[11]   *Brown and Others v Corus (UK) Ltd* [2004] EWCA Civ 374.
[12]   *Poyner v Linde Heavy Truck Division Ltd* LTL 9/1/2004.

8.7 SPECIFIC CONSIDERATIONS FOR VWF CLAIMS

8.7.1 Medical diagnosis

Is there a non-work-related cause for the symptoms?

- Constitutional.
- Hobbies.

8.7.2 Applicable law
- Common law negligence.
- Factories Act 1961.
- Management of Health and Safety at Work Regulations 1992.
- Management of Health and Safety at Work Regulations 1999.
- Workplace (Health, Safety and Welfare) Regulations 1992.
- Provision and Use of Work Equipment Regulations 1992.
- Provision and Use of Work Equipment Regulations 1998.
- Personal Protective Equipment at Work Regulations 1992.
- Manual Handling Operations Regulations 1992.
- Control of Vibration at Work Regulations 2005.

8.7.3 Exposure

Time of exposure?

- differing states of knowledge of the risks from exposure;
- evidence of employer's actual knowledge of risks;
- prolonged period for development of disease, particularly with lower degree of exposure.

Where did exposure occur?

- not likely to be critical.

8.7.3.1 Type of work and machinery and tools used

Length of exposure.

Protective equipment:

- gloves.

8.7.4 Causation

Did that degree of exposure create at the time a foreseeable risk of injury; and/or was there a breach of statutory duty at that time?

8.7.5   Apportionment of damages

Will there be apportionment in respect of non-actionable 'innocent' exposure and 'guilty' exposure?

8.7.6   Limitation

When was the tort completed – onset of symptoms; and/or when was any breach of statutory duty actionable?

Limitation Act 1980:

- section 11 (limitation period);
- section 14 (date of knowledge); and
- section 33 (discretion to waive time-limits).

8.7.7   Medical prognosis

How is the diagnosed condition likely to progress?

8.7.8   Damages
- General damages.
- Handicap on the labour market; inability to work with vibrating machinery.
- Loss of earnings.
- Cost of treatment.

CHAPTER 9

OCCUPATIONAL STRESS CLAIMS

9.1 DEFINING 'STRESS'

Stress is now the second most commonly reported work-related illness. The most recent data available from the Health and Safety Executive (HSE) is that in 2009/2010 9.8 million working days were lost due to stress and the costs to society are about £4 billion per year. The issue of stress at work has, unsurprisingly, been receiving increasing attention from the courts and the government as its impact is felt on the workforce and productivity. A consensus is slowly emerging as to the definition of stress, what might cause it and ways to reduce it.

The starting point in defining stress is in making the distinction between pressure and stress. As the HSE in its guidance booklet *Stress at Work* (1995) put it:

> 'There is no such thing as a pressure-free job. Every job brings its own set of tasks, responsibilities and day-to-day problems, and the pressures and demands these place on us are an unavoidable part of working life. We are, after all, paid to work and to work hard, and to accept the reasonable pressures which go with that.'

Stress arises when a person experiences too much pressure and is unable to cope. In the same guidance booklet, the HSE defined stress as: 'the reaction people have to excessive pressures or other types of demand placed upon them. It arises when they worry that they can't cope. It can involve both physical and behavioural effects, but these are usually short-lived and cause no lasting harm; when the pressures recede, there is a quick return to normal'. The most recent definition on the HSE website is as follows: 'By the term work-related stress we mean the process that arises where work demands of various types and combinations exceed the person's capacity and capability to cope.'

Stress is therefore a reaction, not an illness in itself. It is when stress results in illness that the possibility of an actionable claim arises. Its effects can be shown in physical disorders, such as ulcers, heart disease or hypertension and in psychiatric disorders, such as anxiety and depression. While there should be no distinction in principle to the approach to be taken to injury caused by stress at work, whether physical or psychiatric, most occupational stress claims concern psychiatric illness.

When considering the point at which stress becomes a psychiatric illness, as the Court of Appeal recognised in the leading case of *Sutherland v Hatton*,[1] the dividing line between a 'normal but unpleasant state of mind or emotion and a recognised psychiatric disorder' is itself not easy to draw. Generally, psychiatric illnesses cannot be seen, scanned or measured physically (although currently research is being carried out into measuring small chemical changes, and the future may hold greater certainty). What can be seen are the *effects* of psychiatric illness. Psychiatrists cannot presuppose a standard or normal state of mental health. The best that can be achieved is some average standard of functioning. A person falling outside that standard can then be said to be suffering from a psychiatric condition. Certain criteria are now recognised by the psychiatric profession: the *American Diagnostic and Statistical Manual of Mental Disorder*; the DSM-IV (1994); and the World Health Organisation's *ICD-10 Classification of Mental and Behavioural Disorders* (1992). In short, these provide checklists of symptoms that help to define psychiatric conditions. The controversy over the definitions in the forthcoming DSM-V – expected in 2013 – suggests that agreement about the classification of mental disorders and their diagnostic criteria is far from settled.

9.2 GENERAL PRINCIPLES

Claims for injury caused by stress at work are governed by the common law and, in principal, no special control mechanisms apply. All employers have a duty to take reasonable care for the safety of their employees. If a failure to take the care which can reasonably be expected in the circumstances results in damage, then a claim can be made out. The ordinary principles of employer's liability apply.

However, the Court of Appeal in *Sutherland v Hatton* recognised that such claims require particular care in determination, as they give rise to some difficult issues – in particular in relation to foreseeability – but also to breach of duty and causation. The Court of Appeal therefore provided guidance to be followed when determining claims for occupational stress. These are set out in detail below.

In addition to the common law principles, breaches of the *Management of Health and Safety at Work Regulations 1999* – and in particular breaches of Regulation 3(1)(a) (duty to carry out a risk assessment); Regulation 6 (duty to provide health surveillance); and Regulation 10 (duty to provide information to employees about the risks identified by the assessment) can be relied upon in appropriate circumstances.

---

[1]   [2002] EWCA Civ 76.

In 2001 the HSE published some basic guidance entitled: 'Tackling Work-Related Stress', to assist in the process of risk assessment. This guidance has evolved to become the 'Management Standards' approach to helping employers manage the causes of work-related stress. The Management Standards do not have legal force but are to assist employers in complying with their legal duties. They are available on the HSE website.

Where injury is caused by excessive working hours, the court may have regard to the provisions of the Working Time Regulations 1998. In *Packenham-Walsh v Connell Residential*,[2] while the Court of Appeal noted that the defendant's failure to keep records in accordance with the provisions of the Regulations and its apparent lack of awareness of the consequences of the Regulations did not, in themselves, establish a breach of the Regulations, they did provide a 'favourable background' against which to assess whether or not there had been a breach of duty.

9.3   THE GUIDANCE

The leading case on the general principles to be applied in claims for injury arising out of stress at work remains *Sutherland v Hatton*. The 16 point check-list set out by Hale LJ was subsequently approved by the House of Lords in *Barber v Somerset County Council*,[3] as providing 'a valuable contribution to the development of the law' although the House of Lords was clear that it was to be treated as guidance only and that each case depended upon its own facts.

The following 'practical propositions' were suggested by the court as guidance:

(1)   There are no special control mechanisms applying to claims for psychiatric (or physical) illness or injury arising from the stress of doing the work the employee is required to do. The ordinary principles of employer's liability apply.
(2)   The threshold question is whether the kind of harm suffered by a particular employee was reasonably foreseeable. There must be: (a) an injury to health (as distinct from occupational stress); which (b) is attributable to stress at work (as distinct from other factors).
(3)   Foreseeability depends upon what the employer knows (or ought reasonably to know) about the individual employee. Because of the nature of mental disorder, it is harder to foresee than physical injury, but may be easier to foresee in a known individual than in the population at large. An employer is usually entitled to assume that the employee can withstand the normal pressures of the job unless the employer knows of some particular problem or vulnerability.

---

[2]   [2006] EWCA Civ 90.
[3]   [2004] 2 All ER 385.

(4) The test is the same whatever the employment: there are no occupations which should be regarded as intrinsically dangerous to mental health.

(5) Factors likely to be relevant in answering the threshold question include the following:

(a) The nature and extent of the work done by the employee. Is the workload heavier than is normal for the particular job? Is the work particularly intellectually or emotionally demanding for the employee? Are demands made of the employee unreasonable when compared with demands made of others in the same or comparable jobs, or are there signs that others doing the same job are suffering harmful levels of stress? Is there an abnormal level of sickness or absenteeism in the same job or the same department?

(b) Signs from the employee of impending harm to health. Does the employee have a particular problem or vulnerability? Has he already suffered from illness attributable to stress at work? Have there recently been frequent or prolonged absences which are uncharacteristic of him? Is there reason to think that these are attributable to stress at work, for example because of complaints or warnings from him or others?

(6) The employer is generally entitled to take what it is told by its employee at face value, unless it has good reason to think to the contrary. It does not generally have to make searching enquiries of the employee or seek permission to make further enquiries of his medical advisers.

(7) The indications of impending harm to health arising from stress at work must be plain enough for any reasonable employer to realise that it should do something about it.

(8) The employer is only in breach of duty if it has failed to take the steps that are reasonable in the circumstances, bearing in mind the magnitude of the risk of harm occurring, the gravity of the harm which may occur, the costs and practicability of preventing it, and the justifications for running the risk.

(9) The size and scope of the employer's operation, its resources and the demands it faces are relevant in deciding what is reasonable; these include the interests of other employees and the need to treat them fairly, for example in any redistribution of duties.

(10) An employer can only reasonably be expected to take steps that are likely to do some good. The court will probably require expert evidence on this.

(11) An employer that offers a confidential advice service, with referral to appropriate counselling or treatment services, is unlikely to be found to be in breach of duty.

(12) If the only reasonable and effective step would have been to dismiss or demote the employee, the employer will not be in breach of duty in allowing a willing employee to continue in the job.

(13) In all cases, therefore, it is necessary to identify the steps which the employer both could and should have taken before finding it to be in breach of its duty of care.

(14) The claimant must show that the breach of duty has caused or materially contributed to the harm suffered. It is not enough to show that occupational stress has caused the harm.

(15) Where the harm suffered has more than one cause, the employer will be liable only for that proportion attributable to its wrongdoing, unless the harm is truly indivisible. It is for the defendant to raise the question of apportionment.

(16) The assessment of damages will take account of any pre-existing disorder or vulnerability and of the chance that the employee would have succumbed to a stress-related disorder in any event.

While it is safe to assume that the court will have careful regard to the guidance given in *Sutherland v Hatton*, it has not been followed in all cases. In addition, certain aspects of the guidance require further comment. The relevant issues are discussed below, grouped under the headings 'Foreseeability' (*Hatton* guidance paragraphs (2) to (7)); 'Breach of duty' (*Hatton* guidance paragraphs (8) to (13)); and 'Causation & apportionment' (*Hatton* guidance paragraphs (14) to (16)). It should be noted that, of course, the three elements do not, as pointed out by Hale LJ, 'exist in separate compartments'. In particular: 'foreseeability of what might happen if care is not taken is relevant at each stage of the enquiry.'

9.4 FORESEEABILITY

Paragraphs (2) to (7) of the guidance in *Sutherland v Hatton* deal with the issue of foreseeability. This is covered in detail at Chapter 2 above, which should be read together with this section. For a recent case in which the Court of Appeal appeared to take a rather less stringent approach to the issue of foreseeability see *Dickins v O2 Plc*.[4]

9.4.1 Knowledge about employee

What is an employer entitled to assume about the health of its employee and to what extent is it bound to investigate further? The Court of Appeal in *Sutherland v Hatton* stated that unless the employer knows of some particular problem or vulnerability, it is usually entitled to assume that the employee is up to the normal pressures of the job. Generally, an employer is entitled to take what he is told by or on behalf of the employee at face value. In cases of doubt an employer could suggest that the employee

---

[4]   [2008] EWCA Civ 1144.

consult his own doctor or an occupational health service. However, an employer should not, without a very good reason, seek the employee's permission to obtain further information from his medical adviser since this may amount to an unacceptable invasion of the employee's privacy. It should be noted that the Management Standards require the employer to have systems in place to ensure that employees' concerns about their work or ability to cope can be addressed.

9.4.2   Evidential value of a GP certificate

In *Sutherland v Hatton* the defendants argued that an employer is entitled to take the expiry of a GP's certificate as implicitly suggesting that the employee is fit to return to work and even that he is no longer at risk of suffering the same sort of problem again. The Court of Appeal did not accept this submission, saying that a GP's certificate is limited in time, but that many disorders are not self-limiting and may linger on for some considerable time. An employee who is anxious to return to work, for whatever reason, may not go back to his GP for a further certificate when the existing one expires. Even if the employee is currently fit for work, the earlier time-limited certificate carries no implication that the same or a similar condition will not recur.

The Court of Appeal considered that more relevant than the expiry of the GP's certificate were the actions of the employee. An employee who returns to work after a period of sickness without making further disclosure or explanation to his employer is usually implying that he believes himself fit to return to the work that he was doing before. The employer is usually entitled to take that at face value unless it has other good reasons to think to the contrary.

It should be noted that where an employee, on a return to work or otherwise, provides confidential information to an occupational health or counselling service provided by the employer, the employer cannot be fixed with knowledge. If such information is, however, provided to a manager upon a return to work after sickness absence – for example, at a return to work interview – that will be a different matter entirely.

9.4.3   Inherently stressful occupations

The Court of Appeal in *Sutherland v Hatton* was unwilling to categorise particular jobs as inherently more stressful than others. It noted that some people thrive on pressure whereas others experience harmful levels of stress in jobs that many would not regard as stressful at all. The Court of Appeal did at least recognise the argument that stress was so prevalent in some employments, of which it singled out teaching as one, and employees so reluctant to disclose it, that all employers should have in place systems to detect it and prevent it from developing into actual harm. However, there were policy considerations weighing against singling out particular occupations – for example, benefits such as longer holidays or earlier retirement might be at threat – so that this was a matter best left to regulations imposing specific statutory duties. In the meantime, the ordinary law of negligence applied.

9.4.4 The Management Standards

The Management Standards do recognise six key areas of work that can have a negative impact upon employee health if not properly managed. In each case, a standard is provided which, if not adequately adhered to, is likely to increase the risk of stress.

(1) DEMANDS: these include 'workload, work patterns and the work environment'. The standard is that there should be 'adequate and achievable demands in relation to agreed hours of work', with people's skills and abilities matched to those demands.
(2) CONTROL: namely 'how much say the person has in the way they do their work'. The standard is for workers to have control over their pace of work, their work patterns and when breaks can be taken.
(3) SUPPORT: this includes the 'encouragement, sponsorship and resources provided by the organisation, line management and colleagues'. The standard is for the organisation to have policies and procedures in place to enable managers to support their staff, including providing regular and constructive feedback; employees supporting their colleagues; and employees knowing what support is available and how to access it.
(4) RELATIONSHIPS: this includes 'promoting positive working to avoid conflict and dealing with unacceptable behaviour'. The standard is directed at ensuring that employees are not subjected to unacceptable behaviour, such as bullying and are encouraged to report such behaviour.
(5) ROLE: namely 'whether people understand their role within the organisation and whether the organisation ensures that the person does not have conflicting roles'. The standard is making sure, as far as possible, that individuals understand their roles and responsibilities and that the different requirements placed upon employees are compatible.
(6) CHANGE: this deals with 'how organisational change (large or small) is managed and communicated to the organisation'. The standard is making sure that employees are informed and consulted in a timely manner in relation to changes which might affect them, including having access to relevant support and training.

The courts have not yet considered the Standards in any reported case but they are clearly relevant to the issue of foreseeability as well as breach of duty.

9.5 BREACH OF DUTY

9.5.1 The test of reasonableness

Paragraphs (8) to (13) of the guidance in *Sutherland v Hatton* deal with the issue of breach of duty. The Court of Appeal emphasised that, in every case, it is necessary to consider what the employer not only could have done, but what it should have done. A distinction was drawn between the provision of such comparatively simple things as gloves, goggles, earmuffs or non-slip flooring in respect of physical injuries, and the steps that might be taken in respect of stress injuries, for example allowing the employee a sabbatical, transferring him to other work, redistributing the work, providing the employee with some temporary extra help, arranging treatment or counselling, and providing buddying or mentoring schemes to encourage confidence, etc.

In all cases it will be necessary to consider how reasonable it was to expect the employer to provide such help. As in other areas of negligence, the size and scope of the employer's operation will be relevant, as will its resources, whether in the public or private sector, and the other demands placed upon it. Among the matters to be considered are the interests of other employees in the workplace. It may not be reasonable to expect an employer to rearrange the workload in favour of one employee in a way which prejudices others.

The usual test of reasonableness is to be applied – and indeed the Court of Appeal expressly set out the oft-repeated summary of Swanwick J in *Stokes v Guest, Keen Nettlefold (Nuts and Bolts) Limited*,[5] at p 1783 D–E namely: 'What is reasonable depends upon the foreseeability of harm, the magnitude of the risk of that harm occurring, the gravity of the harm, the cost and practicability of preventing it, and the justifications for running the risk.'

The problem with this is of course that the gravity of the harm is not much of a variable. Even psychiatrists can only guess at the prognosis for recovery in the early stages of mental illness. It is arguable that there could never be justification for running the risk that an employee will suffer a depression from which he will never recover. This difficulty might be countered if the step contended for would be straightforward. For example, in *Dickins v O2 Plc*,[6] the Court of Appeal found that, once it was clear that the employee was under extreme stress, she should have been granted time off when she first requested it and an immediate referral to occupational health should have been made.

---

[5]   [1968] 1 WLR 1776.
[6]   [2008] EWCA Civ 1144.

The Court of Appeal in *Sutherland v Hatton* emphasised that the employer can only reasonably be expected to take steps that are likely to do some good. It suggested that this was a matter on which the court was likely to require expert evidence. Bearing in mind it is likely that a psychiatrist will have been instructed to deal with the medical issues in any event, it is always a sensible step to ask the psychiatrist at an early stage whether the measure contended for – whether it be the provision of counselling, the reduction of working hours and so forth – would have made a difference.

9.5.2 Provision of occupational health or counselling service

Hale LJ stated in *Sutherland v Hatton* that an employer who offers a confidential advice service, with referral to appropriate counselling or treatment services, is unlikely to be found in breach of duty. The only exception was where the employer has been placing totally unreasonable demands on an employee in circumstances where the risk of harm was clear.

In *Intel Corporation (UK) Limited v Daw*[7] – a case involving excessive hours and conflicting pressures – the employee successfully argued that the provision of a counselling service made no difference to her workload and the serious management failings. The Court of Appeal held that the consequences of the employer's failure to take action, in essence to reduce her workload, were 'not avoided by the provision of counsellors who might have brought home to management that action was required. On the judge's findings the managers knew it was required'. The Court of Appeal cautioned that reference to the provision of counselling services in *Sutherland v Hatton* did not make such services a universal panacea by which employers could discharge their duty of care in all cases. It also cautioned against rigid adherence to the principles in *Sutherland v Hatton* – noting that, while they provided useful guidance, it was for the trial judge to determine each case on its own merits.

9.5.3 Demotion/leaving the job

In *Sutherland v Hatton* the Court of Appeal suggested that where the only reasonable and effective step would be to dismiss or demote the employee, the employer will not be in breach of duty in allowing a willing employee to continue in the job. Reference was made to *Withers v Perry Chain Co Ltd*,[8] in which Devlin LJ stated:

> 'The relationship between employer and employee is not that of schoolmaster and pupil ... The employee is free to decide for herself what

---

[7]   [2007] EWCA Civ 70.

[8]   [1961] 1 WLR 1314 at 1320.

> risks she will run ... if the common law were otherwise it would be oppressive to the employee by limiting his ability to find work, rather than beneficial to him.'

The Court of Appeal formulated the proposition that if there is no alternative solution, it is for the employee to decide whether to carry on in the same employment and take the risk of a breakdown in his health, or to leave the employment and look for work elsewhere.

In *Intel Corporation (UK) Limited v Daw*,[9] the Court of Appeal appeared to distance itself from this proposition. In *Daw*, the employer was aware of serious management failings which led to the claimant being overworked but persuaded her to stay in the job on the assurance that assistance would be provided, which was not fulfilled. Pill LJ said of the allegation that she should have decided then to leave:

> 'The fact that the respondent did not give up her job when the stresses grew did not, in present circumstances, eliminate the duty of care owed to her. It is not a rule of law that an employee who does not resign when stresses at work are becoming excessive necessarily loses a right of action against her employer.'

9.6   CAUSATION AND APPORTIONMENT

Paragraphs (13) to (16) of the guidance in *Sutherland v Hatton* deal with the issues of causation and apportionment. These are covered in detail at Chapter 3 above, which should be read together with this section.

It of course remains the position that, having shown a breach of duty, it is still necessary to establish that the breach caused the harm suffered.

Many stress-related illnesses are likely to have a number of stressors present. The Court of Appeal in *Sutherland v Hatton* determined that 'in principle a wrongdoer should pay only for that proportion of the harm suffered for which he by his wrongdoing is responsible'. Where the harm was truly indivisible but due to a number of extrinsic causes, a tortfeasor who had made a material contribution was liable. However, it was suggested that a 'sensible attempt' should then be made to apportion liability accordingly. It is for the defendant to raise the issue of, and establish a case for, apportionment.

In *Dickins v O2 Plc*,[10] Smith LJ cast doubt on this approach, noting that Hale LJ's remarks as to apportionment were obiter only – apportionment did not arise in any of the four appeals under consideration and the House of Lords in *Barber* expressly declined to endorse that aspect of the guidance, stating that they had heard no argument on the topic. Smith LJ

---

[9]   [2007] EWCA Civ 70.
[10]   [2008] EWCA Civ 1144.

went on, at paragraph 46, to provide her own 'provisional view', given in the absence of argument and also obiter that, 'in a case which has had to be decided on the basis that the tort has made a material contribution but it is not scientifically possible to say how much that contribution is (apart from the assessment that it was more than de minimis) and where the injury to which that has led is indivisible, it will be inappropriate simply to apportion damages across the board'. At the time of publication, the point is clearly ripe for taking.

Where the tortfeasor's breach of duty has exacerbated a pre-existing disorder or accelerated the effect of a pre-existing vulnerability, then in any event the award for general damages some heads of special damage might well need to be adjusted to account for future risk.

9.7 ALTERNATIVE CAUSES OF ACTION

This chapter deals with claims at common law – and to a limited extent for breach of statutory duty – for injuries caused by stress at work. There are a number of other potential causes of action and those involved in such claims should be astute to the possibilities at the outset. In particular, early decisions need to be made as to whether or not such claims might be better pursued in the employment tribunal. The broad alternative or indeed cumulative causes of action are dealt with briefly below.

9.7.1 Protection from Harassment Act 1997

Claims for stress caused by bullying and harassment in the workplace might also be pursued under the Protection from Harassment Act 1997. In *Majrowski v Guy & St Thomas' NHS Trust*,[11] the House of Lords held that the Act created a statutory tort for which an employer could be held vicariously liable. There is a six-year limitation period for bringing proceedings under the Act, which runs from the date of the loss. There is a requirement to show a course of conduct which crosses the boundary line from 'conduct which is unattractive, even unreasonable' to 'conduct which is oppressive and unacceptable'.

The House of Lords in *Majrowski* held that to cross that line, 'the gravity of the misconduct must be of an order which would sustain criminal liability'. Initially the courts focused on this sentence in a way that severely restricted the ability of claimants to bring a claim under the Act: see, for example, the case of *Conn v Sutherland*.[12] In recent years, however, the Court of Appeal has resiled from what appears to be the high water mark of *Conn*. The case of *Veakins v Kier Islington Limited*,[13] represents a

---

[11] [2006] UKHL 34.
[12] [2007] EWCA Civ 1492.
[13] [2009] EWCA Civ 1288.

considerably softened approach and suggests that the Act may again provide a useful avenue for claimants.

Note that if the harassing conduct is on one of the six prohibited grounds of discrimination – namely sex, race, disability, age, religion and sexuality – consideration should be given to running the claim in the employment tribunal in the alternative.

9.7.2   Breach of contract/implied duty of trust and confidence

There is a developing body of case law based on the employer's breach of the implied duty of trust and confidence. The term remains as defined in *Mahmud v BCCI*,[14] namely that, 'the employer shall not, without reasonable and proper cause, conduct itself in a manner calculated and likely to destroy or seriously damage the relationship of confidence and trust between employer and employee'.

The term was relied upon successfully, for example, in *Gogay v Hertfordshire County Council*,[15] where a social worker suffered psychiatric injury after being suspended on allegations of sexual abuse without reasonable or proper cause.

Where psychiatric injury is however caused by termination of employment, as opposed to pre-termination breaches, there can be no recovery in the civil courts: see *Johnson v Unisys*[16] and *Eastwood v Magnox Electric Plc*.[17]

9.7.3   Disability discrimination

Where stress causes a person to suffer from a physical or mental impairment which falls within the definition of disability in the Equality Act 2010 – namely an: 'impairment which has a substantial and long-term adverse impact on his or her ability to carry out normal day-to-day activities' then it is unlawful for an employer to discriminate against the employee on grounds of or for something arising in consequence of the disability – such as sickness absence. Perhaps more to the point in the present context, there is a duty on the employer to make reasonable adjustments in relation to employment. These might include, for example, altering working hours or providing supervision or flexible working. There are also important distinctions with the common law. For example, the Employment Code, at paragraph 5.17, makes clear that if an in-house occupational health adviser knows about the disability – for example, depression – the employer will not usually be able to claim that they did not know about the disability.

---

[14]   [1997] ICR 606.
[15]   [2000] IRLR 703.
[16]   [2001] 2 WLR 1076, HL.
[17]   [2004] UKHL 35, HL.

If representing a claimant who might fall within the definition – and this is likely to involve the majority of those suffering from stress-related psychiatric injury – it is important to consider, at the outset, whether there is the possibility of an alternative or cumulative claim in the employment tribunal.

Note that there are much tighter time limits in the employment tribunal, with limitation expiring three months from the date of the act complained of or, if there has been a continuing act, from the last act complained of. The general rule in the employment tribunal remains that no costs are recoverable.

9.8 SPECIFIC CONSIDERATIONS FOR WORK-RELATED STRESS CLAIMS

9.8.1 Medical diagnosis

Type of medical condition.

Is there an alternative cause for the condition?

- Constitutional.
- Financial problems.
- Family or marital problems.

9.8.2 Applicable law
- Common law negligence.
- Management of Health and Safety at Work Regulations 1999.
- Working Time Regulations 1998.
- Management Standards.

9.8.3 Exposure

Time of exposure:

- may have been prolonged;
- symptoms often arise after an increase in work, or change in working pattern.

Where did exposure occur?

- not usually critical.

Type of work:

- important to describe and understand the detail of the work.

Foreseeability:

- was the employer put on notice of a foreseeable risk of injury?

9.8.4   Causation
- Did the work cause the condition?
- Was there another cause of the condition?

9.8.5   Apportionment of damages

If there is more than one factor creating symptoms there is likely to be apportionment.

9.8.6   Limitation

When was the tort completed? Onset of symptoms.

Limitation Act 1980:

- s 11 (limitation period);
- s 14 (date of knowledge); and
- s 33 (discretion to waive time-limits).

9.8.7   Medical prognosis
- How is the diagnosed condition likely to progress?
- What are the chances of recurrence?

9.8.8   Damages
- General damages.
- Handicap on the labour market.
- Loss of earnings.
- Cost of medical treatment, counselling, psychotherapy.

9.8.9   Alternatives to common law claim
- Protection from Harassment Act 1997.
- Contractual claim including breach of the implied duty of trust and confidence.
- Disability discrimination and the Equality Act 2010.

PART 3

STATUTORY BASIS OF CLAIM

CHAPTER 10

GENERAL STATUTORY DUTY

10.1 INTRODUCTION

Where an occupational disease has a long latent period before producing symptoms the statutory duties which were in existence at the time of the exposure will be relevant. What follows is a selection of the most important statutory provisions. Although it may be useful to consult old textbooks containing texts of the statutory provisions, the basic source must be the statutes and regulations themselves.

The following provisions may be of use in cases where exposure occurred many years ago:

Regulations	In force	Status
Shipbuilding Regulations 1931, reg 18	1 July 1931	Revoked 31 March 1961
Factories Act 1937, ss 4(1), 47(1)	1 July 1938	Revoked 31 March 1962
Building (Safety, Health and Welfare) Regulations 1948, reg 82	1 October 1948	Revoked 28 February 1962
Shipbuilding and Ship-Repairing Regulations 1960, regs 53(1), 76(1)	31 March 1961	Revoked 5 December 1988
Construction (General Provisions) Regulations 1961, reg 20	1 March 1962	In force, amended by SIs 1974/1681, 1984/1593, 1988/1657, 1989/635, 1989/682, 1992/2932, 1992/2993, 1996/94

Factories Act 1961, ss 29(1), 41(1), 63	1 April 1962	Revoked 31 December 1992
Construction (Working Places) Regulations 1966	1 August 1966	1 September 1996
Control of Substances Hazardous to Health Regulations 1988	1 October 1989	Revoked 15 January 1995
Management of Health and Safety at Work Regulations 1992	1 January 1993	Revoked 2 December 1999
Provision and Use of Work Equipment Regulations 1992	1 January 1993	Revoked 4 December 1998
Workplace (Health, Safety and Welfare) Regulations 1992	1 January 1993	In force, amended by SIs 1995/2036, 1996/1592, 1999/2024
Control of Substances Hazardous to Health Regulations 1994	16 January 1995	Revoked 24 March 1999
Provision and Use of Work Equipment Regulations 1998	5 December 1998	In force, amended by SIs 1999/860, 1999/2001, 2001/1701
Control of Substances Hazardous to Health Regulations 1999	25 March 1999	Revoked, with savings 20 November 2002
Management of Health and Safety at Work Regulations 1999	29 December 1999	In force
Control of Substances Hazardous to Health Regulations 2002	21 November 2002	In force, amended by SI 2003/978

The older legislation generally provided no specific guidance as to the limits of exposure. The definition usually involved an assessment of the degree of danger rather than setting a guideline or limit which should not be exceeded. Thus, section 63 of the Factories Act 1961 referred to 'any dust or fume or other impurity of such a character and to such extent as likely to be injurious or offensive to the persons employed'. This permitted 'safe' levels of exposure to change over time as greater knowledge of the relative dangers became available. For example, asbestos exposure changed from 177 particles per cc (before 1968) to 0.2 and 0.5 fibre/ml long-term limits some 20 years later. More recent Regulations (for example the Noise at Work Regulations 1989) dealing with specific substances usually set out exposure limits and the task is thus simplified. However, examples of flexible interpretation remain, for example in the Control of Substances Hazardous to Health Regulations.

10.2   STATUTES OF GENERAL APPLICATION

10.2.1   Shipbuilding Regulations 1931, reg 18

These Regulations applied to the construction and repair of ships in shipbuilding yards. 'Premises' were defined as those in which any ships, boats or vessels used in navigation were made, finished or repaired. The Regulations did not apply to the construction of fixed structures such as sea forts. The Regulations provided for the removing of fumes or gas where painting, oxy-acetylene burning, electric welding and rivetting were being carried out. They remained in force until 31 March 1961 when they were revoked by the Shipbuilding and Ship-repairing Regulations 1960.

10.2.2   Factories Act 1937

The provisions of the Factories Act 1937 applied between 1 July 1938 and 31 March 1962. The Act and the subsequent 1961 Act applied to a variety of premises, not all of which are likely to be thought of as a factory in a traditional sense.

Section 151 states:

'(1)   Subject to the provisions of this section, the expression "factory" means any premises in which, or within the close or curtilage or precincts of which, persons are employed in manual labour in any process for or incidental to any of the following purposes, namely:
(a)   the making of any article or of part of any article; or
(b)   the altering, repairing, ornamenting, finishing, cleaning, or washing, or the breaking up or demolition of any article; or
(c)   the adapting for sale of any article;
being premises in which, or within the close or curtilage or precincts of which, the work is carried on by way of trade or for purposes of gain and to or over which the employer of the persons employed therein has the right of access or control:
And (whether or not they are factories by reason of the foregoing definition) the expression "factory" also includes the following premises in which persons are employed in manual labour, that is to say:

(i)   any yard or dry dock (including the precincts thereof) in which ships or vessels are constructed, reconstructed, repaired, refitted, finished or broken up;

(ii)   any premises in which the business of sorting any articles is carried on as a preliminary to the work carried on in any factory or incidentally to the purposes of any factory;

(iii)   any premises in which the business of washing or filling bottles or containers or packing articles is carried on incidentally to the purposes of any factory;

(iv)   any premises in which the business of hooking, plaiting, lapping, making-up or packing of yarn or cloth is carried on;

(v)   any laundry carried on ancillary to another business, or incidentally to the purposes of any public institution;

(vi)   any premises in which the construction, reconstruction or repair of locomotives, vehicles or other plant for use for transport purposes is carried on as ancillary to a transport undertaking or other industrial or commercial undertaking, not being any premises used for the purpose of housing locomotives or vehicles where only cleaning, washing, running repairs or minor adjustments are carried out;

(vii)   any premises in which printing by letterpress, lithography, photogravure, or other similar process, or bookbinding is carried on by way of trade or for purposes of gain or incidentally to another business so carried on;

(viii) any premises in which the making, adaptation or repair of dresses, scenery or properties is carried on incidentally to the production, exhibition or presentation by way of trade or for purposes of gain of cinematograph films or theatrical performances, not being a stage or dressing-room of a theatre in which only occasional adaptations or repairs are made;

(ix)   any premises in which the business of making or mending nets is carried on incidentally to the fishing industry;

(x)   any premises in which mechanical power is used in connection with the making or repair of articles of metal or wood incidentally to any business carried on by way of trade or for purposes of gain;

(xi)   any premises in which the production of cinematograph films is carried on by way of trade or for purposes of gain, so, however, that the employment at any such premises of theatrical performers ... shall not be deemed to be a factory;

(xii)   any premises in which articles are made or prepared incidentally to the carrying on of building operations or works of engineering construction, not being premises in which such operations or works are being carried on;

(xiii) any premises used for the storage of gas in a gasholder having a storage capacity of not less than five thousand cubic feet.'

Section 4(1) of the Act stated:

'Effective and suitable provision shall be made for securing and maintaining by the circulation of fresh air in each work room the adequate ventilation of the room and for rendering harmless so far as practicable, all fumes, dust and other impurities that may be injurious to health generated in the course of any process or work carried on in the factory.'

The test under section 4 was whether the dust, fume and other impurity was injurious. The obligation was to render the dust harmless so far as practicable. There was no requirement that the dust be removed entirely. It will be appreciated that the defining words 'that may be injurious' require judgment in the circumstances and are not susceptible of precise measurement. Factual evidence may need to be supported by expert evidence. It is for the defendants to prove that it was not practicable to take measures and it should be pleaded as an issue in the case.[1]

Section 47(1) required practicable measures to prevent inhalation:

'In every factory in which, in connection with any process carried on there is given off any dust or fume or other impurity of such a character and to such extent as to be likely to be injurious or offensive to the person employed or any substantial quantity of dust of any kind all practicable measures shall be taken to protect the person employed against inhalation of the dust or fume or other impurity and to prevent its accumulating in any work room and in particular, where the nature of the process makes it practicable, exhaust appliances shall be provided and maintained, as near as possible to the point of origin of the dust or fume or other impurity, so as to prevent it entering the air of any work room.'

The test under section 47 of the Act was, like section 4, whether the dust, fume and other impurity was injurious, but it also applied to dust, fume and other impurity that was 'offensive', and to dust of any kind where there was a 'substantial quantity'. It will be appreciated that these defining words are not capable of precise measurement. Factual evidence may need to be supported by expert evidence.

Sections 4 and 47 were breached where a painter working on board ships during their construction was exposed to asbestos.[2]

Debate has arisen as to whether the occupier needs to have knowledge that the substance is 'injurious', ie whether this is an objective or a subjective test. In *Charles v Preston and Thomas Limited*,[3] a breach of section 47 was found where manufacturers of fish and chip cooking ranges required workers to handle asbestos-insulating panels and to cut them into shape and fit them in the cooking ranges. On the other hand, a pipe fitter who was exposed to asbestos lagging at a steel works failed to establish any breach of the Factories Act 1937.[4] This decision was based in part on the concept that the sections were not relevant to the work the

---

[1]   *Nimmo v Alexander Cowan and Sons Limited* [1968] AC 107; *Bowes v Sedgefield District Council* [1981] ICR 234, CA.

[2]   *Bryce v Swan Hunter Group* [1987] 2 Lloyd's Rep 426.

[3]   (Unreported) 14 May 1993.

[4]   See *Banks v Woodhall Duckham Limited* (unreported) 30 November 1995, CA.

pipe fitter was doing and so offered him no protection. It was held that there was no evidence that the exposure was to such an extent or of such a character as to be likely to be injurious, that the activities of asbestos lagging were not 'a process carried on in a factory' because the factory manufactured steel and that the plaintiff was not a person employed within the meaning of section 47 because the words 'person employed' in that section relate back to the words found earlier, namely 'in connection with any process'.

However, in a more recent case, it was held that the duty under section 47 applied to persons who worked in other parts of the premises.[5] In that case the claimant worked in the accounts department of a power plant.

10.2.3   Building (Safety, Health and Welfare) Regulations 1948

These Regulations applied between 1 October 1948 and 28 February 1962. They applied to the construction, structural alteration, repair or maintenance and demolition of a building, and the preparation for, and laying the foundation of, an intended building. For the purposes of reg 2, the following were not 'buildings': docks, harbours, wharves, quays, piers, sea defence works, lighthouses at sea, river works, canals, dams, reservoirs, aqueducts, viaducts, bridges, tunnels, sewers, pipelines, filter beds, gasholders, pole or lattice work designed solely for the support of machinery, plant or electric lines.

Regulation 82 stated:

> 'Where in connection with any grinding cleaning, spraying or manipulation of any material there is given off any dust or fume of such a character and to such extent as to be likely to be injurious to the health of persons employed all reasonably practicable measures shall be taken either by securing adequate ventilation or by the provision and use of suitable respirators or otherwise to prevent inhalation of such dust or fume.'

In *Morrison v Central Electricity Generating Board and Babcock & Wilcox Limited*[6] reg 82 was held to apply to a fitter working in a power station employed by contractors engaged in erecting, testing and maintaining soot blowers, which was held to be part of the 'construction' of the building. However, there was no breach of reg 82 because the degree of asbestos exposure suffered by the plaintiff when working in the vicinity of asbestos laggers was not proved to have been known to be 'likely to be injurious' at the date of the exposure.

---

[5]   *Anderson v RWE Npower plc* (LTL 20/5/2010).
[6]   (Unreported) 15 March 1986.

It is for the defendants to prove that it was not practicable to take measures, and this should be pleaded as an issue in the case.[7]

10.2.4 Shipbuilding and Ship-Repairing Regulations 1960

These Regulations came into force on 31 March 1961. Regulation 53(1) was of general application in that it applied to any dust, fume or impurity that was likely to be injurious. The test was based on the available knowledge at the time of the exposure. It is for the defendants to prove that it was not practicable to take measures, and this should be pleaded as an issue in the case.[8] Regulation 53(1) states:

'Where in connection, with any process carried or on board in or on the outside of a vessel or part of a vessel there is given off any dust or fume or other impurity of such a character and to such extent as to be likely to be injurious to the persons employed all practicable measures shall be taken to protect the persons employed against inhalation, of the dust or fume or other impurity and in particular, where practicable exhaust appliances shall be provided and maintained as near as possible to the point of origin of dust or fume or other impurity to protect such persons against such inhalation.'

Regulation 76(1) applies to asbestos generally, and by reg 76(1)(e) to dust of a character likely to be injurious:

'Breathing apparatus of a type approved for the purpose of this Regulation shall be provided and maintained for the use of every person employed in any of the following kind of work:
(a)   the application of asbestos by means of a spray;
(b)   the breaking down for removal of asbestos lagging;
(c)   the cleaning of sacks or other containers which have contained asbestos;
(d)   the cutting of material containing asbestos by means of portable driven saws;
(e)   the scaling, scuffing or cleaning of boilers, combustion chambers or smoke boxes, where his work exposes him to dust of such a character and to such an extent as to be likely to be injurious or offensive to persons employed in such work.'

10.2.5 Factories Act 1961

The following sections of the 1961 Factories Act were in force between 1 April 1962 and 31 December 1992.

Section 29(1) provided:

---

[7]   *Nimmo v Alexander Cowan and Sons Limited* [1968] AC 107; *Bowes v Sedgefield District Council* [1981] ICR 234, CA.
[8]   *Nimmo v Alexander Cowan and Sons Limited* [1968] AC 107; *Bowes v Sedgefield District Council* [1981] ICR 234, CA.

> 'There shall so far as is reasonably practicable be provided and maintained safe means of access to every place at which any person has at any time to work and every such place shall so far as is reasonably practicable, be made and kept safe for any person working there.'

The provision only applies to the state of the premises and does not apply to the transient condition of the workplace.

When considering whether a workplace was safe the question of reasonable foreseeability does not arise. If, as a matter of objective fact, the place was not safe, there is a breach unless the employer can prove that it was not reasonably practicable to keep the premises safe. It is for the defendants to prove that it was not practicable to take measures, and this should be pleaded as an issue in the case.[9]

Section 41(1) provided:

> 'Effective and suitable provision shall be made for securing and maintaining by the circulation of fresh air in each work room the adequate ventilation of the room and for rendering harmless, so far as practicable all such fumes dust and other impurities generated in the course of any process or work carried on in the factory as may be injurious to health.'

Section 63, which had the same wording as section 47 of the Factories Act 1937 (see above at **10.2.2**), applied to dust, fume and other impurity. The test was whether the dust, fume or impurity was injurious or offensive, or whether it was a substantial quantity of dust of any kind. It is the state of knowledge at the time of exposure that is relevant.[10] The test is not capable of precise measurement, and factual evidence may need to be supported by expert evidence.

In *Banks v Woodhall Duckham*,[11] the Court of Appeal held that the words 'persons employed' meant that the section only protected persons who were actually employed in the dust-making process and not persons who were employed elsewhere but who inhaled the dust. However, the words are capable of another analysis. In *The Estate of Trevor Owen Deceased v IMI Yorkshire Copper*,[12] it was held at first instance that the words 'in connection with any process carried on' referred to the dust produced and not the person operating the process.

10.2.6 Construction (General Provisions) Regulations 1961

Regulation 20 came into force on 1 March 1962, and states:

---

[9] *Nimmo v Alexander Cowan and Sons Limited* [1968] AC 107; *Bowes v Sedgefield District Council* [1981] ICR 234, CA.

[10] See *Asmussen v Filtrona UK Ltd* [2011] EWHC 1734.

[11] (Unreported) 30 November 1995.

[12] (Unreported) 15 June 1995.

'Where in connection with any grinding cleaning, spraying or manipulation of any material, there is given off any dust or fume of such a character and to such extent as to be likely to be injurious to the health of persons employed all reasonably practicable measures shall be taken either by securing adequate ventilation or by the provision and use of suitable respirators or otherwise to prevent inhalation of such dust and fume.'

Regulation 20 is in the same terms as the previous reg 82 of the Building (Safety, Health and Welfare) Regulations 1948 (see above at **10.2.3**) and the same considerations apply. It is for the defendants to prove that it was not practicable to take measures, and this should be pleaded as an issue in the case.[13]

10.2.7 Construction (Working Places) Regulations 1966

These Regulations were in force between 1 August 1966 and 1 September 1996.

Regulation 6(2) stated:

'Without prejudice to the other provisions of these Regulations, every place at which any person at any time works shall, so far as is reasonably practicable, be made and kept safe for any person working there.'

The provision applies only to the state of the premises and not to the transient condition of the workplace.

When considering whether a workplace was safe the question of reasonable foreseeability does not arise. If as a matter of objective fact the place was not safe there is a breach unless the employer can prove that it was not reasonably practicable to keep the premises safe. This defence needs to be pleaded and supported with evidence (see cases mentioned above).

10.2.8 Control of Substances Hazardous to Health Regulations 1988, 1994, 1999 and 2002

Depending on the date or dates of exposure, it may be necessary to rely upon the provisions of all four sets of Regulations. However, the time between exposure and the onset of symptoms is usually fairly short in cases where these Regulations are likely to apply.

The Control of Substances Hazardous to Health Regulations 1988 applied from 1 October 1989. The 1994 Regulations made minor alterations to the 1988 Regulations and applied from 16 January 1995.

---

[13]   *Nimmo v Alexander Cowan and Sons Limited* [1968] AC 107; *Bowes v Sedgefield District Council* [1981] ICR 234, CA.

The 1999 Regulations came into force on 25 March 1999. The 2002 Regulations have applied from 21 November 2002.

A precedent based on the 2002 Regulations is included in Appendix 1. What follows is a summary of the provisions of the 2002 Regulations, but it is recommended that the source material is consulted. If reliance is to be placed on the 1988, 1994 or 1999 Regulations, the source Regulations must be considered in order to identify and apply the variations in the provisions.

Regulation 3 imposes duties on an employer in respect of his employees in the following areas: prohibition of certain substances; assessment of health risks; prevention or control of exposure to substances hazardous to health; monitoring; health surveillance and provision of information, instruction or training. Regulation 3 also imposes duties on an employer in respect of persons other than his employees, whether or not at work, who may be affected by the work carried on by the employer. In these circumstances employers' duties are less onerous. In particular they are subject to the lower standard of reasonable practicability, and there is no duty to provide health surveillance or information, instruction or training.

By reg 8(2) employees are required to make full and proper use of any control measure, personal protective equipment or other thing or facility provided by the employer pursuant to the duties imposed by the Regulations. The employee is also under a duty to report any defect in any of these things.

The Regulations do not apply where the provisions of the Mines and Quarries Act 1954, the Coal Mines (Respirable Dust) Regulations 1975, the Control of Lead at Work Regulations 1998 and 2002 and the Control of Asbestos at Work Regulations 1987 and 2002 apply. The Regulations do not apply to substances that are radioactive, explosive or flammable, or where the substance is at a high or low temperature or under high pressure, in which circumstances other regulations may apply, such as the Provision and Use of Work Equipment Regulations 1992 and 1998. Finally, the Regulations do not apply where the substance is administered in the course of medical treatment.

Substances hazardous to health are defined in reg 2, which states:

> "'Substance hazardous to health" means a substance (including any preparation) –
> (a) which is listed in Part I of the approved supply list as dangerous for supply within the meaning of the Chemicals (Hazard Information and Packaging for Supply) Regulations and for which an indication of danger specified for the substance in Part V of that list is very toxic, toxic, harmful, corrosive or irritant;
> (b) for which the Health and Safety Commission has approved a maximum exposure limit or an occupational exposure standard;

(c) which is a biological agent;
(d) which is dust of any kind, except dust which is a substance within paragraph (a) or (b) above when present at a concentration in air equal to or greater than –
   (i) 10 mg/m^3 as a time-weighted average over an 8-hour period of total inhalable dust; or
   (ii) 4 mg/m^3 as a time-weighted average over an 8-hour period of respirable dust;
(e) which, not being a substance falling with sub-paragraphs (a) to (d), because of its chemical or toxicological properties and the way in which it is used or is present at the workplace creates a risk to health.'

The final subparagraph was worded differently in the preceeding Regulations and instead read: 'not being a substance mentioned in sub-paragraphs ... above, which creates a hazard to the health of any person which is comparable with the hazards created by substances mentioned in those sub-paragraphs'.

Whereas the earlier Regulations referred to 'total inhalable dust' (which was airborne material capable of entering the nose and mouth during breathing and was thereby available for deposition in the respiratory tract), BS EN 481 1993 now refers to 'inhalable dust'.

The substances listed in (a) and (b) above are too numerous to be included in this work, and should be consulted according to the circumstances.

It will be appreciated that the services of a suitably qualified expert will often be required, especially when considering category (d) 'dust of any kind', where it is necessary to have measurements of concentration in air equal to or greater than 10 mg/m^3 of total inhalable dust as a time-weighted average, or 4 mg/m^3 of respirable dust over a time-weighted average in an 8-hour period.

Regulation 6 requires an assessment of health risks where work is liable to expose employees to a substance hazardous to health. The work cannot be carried out until a suitable and sufficient assessment of the risks to health and the steps required to meet the requirements of the Regulations has been made. The assessment must be reviewed if there is reason to suspect that it is no longer valid or that there has been a significant change in the work to which the assessment relates. In *Naylor v Volex Group*,[14] an environmental consultant raised serious concerns about the previous method of assessment in respect of the fumes from soldering. Failure to carry out a reassessment was a breach of statutory duty.

Under reg 7, the employer must ensure that the exposure of his employees to substances hazardous to health is either prevented or, where this is not reasonably practicable, adequately controlled, see *Dugmore v Swansea*

---

[14] LTL 14/2/2003.

NHS Trust & Morriston NHS Trust.[15] The duty is to prevent exposure unless it is not reasonably practicable to do so. Then, the duty is to provide adequate control. This duty is not subject to the qualification of reasonable practicability, and is a strict duty, measured by the standard of adequacy.

The prevention or adequate control of the exposure to substances hazardous to health must be secured by measures other than the provision of personal protective equipment, so far as is reasonably practicable. This limitation of 'reasonable practicability' requires a balance to be struck between the incidence and degree of risk, on the one hand, and the cost in time, effort or money, on the other. Cases dealing with this phrase in other health and safety legislation will be relevant to illustrate the operation of the exercise.

If it is 'reasonably practicable' to do so, the employer's first act should be to control the process or substance hazardous to health by, for example, closing off the process or machine, or by providing suitable exhaust ventilation.

At the very least, the employer should provide protective clothing or suitable masks or respirators. This protective equipment must adequately control exposure to the hazardous substances. 'Adequate' is defined as meaning 'adequate having regard to the nature of the substances and the nature and degree of exposure'. Where protective equipment is provided it must be suitable for the purpose and comply with any applicable provisions of the Personal Protective Equipment Regulations 2002. Respiratory equipment shall be of a type approved by, or conform to a standard approved by, the Health and Safety Executive (HSE).

The control of exposure by inhalation to a substance to which a maximum exposure limit applies (specified in Sch 1) will be treated as adequate only if the level of exposure is reduced below the maximum exposure limit and then further reduced so far as is reasonably practicable. It is to be noted that there are two distinct elements here. The requirements of the regulation are not met if exposure is above the maximum exposure limit, whatever the cost in time, effort or money.

The Regulations require that the control of exposure by inhalation of a substance for which there is an occupational exposure standard will be treated as adequate only if the occupational exposure standard is not exceeded, or, if it is exceeded, where the employer identifies the reasons for the standard being exceeded and takes appropriate action to remedy the situation as soon as is reasonably practicable. It is suggested that this exception covers circumstances where an unforseen event has increased exposure beyond the standard.

---

[15]   [2003] ICR 574.

Carcinogenic substances are defined by reg 2 either by reference to the provisions of the Chemicals (Hazard Information and Packaging for Supply) Regulations 1994 or as listed in Sch 8 of the Control of Substances Hazardous to Health Regulations. Where it is not reasonably practicable to prevent exposure by using an alternative substance or process, control must be achieved by total enclosure of the process and handling systems, and where that is not reasonably practicable, the use of plant, processes and systems of work which minimise exposure. The quantities of carcinogens must be limited, the number of persons who might be exposed kept to a minimum, and eating, drinking and smoking in areas that may be contaminated must be prohibited. Hygiene measures, including adequate washing facilities and regular cleaning of the facilities, must be provided. Areas that may be contaminated must be designated, and warnings signs displayed.

Regulation 8 sets out a duty on the employer, as follows:

'(1) Every employer who provides any control measure, other thing or facility in accordance with these Regulations shall take all reasonable steps to ensure that it is properly used or applied as the case may be.'

A complimentary duty is imposed on the employee to make full and proper use of any control measure, other thing or facility provided pursuant to the Regulations. The employee must take all reasonable steps to ensure that the control measure is returned after use to any accommodation provided for it, and to report any defect in it forthwith to his employer.

Under reg 9 the employer must ensure that the control measure is maintained in an efficient state, in efficient working order and in good repair. This is a strict liability duty. 'Efficient' is to be considered in the context of health and safety. Local exhaust plant must be examined and tested at least once every 14 months, unless another interval is specified in Sch 4 to the Regulations. Where respiratory protective equipment (other than disposable equipment) is provided the employer must ensure that thorough examinations and, where appropriate, tests of that equipment are carried out at suitable intervals. What is a suitable interval will depend upon the circumstances. There is duty on the employer to keep personal protective equipment in a clean condition.

Regulation 10 requires monitoring to ensure the maintenance of adequate control of exposure to substances hazardous to health, or to protect the health of employees. The employer must use a suitable procedure, which will depend in part upon the degree of risk. Certain specified substances and processes require monitoring at specified intervals. The results of monitoring must be recorded and kept for at least five years. Where monitoring is representative of the personal exposure of certain employees, those records must be kept for at least 40 years. These records may be important documents for the purposes of disclosure.

Regulation 11 requires suitable health surveillance where it is appropriate for the protection of the health of employees who are, or are liable to be, exposed to substances hazardous to health. Medical surveillance is required for specified substances or processes. An employer may be obliged to continue medical surveillance after cessation of employment where the employment medical adviser so advises. A health record containing particulars approved by the HSE must be kept in respect of each employee under surveillance for at least 40 years. Where an employer goes out of business it must notify the HSE and offer up its records.

An employee has the right to access his health record on the giving of reasonable notice. An employment medical adviser or appointed doctor may also inspect the workplace or any record kept for the purpose of the Regulations.

The provision of information, instruction and training is covered by reg 12. Where exposure to a substance hazardous to health is possible the employer must provide the employee with such information, instruction and training as is suitable and sufficient for the employee to know the risks to health created by such exposure, and the precautions which should be taken. This must include information on the results of any monitoring and the collective results of any health surveillance. If the maximum exposure limit of a substance specified in Sch 1 has been exceeded, the employee or his representative must be informed.

By reg 13 the employer must have relevant procedures in place for dealing with accidents, incidents and emergencies.

10.2.9   Management of Health and Safety at Work Regulations 1992 and 1999

The 1992 Regulations came into force on 1 January 1993 and were replaced by the 1999 Regulations on 29 December 1999.

Regulation 3 imposes a duty on the employer to make an assessment of the risks to the health and safety of employees, which may be important in relation to the issue of foreseeability. Before 27 October 2003 there was no civil remedy for breach of the Regulations, but they did set the standard for negligence. For events occurring after 27 October 2003, breach of the Regulations will give rise to a breach of duty by an employer in respect of persons in his employment. Regulation 6 of the Management of Health and Safety at Work and Fire Precautions (Workplace) (Amendment) Regulations 2003 states:

'Breach of a duty imposed on an employer by these Regulations shall not confer a right of action in any civil proceedings insofar as that duty applies for the protection of persons not in his employment.'

Examples of both types of pleadings are provided in Appendix 1.

Following a risk assessment under reg 3, reg 4 of the 1999 Regulations states:

'Where an employer implements any preventative and protective measures he shall do so on the basis of the principles specified in Schedule 1 to these Regulations.'

Schedule 1 sets out the general principles of prevention as follows:

(a) avoiding risks;
(b) evaluating the risks which cannot be avoided;
(c) combatting the risks at source;
(d) adapting the work to the individual, especially as regards the design of workplaces, the choice of work equipment and the choice of working and production methods, with a view, in particular, to alleviating monotonous work and work at a predetermined work-rate and to reducing their effect on health;
(e) adapting to technical progress;
(f) replacing the dangerous by the non-dangerous or the less dangerous;
(g) developing a coherent overall prevention policy which covers technology, organisation of work, working conditions, social relationships and the influence of factors relating to the working environment;
(h) giving collective protective measures priority over individual protective measures; and
(i) giving appropriate instructions to employees.

It is to be noted that these principles were not included in the 1992 Regulations.

Regulation 4 of the 1992 Regulations and reg 5 of the 1999 Regulations provide a general requirement to make and give effect to such arrangements as are appropriate (having regard to the nature of the employer's activities and the size of the undertaking) for the effective planning, organisation, control, monitoring and review of the preventive and protective measures.

Regulation 6 of the 1999 Regulations states:

'Every employer shall ensure that his employees are provided with such health surveillance as is appropriate having regard to the risks to their health or safety which are identified by the assessment.'

Thus the requirement to provide health surveillance is qualified by the test of appropriateness. It could be argued that it is not appropriate to put in place health surveillance, for example, shortly after exposure to asbestos because there is a long latent period before the disease creates signs or symptoms. On the other hand, sensitisation to substances causing asthma, for example, can occur immediately or in a very short period of time. In asthma cases the provisions of the Control of Substances Hazardous to Health Regulations are more likely to have specific application. Testing for deteriorating hearing levels may be relevant to prevent further damage by removing a vulnerable employee from the excessive noise. Even if an employee is unduly sensitive to noise, such sensitivity being unforeseeable, once the sensitivity is known the employee could be protected from further damage. Health surveillance could also be relevant where there is known exposure to high stress levels.

Regulation 13 of the 1999 Regulations states:

'(1)   Every employer shall, in entrusting tasks to his employees, take into account their capabilities as regards health and safety.
(2)   Every employer shall ensure that his employees are provided with adequate health and safety training–
(a)   on their being recruited into the employer's undertaking; and
(b)   on their being exposed to new or increased risks because of –
(i)   their being transferred or given a change of responsibilities within the employer's undertaking;
(ii)   the introduction of new work equipment into or a change respecting work equipment already in use within the employer's undertaking;
(iii) the introduction of new technology into the employer's undertaking; or
(iv)   the introduction of a new system of work into or a change respecting a system of work already in use within the employer's undertaking.
(3)   The training referred to in para (2) shall –
(a)   be repeated periodically where appropriate;
(b)   be adapted to take account of any new or changed risks to the health and safety of the employees concerned; and
(c)   take place during working hours.'

Regulation 13(1), which requires the employer to take into account the varying capabilities of its employees, could be relevant in work-related stress cases and work-related upper limb disorder (WRULD) cases. Not every employee will be suitable for every job. Matters of education, qualifications, experience and general capability may be relevant. The requirements of the job must be taken into account. There is a duty under reg 13 to provide training and instruction in the tasks which are required to be performed. Of course it may be a very relevant matter to consider what an employee can reasonably be expected to know and do by reason of his previous education, qualifications and experience. An important feature is the requirement for the training to be repeated periodically.

10.2.10   Workplace (Health, Safety and Welfare) Regulations 1992

These Regulations came into force on 1 January 1993. Regulation 5 applies to the maintenance of the workplace, and of equipment, devices and systems which are used as part of the workplace (eg ventilation systems). Regulation 5 provides:

'(1)   The workplace and the equipment, devices and systems to which this regulation applies shall be maintained (including cleaned as appropriate) in an efficient state, in efficient working order and in good repair.

(2)   Where appropriate, the equipment, devices and systems to which this regulation applies shall be subject to a suitable system of maintenance.

(3)   The equipment, devices and systems to which this regulation applies are –

(a)   equipment and devices a fault in which is liable to result in a failure to comply with any of these Regulations; and

(b)   mechanical ventilation systems provided pursuant to reg 6 (whether or not they include equipment or devices within sub-para (a) of this paragraph).'

The term 'in an efficient state, in efficient working order' relate to matters of health and safety rather than the efficiency of production. The Regulations come with helpful guidance notes.

Regulation 6 applies to ventilation, although there are important exceptions. It states:

'(1)   Effective and suitable provision shall be made to ensure that every enclosed workplace is ventilated by a sufficient quantity of fresh or purified air.

(2)   Any plant used for the purpose of complying with para (1) shall include an effective device to give visible or audible warning of any failure of the plant where necessary for reasons of health or safety.

(3)   This regulation shall not apply to any enclosed workplace or part of a workplace which is subject to the provisions of –

(a)   section 30 of the Factories Act 1961;

(b)   regulations 49–52 of the Shipbuilding and Ship-Repairing Regulations 1960;

(c)   regulation 21 of the Construction (General Provisions) Regulations 1961;

(d)   regulation 18 of the Docks Regulations 1988.'

Regulation 9 relates to cleanliness, requiring that the workplace, furnishings and fittings be kept sufficiently clean.

Regulation 11(1) requires that every workstation must be so arranged that it is suitable for any person at work in the workplace who is likely to work at that workstation and for any work of the undertaking which is likely to be done there. Bad layout can lead to stress, cause incorrect ergonomic positioning and affect exposure to dust or fume or noise. Regulation 11 continues:

'(2)   Without prejudice to the generality of paragraph (1), every workstation outdoors shall be so arranged that –
   (a)   so far as is reasonably practicable, it provides protection from adverse weather;
   (b)   it enables any person at the workstation to leave it swiftly or, as appropriate, to be assisted in the event of an emergency; and
   (c)   it ensures that any person at the workstation is not likely to slip or fall.
(3)   A suitable seat shall be provided for each person at work in the workplace whose work includes operations of a kind that the work (or a substantial part of it) can or must be done sitting.
(4)   A seat shall not be suitable for the purpose of para (3) unless –
   (a)   it is suitable for the person for whom it is provided as well as for the operations to be performed; and
   (b)   a suitable footrest is also provided where necessary.'

10.2.11   Provision and Use of Work Equipment Regulations 1992 and 1998

The 1992 Regulations came into force on 1 January 1993 and were replaced by the 1998 Regulations on 5 December 1998. The Regulations make specific provision for work equipment, which provision will usually be of relevance only in single event accident cases. However, reg 4 of the 1998 Regulations imposes a duty to ensure that the work equipment is so constructed or adapted as to be suitable for the purpose for which it is used or provided. 'Work equipment' has a wide definition and includes not merely machinery, but tools and other items used in the work. Thus reg 4 could have application for work-related upper limb disorder and noise loss claims. The regulation is not qualified by reasonable practicability and so the question is whether the work equipment is 'suitable'. The intended use and the particular features of the work are clearly relevant in these circumstances. Regulation 4 states:

'(1)   Every employer shall ensure that work equipment is so constructed or adapted as to be suitable for the purpose for which it is used or provided.
(2)   In selecting work equipment, every employer shall have regard to the working conditions and to the risks to the health and safety of persons which exist in the premises or undertaking in which that work equipment is to be used and any additional risk posed by the use of that work equipment.
(3)   Every employer shall ensure that work equipment is used only for operations for which, and under conditions for which, it is suitable.
(4)   In this regulation "suitable" –

(a) subject to sub-paragraph (b) [police equipment], means suitable in any respect which it is reasonably foreseeable will affect the health or safety of any person.'

CHAPTER 11

REGULATIONS WITH SPECIFIC APPLICATION

11.1   AT A GLANCE

Regulations	In force	Status
Asbestos Industry Regulations 1931	1 March 1932	Revoked 13 May 1970
Asbestos Regulations 1969	1 May 1970	Revoked 1987
Woodworking Machines Regulations 1974	24 May 1976	Revoked 1989
Control of Asbestos at Work Regulations 1987	1 March 1988	In force, amended by SIs 1988/712, 1992/2966, 1992/3068, 1993/1746, 1994/669, 1994/3247, 1996/2092, 1998/3235
Control of Substances Hazardous to Health Regulations 1988	1 October 1989	Revoked 15 January 1995
Noise at Work Regulations 1989	1 January 1990	In force, amended by SIs 1992/2966, 1996/341, 1997/1993, 1999/2024
Health and Safety (Display Screen Equipment) Regulations 1992	1 January 1993	In force

Manual Handling Operations Regulations 1992	1 January 1993	In force
Control of Substances Hazardous to Health Regulations 1994	16 January 1995	Revoked 24 March 1999
Control of Substances Hazardous to Health Regulations 1999	25 March 1999	In force, amended by SIs 1999/1820, 2000/2831
Control of Asbestos at Work Regulations 2002	21 November 2002	In force
Control of Substances Hazardous to Health Regulations 2002	21 November 2002	In force
Control of Vibration at Work Regulations 2005	6 July 2005	In force
Control of Noise at Work Regulations 2005	6 April 2006	In force

11.2   THE REGULATIONS

11.2.1   Asbestos Industry Regulations 1931

These Regulations came into force on 1 March 1932. Despite the increasing knowledge of the dangers of asbestos, they remained the only statutory protection until 14 May 1970, when they were replaced by the Asbestos Regulations 1969. These Regulations imposed duties on occupiers of factories in respect of a number of defined processes involving asbestos. The duty was limited to the extent that if the processes were carried on only occasionally, and no person was employed for more than eight hours in any week, the Regulations did not apply.

The Regulations applied to the occupiers of any factory or workshop or part of those premises where there was breaking, crushing, disintegrating, opening and grinding of asbestos and the mixing or sieving of asbestos, and all incidental processes involving manipulation of asbestos. The Regulations also applied to the manufacture of asbestos textiles, insulation slabs and sections, and the making or repairing of insulating mattresses composed wholly or partly of asbestos. The activities of sawing, grinding, abrading and polishing asbestos in the dry state were covered in respect of articles composed wholly or partly of asbestos. The Regulations further applied to the cleaning of any chambers, fixtures and appliances used for the collection of asbestos dust from those processes.

The Chief Inspector of Factories was empowered to certify a relaxation or suspension of the Regulations, but it is not clear whether such a power was ever exercised.

'Asbestos' was defined as any fibrous silicate mineral, and any admixture containing any such mineral, whether crude, crushed or opened. Asbestos textiles included any yarn or cloth composed of asbestos or asbestos mixed with any other material.

11.2.1.1   Exhaust draughts

Under reg 1 employers had to provide mechanically powered exhaust draughts to prevent the escape of asbestos dust into the air of any room in which persons worked at defined activities involving asbestos. Thus, manufacturing and conveying machinery for preparing, grinding or dry mixing, spinning and weaving of asbestos and to machines which were fed with asbestos and used for the sawing, grinding, turning, abrading or polishing, in the dry state, or articles composed wholly or partly of asbestos. An exhaust draught was also required for the cleaning and grinding of cylinders and other parts of carding machines, chambers, hoppers and other structures which delivered loose asbestos, asbestos waste sorting and other manipulation of asbestos by hand, including the emptying of sacks, skips or other portable containers and sack-cleaning machines.

The Regulations did not apply to a machine or other plant which did not give rise to asbestos dust, or was so enclosed as to prevent the escape of asbestos dust into the air of the workroom. Similarly an exhaust draught was not required where the asbestos was so wet or so treated with grease or other material as to prevent the evolution of dust.

Regulation 2 required that where mixing or blending of asbestos by hand was carried out (which seems to have been frequently in the first few decades) a mechanically powered exhaust draught had to be provided which was so designed and maintained as to ensure as far as practicable the suppression of dust during the processes. It is to be noted that the duty was limited to one of practicability, not the less onerous requirement of reasonable practicability.

For the making or repairing of insulating mattresses containing asbestos, reg 3 required the provision and maintenance of adequate exhaust and inlet ventilation in accordance with arrangements to be approved in each case. The presence of persons not engaged in filling, beating or levelling of asbestos mattresses was restricted, and a ten-minute pause was permitted before work was resumed, although it is doubtful whether such a pause was sufficient time to allow microscopic asbestos fibres to settle. Floors and benches had to be kept damped down so as to prevent dust arising.

Regulation 9 required the inspection, examination and testing, at least once every six months, of all ventilating plant used for the purpose of extracting or suppressing asbestos

11.2.1.2   Storage

Under reg 4 storage chambers or bins for loose asbestos had to be effectually separated from any workroom, and chambers or apparatus for dust settling and filtering were not allowed in any workroom. Arrangements had to be made to prevent asbestos which had been removed by exhaust apparatus from being drawn back into the air of the workroom.

11.2.1.3   Containment

Regulation 5 required that defined machinery, including machinery used in preparing, grinding, carding, card roller cleaning and sack-cleaning, should be so constructed and maintained that dust or debris containing asbestos could not escape except by an exhaust draught provided in accordance with reg 1.

11.2.1.4   Cleaning

Regulation 6 required that only cleaners be present for the purpose of hand cleaning the cylinders of a carding machine, and forbade, after 1 September 1932, cleaning by hand strickles or other hand tools.

Likely to be of greater relevance is reg 7, which required the floors, work benches and plant to be kept in a clean state and free from asbestos debris, and required suitable arrangements be made for the storage of asbestos not immediately required for use. The floors had to be kept free from any materials, plant or other articles not immediately required for the work carried on and which would obstruct the proper cleaning of the floor. Hand cleaning of sacks was forbidden by reg 8.

Suitable overalls and head coverings had to be provided and maintained for the use of all persons employed in the cleaning of dust settling and filtering chambers, tunnels and ducts. No similar requirement was necessary for other workers not so employed. Regulation 17 required workers to wear the overall and head coverings provided.

11.2.1.5   Breathing apparatus

Regulation 10 provided that breathing apparatus be provided in limited and defined circumstances for every person employed:

(a)   in chambers containing loose asbestos;

(b) in cleaning dust settling or filtering chambers or apparatus;
(c) in cleaning the cylinders, including the doffer cylinders, or other part of a carding machine by means of hand strickles;
(d) in filling, beating, or levelling in the manufacture or repair of insulating mattresses.

11.2.1.6 Persons employed

Under reg 13 workers could not wilfully or negligently disregard any directions given for the purpose of securing the observance of the Regulations or otherwise for the prevention of unnecessary dust. Regulation 14 required workers to make full and proper use of the appliances provided for any of the purposes of the Regulations. Finally, under reg 15 workers were required not to misuse or wrongfully interfere in any way with any appliance provided in pursuance of the Regulations. Workers were required to wear and properly use the breathing apparatus provided.

11.2.2 Asbestos Regulations 1969

These Regulations came into force on 14 May 1970 and remained in force until 1987. They applied to factories, building operations and works of engineering construction. The Factory Inspectorate issued a Technical Data Note setting standards for asbestos dust concentration at 0.2 fibres/ml for crocidolite and 2 fibres/ml for amosite and chrysotile. The duties imposed under the Regulations are absolute. Lack of knowledge that asbestos was present is not a defence since the intention of the Regulations was that an assessment was carried out before works began and any asbestos identified and appropriate steps taken to deal with it.

In *Nurse v Morganite Crucible Limited*,[1] the House of Lords held that the meaning of 'process' in regs 3 and 5 included any operation or series of operations involving some degree of continuity and repetition of a series of acts being an activity of more than minimal duration.

A precedent based on the Regulations is included in Appendix 1.

11.2.3 The Control of Asbestos at Work Regulations 1987

These Regulations were amended in 1992 and 1998.

The Regulations replaced the Asbestos Regulations 1969 and imposed new hygiene levels of 0.5 fibres/ml of air averaged over any continuous period of 4 hours for chrysotile (0.1 fibres over any continuous period of 10 minutes) and 0.2 fibres over any continuous period of 4 hours for other forms of asbestos (0.6 fibres over any continuous period of 10 minutes).

---

[1] [1989] AC 692.

A precedent based on the Regulations is included in Appendix 1.

11.2.4   The Control of Asbestos at Work Regulations 2002

The 2002 Regulations have applied from 21 November 2002. A precedent based on the 2002 Regulations is included in Appendix 1. What follows is a summary of the provisions of the 2002 Regulations, but it is recommended that the source material is consulted. It is to be remembered that there were earlier versions of very similar Regulations in 1988, 1994 and 1999.

Regulation 3 of the 2002 Regulations imposes duties on an employer in respect of his employees in the following areas: prohibition of certain substances; assessment of health risks; prevention or control of exposure to substances hazardous to health; monitoring; health surveillance and provision of information, instruction or training. Regulation 3 also imposes duties on an employer in respect of persons other than his employees, whether or not at work, who may be affected by the work carried on by the employer. In these circumstances employers' duties are less onerous. In particular they are subject to the lower standard of reasonable practicability, and there is no duty to provide health surveillance or information, instruction or training.

By reg 8(2) employees are required to make full and proper use of any control measure, personal protective equipment or other thing or facility provided by the employer pursuant to the duties imposed by the Regulations. The employee is also under a duty to report any defect in any of these things.

The Regulations do not apply where the provisions of the Mines and Quarries Act 1954, the Coal Mines (Respirable Dust) Regulations 1975, the Control of Lead at Work Regulations 1998 and 2002 and the Control of Asbestos at Work Regulations 1987 and 2002 apply. The Regulations do not apply to substances that are radioactive, explosive or flammable, or where the substance is at a high or low temperature or under high pressure, in which circumstances other Regulations may apply, such as the Provision and Use of Work Equipment Regulations 1992 and 1998. Finally, the Regulations do not apply where the substance is administered in the course of medical treatment.

Substances hazardous to health are defined in reg 2, which states:

> "'Substance hazardous to health' means a substance (including any preparation) –
> (a)   which is listed in Part I of the approved supply list as dangerous for supply within the meaning of the Chemicals (Hazard Information and Packaging for Supply) Regulations and for which an indication of

danger specified for the substance in Part V of that list is very toxic, toxic, harmful, corrosive or irritant;

(b) for which the Health and Safety Commission has approved a maximum exposure limit or an occupational exposure standard;

(c) which is a biological agent;

(d) which is dust of any kind, except dust which is a substance within paragraph (a) or (b) above when present at a concentration in air equal to or greater than –

    (i)   10 mg/m^3 as a time-weighted average over an 8-hour period of total inhalable dust; or

    (ii)   4 mg/m^3 as a time-weighted average over an 8-hour period of respirable dust;

(e) which, not being a substance falling with sub-paragraphs (a) to (d), because of its chemical or toxicological properties and the way in which it is used or is present at the workplace creates a risk to health.'

The final sub-paragraph was worded differently in the preceding Regulations and instead read: 'not being a substance mentioned in sub-paragraphs … above, which creates a hazard to the health of any person which is comparable with the hazards created by substances mentioned in those sub-paragraphs.'

Whereas the earlier Regulations referred to 'total inhalable dust' (which was airborne material capable of entering the nose and mouth during breathing and was thereby available for deposition in the respiratory tract), BS EN 481 1993 now refers to 'inhalable dust'.

The substances listed in (a) and (b) above are too numerous to be included in this work, and should be consulted according to the circumstances.

It will be appreciated that the services of a suitably qualified expert will often be required, especially when considering category (d) 'dust of any kind', where it is necessary to have measurements of concentration in air equal to or greater than 10 mg/m^3 of total inhalable dust as a time-weighted average, or 4 mg/m^3 of respirable dust over a time-weighted average in an 8-hour period.

Regulation 6 requires an assessment of health risks where work is liable to expose employees to a substance hazardous to health. The work cannot be carried out until a suitable and sufficient assessment of the risks to health and the steps required to meet the requirements of the Regulations has been made. The assessment must be reviewed if there is reason to suspect that it is no longer valid or that there has been a significant change in the work to which the assessment relates. In *Naylor v Volex Group*,[2] an environmental consultant raised serious concerns about the previous method of assessment in respect of the fumes from soldering. Failure to carry out a reassessment was a breach of statutory duty.

---

[2]   LTL 14/2/2003.

Under reg 7, the employer must ensure that the exposure of his employees to substances hazardous to health is either prevented or, where this is not reasonably practicable, adequately controlled, see *Dugmore v Swansea NHS Trust & Morriston NHS Trust*.[3] The duty is to prevent exposure unless it is not reasonably practicable to do so. Then, the duty is to provide adequate control. This duty is not subject to the qualification of reasonable practicability, and is a strict duty, measured by the standard of adequacy.

The prevention or adequate control of the exposure to substances hazardous to health must be secured by measures other than the provision of personal protective equipment, so far as is reasonably practicable. This limitation of 'reasonable practicability' requires a balance to be struck between the incidence and degree of risk, on the one hand, and the cost in time, effort or money, on the other. Cases dealing with this phrase in other health and safety legislation will be relevant to illustrate the operation of the exercise.

If it is 'reasonably practicable' to do so, the employer's first act should be to control the process or substance hazardous to health by, for example, closing off the process or machine, or by providing suitable exhaust ventilation.

At the very least, the employer should provide protective clothing or suitable masks or respirators. This protective equipment must adequately control exposure to the hazardous substances. 'Adequate' is defined as meaning 'adequate having regard to the nature of the substances and the nature and degree of exposure'. Where protective equipment is provided it must be suitable for the purpose and comply with any applicable provisions of the Personal Protective Equipment Regulations 2002. Respiratory equipment shall be of a type approved by, or conform to a standard approved by, the Health and Safety Executive (HSE).

The control of exposure by inhalation to a substance to which a maximum exposure limit applies (specified in Sch 1) will be treated as adequate only if the level of exposure is reduced below the maximum exposure limit and then further reduced so far as is reasonably practicable. It is to be noted that there are two distinct elements here. The requirements of the regulation are not met if exposure is above the maximum exposure limit, whatever the cost in time, effort or money.

The Regulations require that the control of exposure by inhalation of a substance for which there is an occupational exposure standard will be treated as adequate only if the occupational exposure standard is not exceeded, or, if it is exceeded, where the employer identifies the reasons for the standard being exceeded and takes appropriate action to remedy

---

[3]   [2003] ICR 574.

the situation as soon as is reasonably practicable. It is suggested that this exception covers circumstances where an unforseen event has increased exposure beyond the standard.

Carcinogenic substances are defined by reg 2 either by reference to the provisions of the Chemicals (Hazard Information and Packaging for Supply) Regulations 1994 or as listed in Schedule 8 of the Control of Substances Hazardous to Health Regulations. Where it is not reasonably practicable to prevent exposure by using an alternative substance or process, control must be achieved by total enclosure of the process and handling systems, and where that is not reasonably practicable, the use of plant, processes and systems of work which minimise exposure. The quantities of carcinogens must be limited, the number of persons who might be exposed kept to a minimum, and eating, drinking and smoking in areas that may be contaminated must be prohibited. Hygiene measures, including adequate washing facilities and regular cleaning of the facilities, must be provided. Areas that may be contaminated must be designated, and warnings signs displayed.

Regulation 8 sets out a duty on the employer, as follows:

> '(1)   Every employer who provides any control measure, other thing or facility in accordance with these Regulations shall take all reasonable steps to ensure that it is properly used or applied as the case may be.'

A complimentary duty is imposed on the employee to make full and proper use of any control measure, other thing or facility provided pursuant to the Regulations. The employee must take all reasonable steps to ensure that the control measure is returned after use to any accommodation provided for it, and to report any defect in it forthwith to his employer.

Under reg 9 the employer must ensure that the control measure is maintained in an efficient state, in efficient working order and in good repair. This is a strict liability duty. 'Efficient' is to be considered in the context of health and safety. Local exhaust plant must be examined and tested at least once every 14 months, unless another interval is specified in Schedule 4 to the Regulations. Where respiratory protective equipment (other than disposable equipment) is provided the employer must ensure that thorough examinations and, where appropriate, tests of that equipment are carried out at suitable intervals. What is a suitable interval will depend upon the circumstances. There is duty on the employer to keep personal protective equipment in a clean condition.

Regulation 10 requires monitoring to ensure the maintenance of adequate control of exposure to substances hazardous to health, or to protect the health of employees. The employer must use a suitable procedure, which will depend in part upon the degree of risk. Certain specified substances and processes require monitoring at specified intervals. The results of monitoring must be recorded and kept for at least 5 years. Where monitoring is representative of the personal exposure of certain employees, those records must be kept for at least 40 years. These records may be important documents for the purposes of disclosure.

Regulation 11 requires suitable health surveillance where it is appropriate for the protection of the health of employees who are, or are liable to be, exposed to substances hazardous to health. Medical surveillance is required for specified substances or processes. An employer may be obliged to continue medical surveillance after cessation of employment where the employment medical adviser so advises. A health record containing particulars approved by the HSE must be kept in respect of each employee under surveillance for at least 40 years. Where an employer goes out of business it must notify the HSE and offer up its records.

An employee has the right to access his health record on the giving of reasonable notice. An employment medical adviser or appointed doctor may also inspect the workplace or any record kept for the purpose of the Regulations.

The provision of information, instruction and training is covered by reg 12. Where exposure to a substance hazardous to health is possible the employer must provide the employee with such information, instruction and training as is suitable and sufficient for the employee to know the risks to health created by such exposure, and the precautions which should be taken. This must include information on the results of any monitoring and the collective results of any health surveillance. If the maximum exposure limit of a substance specified in Schedule 1 has been exceeded, the employee or his representative must be informed.

By reg 13 the employer must have relevant procedures in place for dealing with accidents, incidents and emergencies.

11.2.5   Woodworking Machines Regulations 1974

These Regulations were in force from 1974–1989, when they were replaced by the Noise at Work Regulations 1989. The Regulations have no application in forestry work or work on a construction site. Regulation 44 of the Regulations may have application to noise-induced deafness claims where woodworking machines are used in a factory. It states:

> 'Where any factory or any part thereof is mainly used for work carried out on woodworking machines, the following provisions shall apply to that factory or part as the case may be:
> (a)   Where on any day any person employed is likely to be exposed continuously for eight hours to a sound level of 90 dB(A) or is likely to be subject to an equivalent or greater exposure to sound:

> (i)   such measures as are reasonably practicable shall be taken to reduce noise to the greatest extent which is reasonably practicable and
>
> (ii)   suitable ear protectors shall be provided and made readily available for the use of every such person.
>
> (b)   All ear protectors provided in pursuant of the foregoing paragraph shall be maintained and shall be used by the person for whom they are provided in any of the circumstances specified in paragraph (a) of this Regulation.
>
> (c)   For the purposes of paragraph (a) of these Regulations the level of exposure which is equivalent to or greater than continuous exposure for 8 hours to a sound level of 90 dB(A) shall be determined by an approved method.'

The duty is not absolute, but subject to reasonable practicability. To that extent it does not add much to the common law, although there is no need to prove foreseeability.

11.2.6   Noise at Work Regulations 1989

These Regulations came into force on 1 January 1990. They do not apply to sea-going ships, hovercraft or aircraft, but otherwise are of general application. They are not limited to work in a factory. They are not retrospective and only apply to noise exposure from 1990.

The Regulations action levels at a daily personal noise exposure of 85dbA (the first action level) and a daily personal noise exposure of 90dbA (the second action level). The Regulations also set a peak action level of 200 pascals. Where an employee is likely to be exposed to the first action level or above, the employer must ensure that a competent person carries out a noise assessment, and keeps an adequate record of that assessment. The assessment should be reviewed if there has been a significant change in the work or there is reason to suspect that the assessment is no longer valid. Having made the assessment the employer must reduce the risk of damage to hearing to the lowest level reasonable practicable, and, by reg 10, ensure so far as practicable that ear protection is fully and properly used. Where an employee is likely to be exposed to the second action level or above, or to the peak action level, the duty on the employer is to reduce so far as is reasonably practicable the employee's exposure to noise. This duty applies to the source of the noise, and does not relate to providing hearing protection.

Regulation 8 makes provision for ear protection. Where the employee is likely to be exposed to the first action level but not to the second action level, the obligation on the employer is, so far as is practicable, to provide the employee at his request with suitable and efficient personal ear protectors.

Where the employee is likely to be exposed to the second action level or above, or to the peak action level or above, the employer's duty is to provide suitable personal ear protectors which, when properly worn, can reasonably be expected to keep the risk of damage to the employee's hearing to below that arising from exposure to the second action level or the peak action level. The hearing protection must be maintained in an efficient state, in efficient working order and in good repair.

The Regulations require the demarcation of ear protection zones with prescribed signs.

The employer must provide information, instruction and training on the risk of damage, what steps can be taken to minimise the risk and the steps required to obtain personal ear protection.

A precedent based on the Regulations is included in Appendix 1.

11.2.7   Health and Safety (Display Screen Equipment) Regulations 1992

The duties under these Regulations relate not merely to the display screen equipment itself, but also to the workstation as a whole. Display screen equipment is defined as any alphanumeric or graphic display screen regardless of the display process involved. A list of exceptions is then given, which include taxi meters, ticket machines, cash registers and portable systems not in prolonged use. If the claim concerns anything other than a normal keyboard or data input pad, the precise definitions and exceptions given by the Regulations should be checked carefully.

11.2.7.1   *Overlap with other Regulations*

These Regulations cannot be looked at in isolation. The Workplace (Health, Safety and Welfare) Regulations 1992 also apply to workstations (eg regs 6–12, which relate to ventilation, temperature and lighting, cleanliness, room dimensions and space, and the suitability of workstations and seating).

The Regulations apply to workstations which are used by employees (defined as 'users' – see **11.2.7.2** below) whether or not the employer has provided the workstation. The Regulations also apply to workstations provided by the employer for the use of self-employed operators.

11.2.7.2   *Users*

A 'user' is defined in reg 1 as an 'employee who habitually uses display screen equipment as a significant part of his normal work'.

An 'operator' is defined in reg 1 as a 'self-employed person who habitually uses display screen equipment as a significant part of his normal work'. The terms 'habitually' and 'significant part' are not defined.

Thus, the Regulations will apply to an employee who works at home on his employer's business even though the employee is using his own equipment.

11.2.7.3 Self-employed

The Regulations apply to self-employed persons carrying out work for the employer only if the employer provided the workstation. This raises the interesting point as to whether the Regulations will apply where the employer has provided part of the workstation, such as the computor, but the chair, desk and other parts of the workstation are supplied by the self-employed person.

11.2.7.4 Assessments

The employer must make an assessment of the risks to health and safety from the workstation and then reduce the risks to the lowest extent reasonably practicable. These requirements are not the subject of any transitional provisions and have been in force since 1 January 1993.

The employer must perform a suitable and sufficient analysis of the workstations to which the Regulations apply for the purpose of assessing the health and safety risks to which the users and/or operators are exposed. The Guidance Notes produced by the HSE indicate that the principal risks are physical problems, visual fatigue and mental stress. Physical problems encompass everything from neck strain and shoulder tension to uncomfortable legs (caused by lack of a footrest) as well as the hand, wrist and arm problems, formerly known collectively as RSI but now referred to as work-related upper limb disorders (WRULDs).

11.2.7.5 Reassessments

The employer must carry out a reassessment if there is reason to suspect that the first assessment is no longer valid or if there has been a significant change in the matters to which it relates.

Where the assessment or reassessment identifies risks, steps must be taken to reduce those risks to the lowest extent reasonably practicable.

Regulation 3 requires that any workstation first put into use on or after 1 January 1993 must meet the requirements set out in the Schedule to the Regulations. For all pre-1993 workstations the date for meeting the requirements in the Schedule was 31 December 1996.

This obligation applies to workstations operated by 'users' (regardless of who has provided the workstation) and workstations provided by the employer which are used for the purposes of his business by 'operators'.

The requirements in the Schedule are as follows:

(a)   that lighting is adequate;
(b)   that the screen has adequate contrast, no glare or distracting reflections;
(c)   distracting noise is minimised;
(d)   that there is sufficient leg room and clearance to allow postural changes;
(e)   that there is window covering;
(f)   that software is appropriate to task, adapted to the user, provides feedback on system status, and there is no undisclosed monitoring;
(g)   that the screen has a stable image, is adjustable and readable, and is glare/reflection-free;
(h)   that the keyboard is usable, adjustable, detachable and legible;
(i)   that the work surface permits flexible arrangements, is spacious and glare-free;
(j)   that the work chair is adjustable; and
(k)   that a footrest is provided.

Recommendations for seating and posture are:

(a)   that seats are adjustable and provide good lumbar support;
(b)   that there is no excess pressure on underside of thighs and backs of knees;
(c)   that a foot support is provided if needed;
(d)   that there is space for postural change, and that there are no obstacles under desk;
(e)   that the user's forearms are approximately horizontal;
(f)   that there is minimal extension, flexion or deviation of the wrists;
(g)   that the height and angle of the screen allow a comfortable head position;
(h)   that there is space in front of keyboard to support hands/wrists during pauses in keying.

More detail, including two helpful illustrations, is provided in the HSE Guidance Notes.

The requirement under the Schedule is not to provide all the components, but to ensure that, once provided, they meet the criteria set in the Regulations.

11.2.7.6   *Training*

An employer has an obligation under reg 6 to provide adequate health and safety training for 'users' (ie employees who habitually use display screen equipment as a significant part of their normal work). Health and safety training must specifically relate to the use of any workstation upon which the employee may be required to work. Thus, an employee may be a 'user' because of his habitual work on one type of equipment, but will require training on all the equipment upon which he may be required to work even if that period of work is only short. This training is a specific addition to the training required by reg 11 of the Management of Health and Safety at Work Regulations 1992, although there will inevitably be overlap.

If the workstation has been 'substantially modified' then retraining will be required.

11.2.7.7   *Provision of information*

A separate obligation is imposed by reg 7 on an employer to provide both 'users' and 'operators' with adequate information about all aspects of health and safety relating to their workstations, all measures taken by the employer to analyse and reduce the risks, and to ensure that the workstations meet the requirements laid down in the Schedule to the Regulations.

Regulation 7 also requires an employer to ensure that 'users' are provided with adequate information on the measures taken by the employer in planning the daily work routine of users so as to provide breaks (reg 4) and the measures taken to provide training (reg 6(1)).

11.2.7.8   *Breaks*

Under reg 4 an employer must plan the activities of users so that their daily work on display screen equipment is interrupted periodically by such breaks or changes of activity as reduce their workload at that equipment. Whilst the Regulations do not set any particular standard, the Guidance Notes offer suggestions which include 5–10 minutes break per hour away from the screen for intensive users. In *Pickford v Imperial Chemical Industries plc*,[4] the Court of Appeal held that the defendants were negligent in failing to warn the plaintiff of the need to take breaks from prolonged periods of typing. The injury in this case was sustained before the application of the 1992 Regulations.

Regulation 2 requires an employer to perform a suitable and sufficient analysis of workstations for the purpose of assessing health and safety

---

4   [1996] IRLR 622.

risks to which users are exposed. HSE Guidance Note 32 specifically refers to the need to reduce the risk of fatigue and stress. Guidance 33 also refers specifically to software ergonomics in relation to the risk of stress.

11.2.8   Control of Substances Hazardous to Health Regulations 1988, 1994, 1999 and 2002

It may be necessary to rely upon the provisions of all four (or perhaps earlier) sets of the Regulations, depending on the dates of exposure to hazardous substances. Having said that, the time between exposure and the onset of symptoms is usually relatively short in cases where these Regulations are likely to apply.

The 1988 Regulations applied from 1 October 1989. The 1994 Regulations made minor alterations to the 1988 Regulations and applied from 16 January 1995. The 1999 Regulations came into force on 25 March 1999 and were replaced by the 2002 Regulations on 21 November 2002.

Commentary on the main current provisions of the Regulations is set out in Chapter 10. A precedent based on the Regulations is included in Appendix 1.

11.2.9   Manual Handling Operations Regulations 1992[5]

The Manual Handling Operations Regulations 1992 came into force on 1 January 1993. The definition of 'manual handling operations' is any transporting or supporting of a load (including the lifting, putting down, pushing, pulling, carrying or moving thereof) by hand or by bodily force. Whilst the Regulations have an obvious application to 'lifting cases' they can have application in WRULDs claims.

The essence of the Regulations is contained in regs 4 and 5. Regulation 5 requires each employee to make full and proper use of any system of work provided for his use by his employer in compliance with the Regulations. Regulation 4 contains the heart of the Regulations and has given rise to a significant number of judicial decisions which are important for the principles, but which do not contain helpful illustrations of WRULD claims.

11.2.9.1   *Regulation 4 – duties of employers*
'(1)   Each employer shall –
(a)   so far as is reasonably practicable, avoid the need for his employees to undertake any manual handling operations at work which involve the risk of their being injured; or

---

[5]   SI 1992/2793.

(b) where it is not reasonably practicable to avoid the need for his employees to undertake any manual handling operations at work which involve a risk of their being injured –

(i) make a suitable and sufficient assessment of all such manual handling operations to be undertaken by them, having regard to the factors which are specified in column 1 of Schedule 1 to these Regulations and considering the questions which are specified in the corresponding entry in column 2 of that Schedule,

(ii) take appropriate steps to reduce the risk of injury to those employees arising out of their undertaking any such manual handling operations to the lowest level reasonably practicable, and

(iii) take appropriate steps to provide any of those employees who are undertaking any such manual handling operations with general indications and, where it is reasonably practicable to do so, precise information on –

(aa) the weight of each load, and

(bb) the heaviest side of any load whose centre of gravity is not positioned centrally.

(2) Any assessment such as is referred to in paragraph (1)(b)(i) of this regulation shall be reviewed by the employer if –

(a) there is reason to suspect that it is no longer valid; or

(b) there has been a significant change in the manual handling operations to which it relates;

and where as a result of any such review changes to an assessment are required, the relevant employer shall make them.'

The assessment required by the Management of Health and Safety at Work Regulations 1999[6] (and 1992) should have indicated work activities which entail a risk of injury from manual handling. Not every risk is covered by the Regulations; the risk must be 'real' and the asessment should be conducted with a 'degree of realism'.[7] Then it should be determined whether the manual handling task can be avoided, subject to the standard of reasonable practicability.

If it is not reasonably practicable to avoid the manual handling task then a more detailed assessment is required. That assessment should utilise the factors set out in Sch 1 which have five main factors for consideration. The assessment should look at the tasks, the loads, the working environment, individual capability and whether movement is hindered by clothing or personal protective equipment. The first four factors set out a number of questions which should guide the assessment.

The tasks – do they involve:

- holding loads away from trunk?
- twisting?

---

[6] SI 1999/3242.

[7] *Koonjul v Thameslink Healthcare Services* [2000] PIQR P123.

- stooping?
- reaching upwards?
- large vertical movement?
- long carrying distances?
- strenuous pushing or pulling?
- unpredictable movement of loads?
- repetitive handling?
- insufficient rest or recovery?
- a work rate imposed by a process?

The loads – are they:

- heavy?
- bulky/unwieldy?
- difficult to grasp?
- unstable/unpredictable?
- intrinsically harmful (eg sharp or hot)?

The working environment – are there:

- constraints on posture?
- poor floors?
- variations in levels?
- hot/cold/humid conditions?
- strong air movements?
- poor lighting conditions?

Individual capability – does the job:

- require unusual capability?
- hazard those with a health problem?
- hazard those who are pregnant?
- call for special information/training?

A failure to carry out a risk assessment does not mean that an employer can avoid his obligations under the Regulations.[8]

Having made that assessment the employer must take appropriate steps to reduce the risk of injury from the manual handling task to the lowest level reasonably practicable, including the provision of information. Thus, it is to be noted that the obligations under the Regulations are not absolute. Causation remains an important factor; for example, where there was no evidence establishing the benefits that improved training could have achieved, the claim failed.[9]

---

[8]   *Swain v Denso Martin Ltd* [2000] PIQR P51.

[9]   *Warner v Huntingdon District Council* (unreported) 16 May 2002.

11.2.10   The Control of Vibration at Work Regulations 2005

The Regulations came into force on 6 July 2005. However, for work equipment first provided to employees prior to 6 July 2007 there is an extension of the time taken to eliminate or control vibration where the work equipment does not permit compliance with the exposure limit values.

For hand-arm vibration the daily exposure limit is 5 m/s2 A(8) and the daily exposure action level is 2.5 m/s2 A(8). For whole body vibration the values are 1.15 m/s2 A(8) and 0.5 m/s2 A(8).

Where the work is liable to expose an employee to a risk from vibration, the employer must carry out a suitable and sufficient risk assessment. There is a list of matters which the risk assessment shall consider. A record of the significant findings of the risk assessment shall be made. The employer is required to ensure that risk from exposure to vibration is either eliminated at source or, where that is not reasonably practicable, reduced to as low a level as is reasonably practicable. The general principles of prevention set out in the Management of Health and Safety at Work Regulations 1999, Schedule 1 shall be applied. The duty on the employer is to ensure that his employees are not exposed to vibration above an exposure limit value. If the exposure limit value is exceeded the employer must reduce the exposure to below the limit value, identify the reason for that limit being exceeded and modify the preventative measures taken.

The Regulations make provision for health surveillance. Regulation 8 requires the provision of suitable and sufficient information, instruction and training relating to the risks.

11.2.11   Control of Noise at Work Regulations 2005

These Regulations came into force on 6 April 2006, with the exception of the music and entertainment sectors where a later date of 6 April 2008 applied. They do not apply to sea-going ships, hovercraft or aircraft, but otherwise are of general application to workplaces. They are not retrospective and only apply to noise exposure from 2006 or 2008 as relevant.

The Regulations create a lower exposure action value of a daily or weekly personal noise exposure of 80 dBA and a peak sound pressure of 135 dBC. The upper exposure action values will be 85 dBA and 137 dBC. The exposure limit values are a daily or weekly personal noise exposure of 87 dBA and a peak sound pressure of 140 dBC.

Where an employee is likely to be exposed to noise at or above the lower exposure action level, the employer must make a suitable and sufficient assessment of the risk from that noise. There are detailed requirements for the risk assessment to consider. The employer must record the significant findings of the risk assessment, and the measures which it has taken and which it intends to take to meet the requirements of the Regulations. The assessment should be reviewed if there has been a significant change in the work or there is reason to suspect that the assessment is no longer valid. Having made the assessment the employer must ensure that risk from the exposure is either eliminated or, where that is not reasonably practicable, reduced to a level as low as is reasonably practicable. Where employees are exposed to noise at or above the upper exposure action level of 85 dBA or 137 dBC the employer must take steps to reduce the noise by measures independent of personal hearing protectors. There is a list of the actions which an employer must take to reduce exposure to noise.

Regulation 7 makes provision for ear protection to be made available if there is exposure at or above the lower exposure action level. The means of reducing noise and the hearing protection must be maintained in an efficient state, in efficient working order and in good repair. The Regulations require the demarcation of ear protection zones with prescribed signs. There is a duty imposed on the employee to make use of the hearing protection provided. There are provisions for health surveillance, information, instruction and training.

PART 4

PRACTICAL MATTERS

CHAPTER 12

PRACTICAL MATTERS

12.1   WHICH EMPLOYERS TO SUE

In many occupational illness cases the claimant may have worked for a number of different employers or employers with different names. The first consideration is to decide which of the employers is worth pursuing from the perspective of establishing liability.

If the occupational illness was caused by cumulative exposure to a damaging substance or environmental factor, careful consideration must be given to whether a particular employer is worth pursuing. Defendants will be liable only for that portion of exposure for which they were responsible. Therefore, if the period of exposure was short or the degree of exposure modest with a particular employer, it might not be worth joining that employer to proceedings in terms of time, energy and cost. In addition, it may be much easier from an evidential point of view to make a case against the other employers.

The decision to omit a particular employer from the list of defendants based on the claimant's minimal or infrequent exposure usually takes place at an early stage in the preparation of the claim when the issues and strengths of the case may not be entirely clear. As such, caution must be exercised before making a final decision in this regard. It is important that the claimant provides as much detail about exposure as possible to help in the decision-making process.

These considerations are more likely to arise in claims involving asbestos, noise, vibration white finger (VWF) and possibly occupational asthma, and are less likely to arise in claims involving hazardous substances, work-related upper limb disorders (WRULD) and work-related stress.

12.2   DOES THE EMPLOYER EXIST NOW?

In occupational illness cases it is often the case that the claimant worked many years previously for a company which no longer exists or whose name has changed. Some detective work may be necessary. If a company no longer exists it will be necessary to apply to the court to have the company restored to the Register so that it can be sued.

Historically, the answer has been that the claimant must apply to the companies' court to restore his previous employer company to the Register for the purpose of issuing proceedings and obtaining judgment. This is so even though restoring a defunct company to the Register is costly and time-consuming, and even though the practical implications add nothing of significance to the proceedings. A claimant's right to sue is against the natural or legal person by whom he has been wronged. So, although an insurance company may handle the claim on the defendant's behalf, it has not been possible to claim a right against the insurance company until judgment has been obtained against the defendant.

That is set to change if and when the Third Parties (Rights Against Insurers) Act 2010 (the 2010 Act) comes into force. The 2010 Act will mean that it is not usually necessary for a company that has been removed from the Companies' Register to be reinstated so that proceedings can be brought against it, if the claim will be handled and satisfied by an insurer.

Unfortunately, having received royal assent on 25 March 2010, the commencement date for this Act is still awaited. The Secretary of State for Business, Innovation and Skills announced on 2 June 2010 that all regulation inherited from the last government, including this Act, would be reviewed. No commencement date will be set until that review has been completed.[1] As such, it is not possible to say when, or even if, the 2010 Act will be implemented.

This chapter therefore addresses with applications made to restore a company to the Register under the Companies Act 2006 (the 2006 Act), as well as the practical implications of any implementation of the 2010 Act.

12.3   RESTORATION UNDER THE COMPANIES ACT 2006 (THE 2006 ACT)

Once a company is dissolved, proceedings issued against it are invalid. Until the implementation of the 2006 Act, a claimant would apply under section 651 of the Companies Act 1985 to restore a company to the Register for the purposes of pursuing a personal injury claim against them. The 2006 Act came into force on 1 October 2009: since that date, any application should be made under section 1029 of the 2006 Act.[2] Sections 1029–1032 of the 2006 Act (restoration to Register by the court) apply whether the company was dissolved or struck off the Register

---

[1]   House of Commons Hansard Written Answers Index for 9 June 2010.
[2]   Companies Act 2006 (Commencement No 8, Transitional Provisions and Savings) Order 2008, art 5, Schedule 2, paras 1, 90, 91, but note para 91(4).

before, on or after 1 October 2009.[3] The 2006 Act has made some revision to the process of applying to restore a company to the Register under the Companies Act 1985, although not substantially so. A new administrative restoration to the Register is possible, although may only be used by a former director or member of the company, so is outside the scope of this book.

12.3.1 The application

Under the 2006 Act, an application may be made to the court to restore to the Register a company that has been dissolved, is deemed to have been dissolved or has been struck off the Register, whether or not the company has in consequence been dissolved.[4] An application can be made by any person with a potential legal claim against the company.[5] An application may be made at any time for the purpose of bringing proceedings against the company for damages for personal injury.[6] A restoration to the Register has the practical effect that the resolution is void.

One difficulty with the Companies Act 1985 was that the restoration of a company to the Register would not have retrospective effect so as to validate the proceedings previously commenced against it. Under section 1032 of the 2006 Act, it is made clear that the general effect of an order by the court for restoration to the Register is that the company is deemed to have continued in existence as if it had not been dissolved or struck off the Register, thus validating proceedings commenced against it. The old problem under section 651 of the Companies Act 1985 has therefore been resolved.

12.3.2 The procedure[7]

The application must be made to the Companies Court in the Chancery Division. The Registrar of Companies is named as the defendant and the matter is titled 'in the matter of ... Limited and in the matter of the Companies Act 2006.' The application should make it clear whether the claimant is applying to have a dissolution declared void or a company restored to the Register after being struck off. The application is made using a Part 8 claim form and should be accompanied by a witness statement setting out:

(a) the fact that the claimant was employed by the company and a summary of the asbestos-related disease claim;

---

[3] SI 2008/2860, Schedule 2, paras 1, 90, 91.
[4] Section 1029(1).
[5] Section 1029(2)(f).
[6] Section 1030(3).
[7] See TSol's Guide to Company Restoration http://www.tsol.gov.uk/Publications/Scheme_Publications/company_restoration.pdf.

(b)   a chronology of the company's existence and attach copies of the memorandum and articles and a company search;
(c)   details of the company's insurance at the relevant time; and
(d)   any limitation issues – see *Re Workvale Limited*, below.[8]

The application and witness statement must be served on the Registrar at Companies House in Cardiff and also on the Treasury Solicitor. It is wise also to serve the insurer and the liquidator. Evidence of service should be provided to the court. The Treasury Solicitor usually deals with these applications on behalf of the Registrar. The usual form is for the Treasury Solicitor:

(a)   merely to indicate no objection;
(b)   to require payment of costs; and
(c)   to require the claimant's solicitor to undertake to keep the Registrar informed of the progress of the personal injury case.

12.3.3   The hearing and the order

The court's power to restore is discretionary so application should be made promptly. Return dates for the hearing may take up to three months. The Registrar of the Companies Court in London usually hears restoration cases in chambers once a week on Friday afternoons. Cases are also heard at the District Registries or at a County Court that has the authority to wind up the company. Other parties who are interested should be notified of the hearing date. These include the insurer and the liquidator. The proposed order should be taken to the hearing.

The application may be dealt with on paper so long as the relevant witness statement, proof of service, undertaking and draft order are provided to the court. Paper hearings are generally obtained faster.

Once the order has been made, the applicant must deliver a copy of the court order to the Registrar to restore the company. A company is restored when the order is delivered.

12.3.4   Limitation

Limitation issues may arise within the application to restore. The limitation period does not stop running just because the company has gone into liquidation or been struck off: see *Smith v White Knight Laundry Limited*.[9]

An application for restoration for the purposes of bringing a claim for damages for personal injury can be made at any time, but the court may

---

[8]   (No2) [1992] 1 WLR 416.
[9]   [2002] 1 WLR 616, CA.

not make an order for restoration where it appears that the claim would fail due to limitation. Section 1029 therefore prevents an order for restoration being made by the court where the limitation defence was accrued for the defunct company. The court has power under section 1032(3) to direct that any period between the dissolution (or striking off) of the company and the making of the order is not to count for the purposes of limitation. The effect is akin to an order for relief under section 33 of the Limitation Act 1980.

In *Smith v White Knight Laundry Limited* (considering similar provisions in the 1985 Act) guidance was given on how to deal with limitation-expired cases. Parker LJ stated that the claimant should inform all other potentially interested parties of the issue and should put before the Companies Court all of the evidence that would be relied on in an application for discretion under section 33 of the Limitation Act 1980. If the court is satisfied that the section 33 application to disapply the limitation period is bound to succeed then the company will be restored to the Register. Whether the proof needed of the likely success on section 33 is as high as 'bound to succeed' or as low as 'likely to succeed' is not clear in view of the clash between the words of Parker LJ and those of Harman LJ in *Re Workvale Limited*.

Where the ex-employer is in voluntary receivership the limitation period does not run during the receivership: see *Re T & N Limited*[10] and the Insolvency (Amendment) Rules 2006.

12.4   COMPANIES IN RECEIVERSHIP

When a company is not dissolved, but in receivership, a claimant will need permission to sue either from the receiver or the court: see *Re Atlantic Computer Systems.*[11] Similarly, where a limited company is compulsorily liquidated so that a winding up order is made, no action may be commenced or proceeded with without the court's permission.[12] Where a limited company is the subject of voluntary liquidation or receivership there is no requirement for permission to commence or continue proceedings. Permission is likely to be obtained on terms similar to those required by the court on an application to restore a dissolved company to be restored to the Register.

12.4.1   Retrospective permission to sue

The High Court had previously concluded that permission could be obtained retrospectively.[13] However, in the case of *Re Taylor (a*

---

[10]   [2005] EWHC 2870 Ch.
[11]   [1992] Ch 505 at 529F and cl. 43 (schedule B1) of the Insolvency Act 1986.
[12]   Section 130 Insolvency Act 1986.
[13]   *Re Saunders (a Bankrupt) Bristol and West BS v Saunders* (1997) Ch 60.

bankrupt),[14] this issue was considered again. Judge Kershaw concluded that he need not and should not treat the point as being 'settled at first instance' by *Re Saunders*. When considering the question of whether the Insolvency Act 1986 had the effect of making proceedings against a bankrupt a nullity if started without the requisite permission, he disagreed with Lindsay J in *Re Saunders* that a court can give leave to start proceedings which have already been started. He examined a number of previous cases before reaching his conclusion. His judgment was that the effect of section 285(3)(b) of the 1986 Act is to render any proceedings against a bankrupt by someone who is a creditor in respect of a debt provable in bankruptcy void. He further concluded that something which is void cannot be validated retrospectively.

Both *Re Saunders* and *Re Taylor* are High Court authorities, and the matter has not reached (as of yet) any higher level court. However, for the present, it is likely that the case of *Re Taylor* will be treated as the case to be followed, given the extensive consideration of case law and reasons given for disagreeing with Lindsay J set out in his judgment. Those seeking to apply for permission retrospectively may find they are disappointed. It is therefore very important to address the possibility of the need for permission at a very early stage in the investigation of a claim.

12.5 THIRD PARTIES (RIGHTS AGAINST INSURERS) ACT 2010 (THE 2010 ACT)

The Third Parties (Rights against Insurers) Act 2010, if brought into force, will mean that it is no longer necessary for a company that has been removed from the Companies' Register to be reinstated so that proceedings can be brought against them, as long as the claim will be handled and satisfied by an insurer. It will also repeal the Third Parties (Rights against Insurers) Act 1930 (the 1930 Act) (subject to Schedule 3, paragraph 3, see **12.5.2** below).

Within the context of asbestos claims, this Act should make things considerably easier. The right of a dissolved company (and most insolvent companies) under a contract of insurance will vest in the person to whom the liability of the company was incurred without the need to establish first the company's liability. Liability of the company must be established, however, before the rights against the insurer can be enforced.[15]

12.5.1 How does it work?

The claimant has a right to seek a declaration as to the insured's liability to them. That declaration can either be a declaration of the insured's

---

[14]   [2006] EWHC 3029 (Ch).
[15]   Section 1(3).

liability or a declaration as to the insurer's potential liability, or both.[16] A person is entitled to such a declaration on proof of either the insured's liability or the insurer's potential liability in such proceedings, subject to any defence which the insurer might raise.[17] Where the court makes a declaration, it may give the appropriate judgment against the insurer, which is likely to be a money judgment.[18]

This is an optional mechanism: a claimant may alternatively bring proceedings against the insured before commencing proceedings against the insurer (as they do at present).

12.5.2 When will the Act apply?

The Act applies where the insured becomes a 'relevant person' before as well as on or after the commencement date, or where the liability was incurred before as well as on or after the commencement date. The great majority of claims will therefore be covered by the 2010 Act.

Until the implementation of the 2010 Act, the 1930 Act will remain in force. This will mean that, although an insurer can be required to satisfy a judgment against the insured, it is still necessary to obtain such a judgment before enforcement against the insurer can take place, and therefore still necessary to apply to restore a company to the Register.

Although Schedule 4 of the 2010 Act stipulates that the whole of the 1930 Act will be repealed, paragraph 3 of Schedule 3 of the Act contains an important exception to that rule: although the 2010 Act will apply either where the insured incurs a liability to the third party after the date the Act comes into force or where the insured is subject to an insolvency event after such date, if both of these events occur before the commencement date, the 1930 Act will continue to apply.

12.5.3 Who is a relevant person?

Although the relevant insured person can be an individual, our focus for the purposes of this book is corporate bodies. Such a body is a relevant person if it has been dissolved and has not been restored to the Register or ordered to be restored to the Register.[19] Rights will also transfer where companies are insolvent, or are subject to either voluntary or compulsory winding up.[20]

If a relevant person (see **12.5.5** below) incurs a liability against which they are insured under a contract of insurance, or if a person who is subject to

---

[16] Section 2(2).
[17] Section 2(3).
[18] Section 2(6).
[19] Under section 1025 or 1031 of the 2006 Act.
[20] See section 6 for full details of who can be a 'relevant person'.

such a liability becomes a relevant person, the rights of that relevant person under the contract against the insurer in respect of the liability are transferred to and vest in the person to whom the liability is or was incurred ('the third party').[21] In order to establish liability, both the existence of and amount of liability must be established: such liability can be established by, for instance, a judgment, decree, declaration or enforceable agreement.[22]

12.5.4   Defences and limitations

Where proceedings are brought for a declaration as to the insured's liability to the person, the insurer may rely on any defence on which the insured could rely had the proceedings been brought against the insured.[23] However, ability of the insurer to rely on certain technical defences is limited (eg defences based on requirements in the policy for the insured to supply information or that the insured should first pay the sums due to the claimant before the insurer's liability arises).

Potential grounds for an insurer to avoid liability are curtailed within the Act.[24] Notification of the claim or provision of information about the claim by the third party claimant is to be treated as made by the insured, and insurance cannot be avoided for failure to provide information or assistance if that requirement could not be fulfilled because the company was dissolved. An insurer cannot rely on the limitation period relevant to enforcement of the contract of insurance by the insurer to avoid liability to the third party. The insurer's right of set off has the practical effect that the insurer does not have to pay the third party the value of any insurance excess that he would have been entitled to had the claim been made against the insured.[25] Further provisions are made for limits on rights transferred and conditions affecting transferred rights.[26]

Where a person starts proceedings for a declaration after the expiry of the relevant limitation period applicable to an action against the insured, but while such an action is in progress, the insurer may not rely on the expiry of that period as a defence unless the insured is able to rely on it in the action against the insured.[27] Where a person who has already established liability of an insured brings proceedings against the insurer, the 2010 Act does not mean that the person's cause of action against the insurer arose otherwise than at the time when that person established the liability to the insured, for the purposes of limitation.[28]

---

[21]   Third Party (Rights Against Insurers) Act 2010, section 1(1) and (2).
[22]   Section 1(4).
[23]   Section 2(4).
[24]   Section 9.
[25]   Section 10.
[26]   Sections 8 and 9.
[27]   Section 12(1), (2).
[28]   Section 12(4).

12.5.5   Obtaining disclosure from the insurer and third parties

The Act also provides a means by which a potential claimant can obtain information and disclosure,[29] both from someone that the potential claimant reasonably believes is a 'relevant person' and has incurred a liability to him, and from someone who the potential claimant thinks can provide certain information. Relevant other parties could include brokers or former employees as to the insured's insurance position.

A request for such disclosure should be made in writing and the Act specifies the information that may be requested. There is a list of disclosable information within the statute.[30]

12.5.6   Insurer's concession

Until such time as the 2010 Act comes into force, claimants will need to continue to take steps to restore companies to the Register before proceeding with a personal injury claim and the defendant company is no longer on the Register.

However, insurers sometimes purport to concede at the outset of discussions with the claimant, or further down the line, that they are liable to pay damages to the claimant, leading to the question of whether the claimant can rely on this concession and not make the application to apply a defunct company to the Register. This raises a number of interesting questions. Can these concessions be trusted and relied upon and/or will they cause problems in the future? Might this lead to estoppel arguments? Surely there is a problem with a judgment against a company that does not exist, if indeed it can be said that there is a judgment in the circumstances.

12.6   IS THE EMPLOYER WORTH SUING?

If the employer, whether a company, partnership or sole proprietor, has no assets, it will not be worth suing unless an insurance policy was in existence. The smaller the business the less likely it will be that assets and insurance still exist. For example, a retired proprietor of a small plumbing and heating firm may have no worthwhile assets and may never have bothered with the trouble and expense of insurance. The position needs to be investigated.

There can be circumstances where liability for earlier torts can be transferred to another quite different company. This can arises under a

---

[29]   Schedule 1.
[30]   Schedule 1.

transfer agreement between parties, see this illustrated in *Bateman v Danks Holdings Ltd and Bristol & Babcock Ltd.*[31]

A transfer of liability may also occur by operation of law under the provisions of the Transfer of Undertakings (Protection of Employment) Regulations 1981 (TUPE)[32] or from 6 April 2006 by the Transfer of Employment (Protection of Employment) Regulations 2006.[33] Where after 1 April 1982 an undertaking (business) is transferred to another company the liabilities in respect of existing employees is transferred with the business and the original company is no longer liable.

As personal injury lawyers we need now to take some interest in insurance law. An issue may arise in respect of the insurance cover where the exposure was some time ago and the insurers who were on risk at that time are not now the insurers. The question that needs to be considered in these circumstances is whether it is the policy in force at the time of the exposure or the policy in force at the time when the disease developed? This has particular application to asbestos cases.

The dispute stemmed from the different wording of the insurance policies. So the question was which wording triggered liability? That is why the litigation became known as the 'trigger litigation'.

On 8 October 2010 the Court of Appeal handed down a judgment of over 100 pages following many weeks of argument by many interested parties. The case is conveniently known by the name of the lead case, *Durham v BAI (Run Off) Ltd.*[34] It needs to be said straight away that the three judgments each have a slightly different approach and some differing conclusions and there is already talk of an appeal to the Supreme Court. So much insurance money is at stake, that an appeal is almost inevitable. It should also be said that the CA decision does not provide that simple, clear answer which so many of us personal injury lawyers seek.

The answer to which, if any insurance company is liable, is to be found in considering the meaning of phrases such as 'injury or disease sustained or contracted' and 'injury or disease caused'.

Lord Justice Rix gave this summary:

> '"Sustain" means sustain. The phrase "sustaining injury" referred to the time when the injury was first suffered or inflicted and not to the cause of the injury. The phrase "disease contracted" was concerned with the causal origins of disease. But "disease contracted" looks back to causative origins. The ELCIA 1969 policies, by reason of their deeming clause, provide security for employee claimants, but not for the insureds. But I would have

---

[31] [2009] EWHC 2082 (QB), [2009] All ER (D) 66 (Aug).
[32] SI 1981/1794.
[33] SI 2006/246.
[34] [2010] EWCA Civ 1096, [2010] All ER (D) 88 (Oct).

preferred, had precedent allowed me, to respect the commercial purpose of EL insurance, a fortiori during the ELCIA 1969 era, and to vindicate the industry's attitude to such insurance over so many decades, up to Bolton, by acknowledging that, when mesothelioma develops, the "injury" of mesothelioma is sustained, in its origins, at the time when the insult of exposure, which materially increases the risk of developing mesothelioma, occurs.'

However, he goes on to acknowledge the different approaches of the other two Judges of the Court of Appeal:

'Lady Justice Smith has endorsed in full the judgment of the judge, but has done so, not so much on his ex-employee point which drove him to his conclusion that the parties had made a mistake about language but, on the principal ground that the sustained wording should be given the meaning which the users of it at the time of the policies in question and in the factual matrix of those policies understood it to mean, viz as the same as causation wording.

She accepts that nowadays, with the advance of modern medical knowledge, the position would be different. In my respectful judgment, however, subject to estoppel or binding custom, which does not arise, the evidence to which she refers does not support her conclusion. There was no reasonable understanding that sustained meant caused, or that sustained wording had the same effect as caused wording. It was rather that, in a period when the case of mesothelioma was less well known, and in the light of the fact that some 99 per cent of injuries were caused and sustained at the same time, there was a mixture of reasons which led the parties to conclude that the effect of one wording gave the same result as the other. The fact that policies with different wordings were treated the same, does not I fear mean that they had the same meaning. The difference between them has been exposed by the case of mesothelioma (on the Bolton analysis).

Lord Justice Burnton is, I think, in general but not complete agreement with my analysis of the wordings. He disagrees, however, about the Independent wording. He also disagrees (as does Lady Justice Smith, for she agrees with the judge) with my conclusion that ELCIA 1969 requires causation wording. However, he would extend section 1(1) of ELCIA 1969 to ex-employees. Thus where section 1(1) states:

"every employer carrying on business in Great Britain shall insure … against liability for bodily injury or disease sustained by his employees, and arising out of and in the course of their employment in Great Britain in that business"

he would read "employees" as including "ex-employees".

This is a tempting and generous interpretation, but I fear, with respect, that I am unable to agree with it. I do not think that the point was expressly argued by any of the claimants, or conceded by the insurers. But in the written submissions of the Secretary of State, as an interested party, the observation is made that a construction of the section which does not call

for wording on a causation basis may have the result that "ex-employees may
not be covered at all". In my judgment, it is difficult to give to "employees"
a meaning which includes "ex-employees".'

Thus the concern is whether in respect of now defunct companies there is
or was an insurance policy which provides indemnity in the particular
circumstances.

12.7   FINDING THE INSURER

Where the claimant's exposure occurred over a number of years there may
be more than one insurer. Enquiries should be made to the Employers'
Liability Tracing Service (elto.org.uk) which is an independent
not-for-profit organisation set up by the insurance industry to help
claimants find the insurer of their former employer. The ELTO maintains
a complete EL Database of all new and renewed EL policies, all old EL
policies that have new claims made against them, and all successful traces
from the previous Employers' Liability Tracing Service and from ELTO.

APIL also holds a database of insurers. Enquiries made to a trade union,
other local solicitors or other persons known to the claimant may also
produce results.

CHAPTER 13

PRE-ACTION PROTOCOL FOR DISEASE AND ILLNESS CLAIMS

13.1 INTRODUCTION

The Protocol for Disease and Illness Claims came into force in December 2003. The text of the Protocol is set out in Appendix 5. The Protocol does not claim to be a comprehensive code, but provides a framework for the conduct of claims in occupational illness. What follows is a summary of the Protocol, with some comments.

The Protocol applies to disease claims but does not usually apply to any injury caused by an accident or other similar single event. However, in appropriate cases it may be agreed between the parties that the Protocol can be applied where a single event occurs but causes a disease or illness.

The Protocol defines disease as covering any illness, physical or psychological, any disorder, ailment, affliction, complaint, malady, or derangement other than a physical or psychological injury solely caused by an accident or other similar single event.

The Protocol states that it covers disease claims which are likely to be complex and frequently not suitable for fast-track procedures even though they may fall within fast-track limits. The current fast-track limit is £25,000. Claims which may fall within fast-track limits are pleural plaques, noise-induced hearing loss, and vibration white finger (VWF). Claims for work-related upper limb disorders (WRULDs) may also fall within fast-track limits. If these claims are not settled and go to trial, issues of liability and quantum are likely to take 2–3 days, and a fast-track listing with a timetable of one day will be insufficient. Some cases are put in the fast track (with the agreement of the court, the claimant and the defendants) on the basis that they are likely to settle. However, once it appears that a trial is likely, steps should be taken to reallocate the claim and to have a realistic timetable applied.

The aim of the Protocol is to build on and increase the benefits of early but well-informed settlement which genuinely satisfies both parties to the dispute. In particular, it encourages more contact between the parties, better and earlier exchange of information, and better investigation by both sides. The intention is to put the parties in a position where they may be able to settle cases fairly and early without litigation. If litigation is required, the Protocol is intended to enable proceedings to run to the court's timetable. However, if the court has to consider the question of compliance after proceedings have begun, the Protocol will not be concerned with minor infringements.

It has been conceded that the timetable and arrangements for disclosing documents and obtaining expert evidence may need to be varied to suit the circumstances of the case. This is a potential escape route for defendants who have little interest in progressing the matter. If a party considers the detail of the Protocol to be inappropriate he should communicate his reasons to all of the parties at that stage.

It is common practice to expedite hearings where the claimant is suffering from a terminal illness and has a much shortened life-expectancy. Such hearings usually concerns asbestos claims where the claimant has mesothelioma or lung cancer and is anxious to see the conclusion of the litigation and know that he has ordered his affairs rather than leaving his widow or family to bring a fatal accidents claim. It is a matter for the claimant to decide whether he wishes the matter concluded before his death, but it must be remembered that the claim under the Fatal Accidents Act may have a higher monetary value that an earlier claim relying on the 'lost years' yardstick of compensation. Where speedy resolution of the claim is necessary the defendant is expected to treat the matter with urgency.

13.2   OBTAINING HEALTH AND OTHER OCCUPATIONAL RECORDS

In an occupational illness claim it is vital to consider occupational health records, personnel records and other records which employers are required to keep in respect of monitoring and the testing and maintenance of equipment. The Protocol acknowledges that there may be circumstances where potential claimants cannot send a proper letter of claim until the records have been considered. A claimant may request the occupational records, health records and personnel records before composing and sending a letter of claim.

Such requests should alert potential defendants to the fact that a possible disease claim is being investigated. Copy records should be provided within a maximum of 40 days of the request and at no cost. The Protocol suggests that it is good practice for a potential defendant to disclose product data documents identified by a potential claimant at this stage, which may resolve a causation issue. This is a good practice, but with less of a sanction attached to it.

13.3 WHERE THE DEFENDANT HAS DIFFICULTY PROVIDING INFORMATION

The Protocol suggests that only in rare circumstances should a defendant have difficulty in providing information. In such cases the defendant should quickly provide details of what is being done to resolve the difficulty and to provide a reasonable time estimate for doing so. The court also has the power to impose costs sanctions for unreasonable delay in providing records.

13.4 FAILURE TO COMPLY WITH A REQUEST FOR INFORMATION

If the defendant does not provide records within 40 days and fails to give reasons, the claimant may then apply to the court for an order for pre-action disclosure.

13.5 THIRD PARTIES HOLDING RECORDS

Third Party record holders are expected to co-operate with requests for copies of relevant records. Under the Civil Procedure Rules parties may apply to the court for pre-action disclosure by third parties. Third parties may be previous employers who hold records which show the state of the claimant's health at the relevant time. Medical records held by a GP or hospital may also be relevant. GP records will normally be obtained before a decision is taken as to whether to proceed.

Following disclosure of the records, if the claimant decides not to proceed further he must notify any potential defendant who has been put on notice of a possible claim, and to do so as soon as practicable.

13.6 LETTER OF CLAIM

As soon as the claimant has sufficient information to substantiate a realistic claim a letter of claim should be sent to the defendant, who has 3 months from the date of acknowledgement (which must be provided within 21 days) to respond. Thus the defendant has a maximum of 3 months and 3 weeks to respond to the letter of claim.

It is not necessary to have detailed information about the quantum issues at this stage. A letter of claim is set out in Appendix 5 which follows the precedent suggested by the Protocol. The claimant is required to send two copies of the letter of claim to the proposed defendant: one copy for the defendant and the other for his insurer. Presumably the sanction for failure to send two copies is the cost of a photocopy.

The letter of claim should contain a clear, chronological summary of the facts on which the claim is based, including details of the illness alleged, and the main allegations of fault. An employment history should be given, and some indication of the claimant's current condition and prognosis. A medical report can be included but this is not a requirement. An outline of the financial losses likely to be claimed should be provided. The letter of claim should also indicate whether a claim is being made against any other potential defendant, and identify any known insurer involved. There should be sufficient overall information to enable the defendant's insurer/solicitor to commence investigations and to put a broad valuation on the risk. The existence of a conditional fee agreement should be notified, as should the fact that there is a success fee and/or insurance premium. The level of the success fee or cost of the insurance premium should not be provided since these will indicate the claimant's view of the prospects of success.

The letter of claim should identify any relevant documents held by the claimant which are not already in the defendant's possession. Where the action is brought under the Law Reform Act or the Fatal Accidents Acts, relevant documents will normally include copies of a death certificate, a post-mortem report, inquest depositions, and, if in existence at that date, a grant of probate or letters of administration.

13.7 DEFENDANT'S RESPONSE TO LETTER OF CLAIM

The defendant should send an acknowledgement of the letter of claim within 21 calendar days of the date of its posting, identifying the liability insurer (if any) which will be dealing with the matter and, if necessary, identifying specifically any significant omissions from the letter of claim. If no acknowledgement by the defendant or insurer is received within 21 days, the claimant will be entitled to issue proceedings.

The identity of all relevant insurers, if more than one, should be notified to the claimant by the insurer identified in the acknowledgement letter, within one calendar month of the date of that acknowledgement. The slight catch here is the question of who has decided which insurers are relevant. It does not prevent an insurer saying at a later stage that they are not the only insurer.

The defendant or his representative should, within 3 months of the date of the acknowledgement letter, provide a reasoned answer. If the claim is admitted this should be made plain. If only part of the claim is admitted, this should be stated in clear terms indicating which issues of fault and/or causation and/or limitation are admitted and which remain in issue and why:

(a) If the claim is not admitted in full, the reasons for this should be set out and should include comments on the employment status of the

claimant (including job description(s) and details of the depart-
ment(s) where the claimant worked), the allegations of fault,
causation and limitation, and if a synopsis or chronology of relevant
events has been provided and is disputed, the defendant's version of
events.

(b) If the claim is not admitted in full, the defendant should enclose
with his letter of reply documents in his possession which are
material to the issues between the parties and which would be likely
to be ordered to be disclosed by the court, either on an application
for pre-action disclosure or on disclosure during proceedings.
Reference can be made to the documents annexed to the Personal
Injury Protocol.

(c) Where more than one defendant receives a letter of claim, the
timetable will be activated for each defendant by the date on the
letter of claim addressed to it. If any defendant wishes to extend the
timetable because the number of defendants will cause complications, agreement to a different timetable should be sought as soon as
possible.

Where events occurred outside England and Wales and/or where the
defendant is outside the jurisdiction, the time periods of 21 days and 3
months should normally be extended up to 42 days and 6 months.

13.8 SCHEDULE OF SPECIAL DAMAGE

The letter of claim requires an outline of the financial losses likely to be
claimed. A schedule of special damages with supporting documents
should, therefore, be prepared and sent to the defendant as soon as
practicable. This can be a difficult matter to assess since there may be an
advantage in disclosing a more detailed, but still incomplete, schedule as
an aid to settlement negotiations.

13.9 EXPERTS

The Protocol acknowledges that in occupational illness claims expert
opinions will usually be required to deal with three areas of likely
contention between the claimant and the defendant: first, issues of
knowledge, fault and causation; secondly, medical issues of causation,
condition and prognosis; and, thirdly, in larger claims, issues of damages.
Even though some judges seem to consider that issues arising out of
occupational illness claims can be dealt with without expert evidence, it
may be difficult for the average trial judge to fully understand issues such
as: the likely degree of exposure to asbestos dust, or the total noise-dose
of the claimant; the amount of respirable asbestos dust liberated by
pulling old lagging off pipes; the relationship between 90 decibels and 93

decibels; the effect of having two machines each creating 90 decibels of noise; whether typing or keying is a repetitive, forceful action giving rise to a foreseeable risk of injury, etc.

The Protocol states that in disease claims the parties and their advisers should be flexible in their approach to expert evidence. Decisions on whether experts might be instructed jointly, and on whether reports might be disclosed sequentially or by exchange, *should rest with the parties and their advisers*. Sharing expert evidence may be appropriate on various issues including those relating to the value of the claim. However, the Protocol states that it does not attempt to be prescriptive on issues in relation to expert evidence. It is to be hoped that this will bring about some beneficial changes in some attitudes.

The Protocol explicitly recognises that there will be many occasions where a claimant will need to obtain a medical report before issuing a letter of claim. In such cases the defendant will be entitled to obtain its own medical report. The Protocol states that in some instances it may be more appropriate to send the letter of claim before a medical report is obtained, although it should be borne in mind that it may be difficult to write a comprehensive letter of claim before such evidence is available.

Similarly, defendants will usually need to see a medical report or other expert evidence before they can reach a view on causation.

Where the parties agree that nomination of a single expert is appropriate, a list of the name(s) of one or more experts in the relevant speciality whom each party considers suitable to instruct should be exchanged between the parties before either party instructs its expert. Within 14 days either party may indicate an objection to one or more of the named experts, in which case a mutually acceptable expert must be agreed upon. If either party objects to all the listed experts, the parties may then instruct experts of their own choice. The court does not have a role at this stage and is limited to deciding subsequently whether either party had acted unreasonably. It is suggested that the court should be urged not to apply too much hindsight to this exercise.

Some caution needs to be exercised since, if one party does not object to an expert nominated by the other party, he will not be entitled to rely on his own expert evidence unless the first party agrees, or the court so directs, or the first party's expert report has been amended and the first party is not prepared to disclose the original report. If the court is being asked to permit that party to rely on his own expert evidence at such a late stage, it is likely to require a proper explanation as to how the state of affairs arose and may make appropriate costs orders.

Either party may send written questions on the report to the agreed expert, via the solicitors of the party who nominated the expert. The expert should send answers to the questions separately and directly to each party. The cost of a report from an agreed expert will usually be paid by the instructing party; the costs of the expert replying to questions will usually be borne by the party which asks the questions.

The Protocol provides that where the defendant admits liability in whole or in part, before proceedings are issued, any medical report upon which the claimant intends to rely should be disclosed to the defendant, and any medical report upon which the defendant intends to rely should be disclosed to the claimant.

13.10   RESOLUTION OF ISSUES

The main aim of the Protocol is to resolve issues. The revised protocol says that the parties should consider whether some form of alternative dispute resolution would be more suitable than litigation. The court may require the parties to provide evidence that they did consider alternative dispute resolution.

If the claim is going to litigation, steps should be taken to try to resolve as many issues as possible. Part 36 of the Civil Procedure Rules enables claimants and defendants to make formal offers to settle before proceedings are started. The party making the offer must always supply sufficient evidence and/or information to enable the offer to be properly considered.

The Protocol suggests that it will only be necessary to carry out a 'stock take' of the issues in dispute and the necessary evidence where a claim is not resolved. Issues are more likely to be compromised in occupational illness claims than in other personal injury claims. Issues such as the length and degree of negligent exposure and the protective measures which were first available and how long these were used by the claimant can all be the subject of compromise. A proper evaluation of whether a party is likely to be able to prove the maximum/minimum for which it contends is very important. Defendants often want to compromise all the issues by giving an overall discount on the award of damages.

13.11   STARTING PROCEEDINGS

The claimant should delay issuing proceedings for 21 days from disclosure of reports to enable the parties to consider whether the claim is capable of settlement. Where the defendant is insured and the pre-action steps have been conducted by the insurer, the insurer will normally be expected to nominate solicitors to act in the proceedings, and the claimant's solicitor should request that the insurer so nominate 7–14 days before the intended issue date.

CHAPTER 14

EVIDENTIAL MATTERS

14.1   WITNESS STATEMENT

Part 32 of the Civil Procedure Rules requires that witness statements conform to requirements of Practice Direction PD32. The main requirements are set out below.

A witness statement should be headed with the name and number of the proceedings, the court or Division in which the proceedings are being heard, and the names of the parties. At the top right-hand corner of the first page there should be clearly written:

(a)   the party on whose behalf the statement is made;
(b)   the initials and surname of the witness;
(c)   the number of the statement in relation to that witness;
(d)   the identifying initials and number of each exhibit referred to; and
(e)   the date the statement was made.

The witness statement must, if practicable, be in the intended witness's own words. It should be expressed in the first person and should also state: the full name of the witness; his place of residence or, if he is making the statement in his professional, business or other occupational capacity, the address at which he works; the position he holds; the name of his firm or employer; his occupation, or if he has none, his description; and the fact that he is a party to the proceedings or is the employee of such a party if that be the case.

The witness statement must indicate which of the statements in it are made from the witness's own knowledge and which are matters of information or belief, and the source for any matters of information or belief.

Any exhibit used in conjunction with a witness statement should be verified and identified by the witness and remain separate from the witness statement. Where a witness refers to an exhibit or exhibits, he should state, 'there is now shown to me [*description of exhibit*] marked "..."'. The exhibit must be headed with the name of the proceedings and identified by a declaration from the witness. The first page of each exhibit should be marked with the mark referred to in the witness statement.

Where a witness makes more than one witness statement to which there are exhibits, the numbering of the exhibits should run consecutively throughout and not start again with each witness statement.

A witness statement should be produced on durable quality A4 paper with a 3.5 cm margin, be fully legible and typed on one side of the paper only. It should be divided into numbered paragraphs and have all numbers, including dates, expressed in figures.

A witness statement is the equivalent of the oral evidence which that witness would, if called, give in evidence; it must include a statement by the intended witness that he believes the facts in it are true.

Any alteration to a witness statement must be initialled by the person making the statement or by the authorised person where appropriate. A witness statement which contains an alteration that has not been initialled may be used in evidence only with the permission of the court.

14.2 CLAIMANT'S EVIDENCE

It is rare for an occupational illness case to proceed satisfactorily on the oral evidence of the claimant alone. In many cases the claimant's evidence will deal with events which happened many years ago and over a protracted period of time. His recollection will usually only be general rather than specific. He may be able to reconstruct a sequence of the places where he worked, but his memory of the dates or periods of time he spent there will probably be less precise.

The case will begin with a statement from the claimant which sets the basis for the claim. The factual issues which are likely to arise must then be identified and the claimant's statement expanded, partly from his own recollection and partly from the gathering of further evidence. Set out below are examples of statements relating to the main occupational illnesses discussed here, but the intention is to illustrate a method for application to any occupational illness case. The facts may differ, but many of the steps will be the same.

Although it may take a little more time, it is usually helpful to examine the claimant's employment history year by year. In that manner a more detailed picture of the relevant matters will be obtained. If necessary, years should be broken down into smaller sections since some of the work may have been seasonal, such as annual maintenance, or it may have involved more intense periods of effort.

When the maximum detail has been obtained from the claimant it is then possible to consider in what areas evidence will be required from other sources. In practice the gathering of evidence and the expanding of the claimant's statement will take place at the same time, but it is important to step back and take stock of the evidence. The claimant may have strong beliefs which he translates into bold assertions, but which may lack a sound factual basis. The claimant's beliefs must be supported by other evidence.

14.3 REQUIRED DETAILS

Experience has taught defendants to be wary of unsupported assertions that a claimant worked at a certain place for a certain time. Some claimants have falsely asserted that they were employed in a company many years previously knowing that the business has folded and that its tax records do not extend back to the years in which the claimant asserts he was employed. A claimant must therefore prove that he was employed as he claims by providing detail of the workplace and details, for example, of the name of the foreman and workmates. This gives the defendant an opportunity to check the claimant's assertion. In occupational illness cases, liability issues with which the claimant must deal are likely to be:

- where he worked;
- when he worked there;
- the type of product or substance used;
- what work he did;
- what work others did in proximity to him;
- how long during each day he was exposed;
- whether protective measures were taken;
- whether protective equipment was provided and when;
- was he given any instruction or training;
- whether there were any other sources or potential sources of exposure.

The claimant must also deal with the limitation issues as follows:

- When was he first aware of an illness or disability?
- What did he think was the cause of his illness or disability?
- When did he first think that his illness or disability might be caused by something at work?
- What made him think that his illness or disability might be caused by something at work?
- Was he provided with any personal protective equipment and, if so, what did he think was its purpose?
- Did he have health tests at work, if so when, and what did he think was the purpose?
- What was he told about the results of the tests?

- Did he know fellow workers who had brought claims for the same illness or disability?
- Was he a member of a trade union and, if so, did it provide any relevant information and, if so, when?
- When did he first know that he could bring a claim, and what was the source of his knowledge?
- When did he first think that his illness or disability was such that he thought it worth bringing a claim?
- Did he consult a medical adviser about his illness or disability and, if so, when, and what was he told?
- Did he consult anyone else about his illness or disability and, if so, when, and what was he told?

14.3.1   Asbestos

14.3.1.1   Where he worked

The claimant may have worked in a factory or workshop making asbestos products, or cutting asbestos cloth or sheet for installation in products such as ovens. He may have loaded or unloaded raw asbestos in sacks or bags. On the other hand, he may have worked on a host of different construction sites, or carried out maintenance on boilers, for example, in a variety of different buildings.

14.3.1.2   When he worked there

Clearly this starts with basic dates. The tax records will establish employments post-1 April 1962. The claimant may have moved between various factory premises and in some locations there may have been no asbestos exposure. Claimants can be helped to remember dates by reference to events such as when they were married, when their children were born, when their parents died, and even when their football team last won a trophy. This history can then be re-examined by some cross-referencing with the evidence of workmates who may have their own personal reasons for remembering certain dates. The disclosure of documents which reveal dates when machines were changed or new premises occupied can provide an anchor for dates.

14.3.1.3   The type of product or substance used

It may not always be easy to produce evidence that the material used was asbestos rather than something else. Attention must be given to the description of the substances used and the products worked upon. Raw asbestos fibres may be relatively easy to describe, and this can be supplemented by the name on the sack, bag or container. Cement sheet with fibre mixed in may be less obviously asbestos-based. Using information such as the description of the size of an uncut sheet, and whether it had markings or a name stamped upon it, an expert can usually identify the product and state whether it contained asbestos.

14.3.1.4   What work he did

The majority of asbestos cases these days involve the claimant having worked on an asbestos product. Asbestos rope/string or cloth sheet may have been cut or torn and installed in a product to provide insulation. Ovens, toasters, chip-shop fryers, electrical switch gear, railway locomotives and carriages, ducting for cabling, and protective gloves and clothes may all have contained asbestos products. These are only a few examples. Evidence is required to prove the degree of exposure to liberated asbestos fibres which the claimant then inhaled.

14.3.1.5   What work others did in proximity to him

The claimant may not have worked with asbestos himself but alongside or beneath laggers, or alongside factory workers cutting asbestos sheet for installation in the final product. Such exposure may well have been foreseeably likely to cause asbestos disease.

14.3.1.6   How long during each day he was exposed

In the earlier years, exposure may have been small and intermittent, and this may allow the defendant to argue that it was not foreseeable at that date that such minor exposure would cause asbestos disease in later years.

14.3.1.7   Whether protective measures were taken

The machining or cutting of asbestos may have been contained or extraction equipment may have removed asbestos fibres. The type of protective equipment, its function and actual use may all be relevant in establishing whether the protective measures were adequate. Of course, expert evidence may be needed in this respect, but the evidence of the claimant is an essential foundation.

14.3.1.8   Whether protective equipment was provided and when

Questions the claimant must consider are whether he was provided with a mask, and if so what type of mask, and whether this provided a proper seal or whether other protective equipment created gaps around the side. The date when protective equipment was provided can be relevant to the issue of whether at that date more effective protective equipment was available.

14.3.1.9   *Whether there were any other sources or potential sources of exposure*

The usual sources will be other employment or service in the armed forces. The exposure may not have been through working with asbestos itself but, for example, using asbestos cloth in work such as a baker removing trays from a hot oven, or a fireman using an asbestos fire blanket.

14.3.2   Noise

14.3.2.1   *Where he worked*

Establishing where the claimant worked is very important in a noise-induced hearing loss case based on work in a factory because the noise levels may have differed in different departments of the factory. It is necessary to build up a means of assessing the noise-dose sustained over the years. The claimant may have worked on a particular machine or next to noisy equipment, and these details are important.

In cases where the claimant used pneumatic-powered tools on a building site or when digging up roads, location is only important for establishing that he was there when such tools were used. More important is which tools he used and for how long.

14.3.2.2   *When he worked there*

Once again the focus is on building up the evidence of the noise-dose suffered. A claimant may have worked in a noisy location only for a limited time, or he may have worked in the same location but the machines changed in type or in number, thus affecting the noise levels. The claimant may have worked only for a few hours in a certain location, but it was during those hours that the excessive noise was generated, for example on an engine test bed, or at the beginning of a work cycle. It may be helpful in these circumstances to create a diary so that the detail can be established.

14.3.2.3   *The type of tools and machines used*

Although this is a rather obvious category, it is important for building a picture of the noise dosage. Furthermore, it is necessary to identify each machine so that noise levels can be calculated or read from noise surveys which the defendant may have compiled. Where possible, the manufacturer's name and model number of the machine should be used, although in reality such detail is rarely available in relation to very old machines. A cross-check between the names on the documents and the names colloquially used by the workforce may avoid unnecessary duplication of detail.

14.3.2.4 *What work he did*

This evidence may have emerged from examination of where the claimant worked, when and with what tools or machines. However, other important factors may be, for example, whether the claimant was part of a work-gang or team, but not directly involved in using the equipment, or whether he worked at some distance loading or unloading product from the machine and was thus exposed to different noise levels.

14.3.2.5 *What work others did in proximity to him*

This category goes hand-in-hand with the evidence concerning where the claimant worked, what work he carried out, and with what tools and machines.

14.3.2.6 *How long during each day he was exposed*

Time of exposure is very important in noise-induced hearing loss cases. The total noise-dose can differ greatly according to the time of exposure. A claimant who worked an 8-hour shift may have spent time setting up the machine or loading product when the machine was inactive and quiet. For example, noisy welding and hammering may have been interspersed with times when the component was being turned over or repositioned for the next task. A train driver or vehicle driver may have worked an 8-hour shift but have been in the cab for only 5 hours a day.

14.2.3.7 *Whether protective measures were taken*

This is likely to have varied over time. For example, screens and baffles may have been provided at later dates, and machines may have been enclosed and damped against noise.

14.3.2.8 *Whether protective equipment was provided and when*

The discussion here principally concerns ear-plugs and ear muffs. Bilsom wool, foam ear-plugs, wax ear-plugs and ear muffs were likely to have been provided in later years, improving over the years to give better protection. Some of the issues to consider are whether the protection provided was ineffective against very high noise levels, and whether information and instruction was provided to workers to ensure that the protective equipment was properly used.

14.3.2.9 *Whether there were any other sources or potential sources of exposure*

Issues to be considered under this heading are, for example, whether the claimant served in the Armed Forces, his hobbies and other external factors which may have exacerbated his injury, e g going regularly to noisy clubs or bars, etc.

14.3.3 Work-related upper limb disorders (WRULDs)

14.3.3.1 *Where he worked*

The question of where the claimant worked may be of less significance in WRULD claims than the type of work he performed. However, evidence as to location is a helpful building block for the rest of the evidence.

14.3.3.2 *When he worked there*

This may be significant because the work may have changed over the years, or there may have been changes to the way in which the work was performed. Changes in the work rate or in the rotation of tasks may have occurred. The length of time spent on the various tasks may also have changed. Such details must be incorporated into the overall evidence of the work which it is claimed caused injury to the claimant.

14.3.3.3 *What work he did*

The work carried out by the claimant is central to a WRULD claim. This must be identified and examined in detail, stage by stage, in order to provide evidence of the damaging component of the task. For example, a worker may have trimmed pot plants with repeated snips of the secateurs, but the damaging component of the task was holding the plant pot and twisting it around for the trimming process. Taking the same example, one hand may be affected by one medical disorder and the other hand affected by a different medical disorder.

14.3.3.4 *How long during each day he carried out the work*

Injury in WRULD cases usually occurs as a result of repetitive action. A task performed with significant breaks is unlikely to cause injury. Many employers introduced work rotation to reduce the risk of injury to the workforce. The work may have had built-in breaks caused by the need to set up or perform work that did not carry the risk of injury.

14.3.3.5   Whether protective measures were taken

Protective measures in relation to WRULD cases usually involve rotation of the workforce so as to reduce the time spent by an individual on a task which carries risk.

14.3.3.6   Whether there were any other sources or potential sources of exposure

A host of possible other causes could have contributed to or caused the injury, including, for example, playing a musical instrument, knitting, DIY, sport, and a second job.

14.3.4   Vibration white finger (VWF)

14.3.4.1   Where he worked

In VWF cases the claimant may have worked in a factory or workshop, on construction sites, in mines, quarries or in forests, digging up roads for statutory undertakings, or making and mending highways. The question of where the claimant worked is only of significance in looking at other issues. For example, a person who works in a factory making concrete lamp-posts using vibratory tools to remove bubbles from liquid concrete may carry out that work for his 8-hour shift. On the other hand, a man working with road-breaking tools may spend part of his 8-hour shift travelling to and from the site and then perform intermittent tasks.

14.3.4.2   When he worked with vibratory tools or machinery

The amount of time the claimant was exposed to working with vibratory tools or machinery is one of the crucial issues in VWF cases. As observed above, the time of the shift or the time on site only sets the context in which the damaging exposure may have taken place. Workers using jack-hammers to break up tarmacadam may wait for others to shovel out the spoil, or they may be multi-tasking and do the shovelling themselves. In many ways it is almost impossible to have an accurate assessment from the claimant of the time spent working with vibratory tools when such use is intermittent. It is generally assumed that a claimant will over-estimate this time (not necessarily consciously), whilst an engineer will halve the claimant's estimate. Bearing this in mind, the claimant's statement must accurately reflect his true working conditions so as to deflect crude reductions.

14.3.4.3 The type of tools or machinery used

This is relevant to the issue of what frequency of vibration the claimant was exposed to. Different types of tools and equipment produce vibration at different frequencies.

14.3.4.4 Whether protective measures were taken

Protective measures against risk of VWF are damping tools or machinery, rotating work tasks and reducing the time spent with certain tools.

14.3.4.5 Whether protective equipment was provided and when

The claimant may have been provided with padded gloves or similar protective equipment.

14.3.4.6 Whether warnings and instructions were given

Whilst not every workman using vibratory tools or machinery will suffer VWF, some are more susceptible to damage. Workers should be warned to watch out for the onset of symptoms and then seek medical advice, or be instructed to work in a particular way.

14.3.4.7 Whether there were any other sources or potential sources of exposure

Defendants have been known to plead in their defence that the cause of the claimant's injury was due to 'excessive DIY' rather than any work-related task.

14.3.5 Work-related stress

14.3.5.1 What work he did

A work-related stress claim usually has at its heart some change in working practice or some addition to the workload.

14.3.5.2 What the defendant knew

A major evidential problem in establishing foreseeability in work-related stress claims is in proving that the employer knew or ought to have known that the claimant was suffering stress to a degree that it was making him ill. This problem can be exacerbated by the fact that workers who fall ill through stress are generally those who claim to be able to manage the stress created by the work. Such claimants are sometimes labelled 'apparent copers'; they do not complain. They may not be truthful with their GP, who may conclude that the illness is due to factors unrelated to work. In addition, such workers may secretly work at home or arrive at work early, leave late or work in their breaks.

14.3.5.3 *What could have been done to avoid the stresses imposed on the claimant?*

The Court of Appeal in *Sutherland v Hatton*[1] stressed the importance of proving that the stress arose from a breach of duty. This approach was approved by the House of Lords in *Barber v Somerset County Council*.[2]

14.3.5.4 *Causation*

To some degree we are all affected at one time or another with common stressors such as shortage of money, emotional relationships, involvement with the law, illness, illness in a relative or close friend, or death in the family. Children can cause stress to their parents in respect of their development, progress at school, friends, pregnancy, crime, drink and drugs. In other words, stress-related illness can arise from many other causes outside the working environment. Medical evidence is therefore of crucial importance in establishing causation.

A defendant will be anxious to establish other possible causes in order to defeat a claim in its entirety or reduce its contribution to damages. A certain degree of pre-empting is thus advisable. Sources of information relating to cause are many and varied. Evidence may come from witnesses to whom the claimant has confided. The personnel files, occupational health records and works surgery records may all contain information or clues leading to relevant information. The claimant's GP notes are usually the most useful, but the claimant may also have been referred to hospital. Evidence that the claimant has sought counselling is particularly relevant in stress cases.

Obtaining expert evidence will often be an expensive step and may take time, especially in specialised areas where there are limited numbers of suitable experts. Claimants, defendants and their advisers will therefore need to consider carefully how best to obtain any necessary expert help quickly and cost-effectively.

14.4 INVESTIGATING THE CIRCUMSTANCES OF THE CLAIM

In most occupational disease cases the claimant's working history is of great importance. First, the location of the claimant in relation to the source of the excess exposure, whether fume, dust, noise or other, is crucial. Secondly, the length and degree of the exposure must be

---

[1]   [2002] 2 All ER 1.
[2]   [2004] 2 All ER 385.

examined. Consideration must then be given to what protective and preventative measures were in place. Finally, the question of the provision of personal protective equipment should be considered.

Stress cases stand apart from other occupation illnesses in certain respects. Stress claims are not the preserve of any one section of the working population. Claims are made by managers, salesmen, clerical staff, teachers and local authority workers, amongst others. The circumstances of each case will be radically different from others. Although the legal framework may be the same, the factual framework is likely to differ from case to case. It is important, therefore, to establish a clear picture of the workplace and the employee's place in that workplace. The moment of breakdown is often caused by an event which is in reality the 'final straw that broke the camel's back'.

The first task is to understand the structure of the workplace. Stress usually arises from pressure exerted by a more senior employee in the form of excessive demands in respect of the work task. A key to understanding what happened is to understand the structure of the organisation as it relates to the claimant. It is necessary to identify the immediate level of supervisors above the claimant and the supervisors or managers above that level, since added pressure may have been generated at some higher level in the hierarchy.

The second task is to understand the work which the claimant is expected to do. It is important that all the work tasks are considered. It may appear that a claim is based on only one aspect of the work – the frustration with excessive paperwork, for example – which may not be a problem if the employee's time was not taken up with other tasks and commitments.

14.5 DEFENCES

In some cases, for example, defendants have been able to call evidence that the ventilation was adequate. This is clearly a matter of fact and degree and expert evidence is vital so far as each party is concerned in advancing their respective contentions.

A defendant may also claim that it was not reasonably practicable in the circumstances to prevent exposure. This requires consideration of the balance between the incidence of risk, the significance of the possible injury and the cost in terms of money, effort and time in avoiding or reducing the risk. Thus, for example, where only a small number of workers suffered irritation of the eyes, which had no permanent adverse effect, the defendants could argue that nothing needed to be done to protect the workforce as a whole. It will be appreciated that this will give rise to considerable areas of discussion.

14.6 DOCUMENTARY EVIDENCE

In cases where it is alleged that there has been exposure to an excessive or harmful degree, documentation evidence falls into three broad categories.

First, documents which relate to knowledge of the risk may include scientific publications or articles from the Factory Inspectorate or HSE, manufacturers' data sheets, or research papers from an internal department.

The second broad category of documents relates to the degree of exposure, for example where measurements were taken, or relevant entries made in committee minutes.

The third category of documents relates to the claimant personally and may comprise his personnel records, occupational health records, GP notes, hospital notes, and notes from professionals such as counsellors or osteopaths.

Perhaps the most wide-ranging documents relate to stress cases. These include job applications, including previous work histories, pre-employment medicals, contracts of employment, personnel records or human resources records (which should include employee appraisals and promotion records), occupational health records and works surgery records. Other possibly relevant documents are the staff manual or handbook, any work stress health policy, training records, and complaints book/suggestion records.

The Management of Health and Safety at Work Regulations 1992 and 1999 require employers who employ more than five employees to keep records of risk assessments (reg 3(4)).

The Control of Substances Hazardous to Health Regulations require the keeping of records of substances to which employees are exposed, and records of monitoring and health surveillance.

The Provision and Use of Work Equipment Regulations 1992 and 1998 provide that where any machinery has a maintenance log, the log must be kept up to date (reg 6(2) of the 1992 Regulations and reg 5(2) of the 1998 Regulations). The 1998 Regulations contained a new provision requiring an employer to inspect the safety of work equipment and to record and keep on file the result of the inspection until the next inspection. It does not appear that there is a requirement to preserve the old record once the next inspection has taken place.

PART 5

VALUING THE CLAIM

CHAPTER 15

GENERAL DAMAGES

15.1 INTRODUCTION

General damages are awarded for the injury itself, pain, suffering and disability. Awards of damages for handicap on the labour market and for loss of congenial employment are also generally regarded as heads of general damage. These three elements will be considered below.

Interest on general damages is awarded at 2 per cent simple interest from the date of the service of proceedings.

Bereavement damages were introduced by the Fatal Accidents Act 1976. For causes of action accruing on or before 31 March 2002 the award is £7,500. For causes of action accruing on or after 1 April 2002 the award is £10,000. For causes of action accruing on or after 1 January 2008 the award is £11,800. Interest on bereavement damages are awarded at the full interest rate from the date of the death.

15.2 PROVISIONAL DAMAGES

Instead of one final assessment of damages, a claimant may apply for an award of provisional damages in certain circumstances. A claim for provisional damages may be made where it is proved, or admitted, that in the future the claimant may develop some serious disease or suffer some serious deterioration in his health. An award of provisional damages is likely to be most relevant in asbestos cases, but may be relevant to other cases of occupational illness.

Section 31(a) of the Senior Courts Act 1981 sets out the criteria for an award of provisional damages:

> 'this section applies to an action for damages for personal injuries in which there is proved, or admitted to be a chance that at some definite or indefinite time in the future the injured person will as a result of the act or admission which gave rise to the cause of action, develop some serious disease or suffer some serious deterioration in his physical or mental condition.'

It is a matter for the claimant in the first instance to decide whether he wishes to apply for provisional damages. He may prefer an award of damages, enhanced to take account of the future risk, and be content to bear the risk himself. Of course there is no certainty that the court will make an order, and in a significant number of cases the court has declined to do so, even in circumstances which seem most appropriate.[1]

A claim for provisional damages must be set out in the particulars of claim. It must be stated that the claimant is seeking an award of provisional damages and that there is a chance that at some future date the claimant will develop some serious disease or suffer some serious deterioration in his physical or mental condition, specifying what that might be. A precedent relating to asbestos-related disease is set out in Appendix 1.

If the court is satisfied that the criteria are met, an award will be made on the basis that the serious disease or serious deterioration does not occur. The court will then direct the period of time in which an application for further damages may be made, which period is usually for the claimant's life (shorter periods are less usual). The court may specify different periods of time for different conditions. If the court does order a period shorter than the claimant's life the claimant may make an application for the period of time to be extended, which will need to be supported by appropriate medical evidence.

At the time of the judgment for provisional damages the court will give directions as to which documents are to be filed and preserved so as to form a case file for a future application. The documents will be listed in a schedule forming part of the judgment. The case file should include a copy of the original judgment, the pleadings or statements of case, a transcript of the judge's reasoned judgment, and all medical reports upon which reliance was placed. Where the court considers it necessary it will order that the file should include a transcript of the relevant parts of the evidence and any relevant witness statements. The file may be added to as a result of subsequent applications. The court will retain the case file and the parties should also keep a copy of the documents in the case file. An issue as to causation of any future disease may be left for determination in the future, when some matters may be clearer or the medical evidence may have advanced.

There is some support for the contention that a claimant may apply for a declaration that his dependants could bring a claim for a further award even though the claimant has died in the interim,[2] since the death of the claimant may otherwise extinguish the right. However, the Court of Appeal in *Middleton v Elliott Turbomachinery Ltd* did not feel that it was appropriate to make such a declaration in that case.

---

[1]   See, e g *Moses v County Durham Health Authority and Others* (unreported) 25 June 2002.

[2]   *Middleton v Elliott Turbomachinery Ltd* (1980) *The Times*, October 20.

Before applying for a further award of damages the claimant must give 28 days' written notice to the defendant and its insurers, if known. The claimant then has 21 days after the 28-day period to apply to the court for directions.

The defendant can make a Part 36 offer specifying that it is in full and final satisfaction of the present and future claims. Alternatively, the defendant can make a provisional Part 36 offer stating it to be on the basis that the claimant will not develop the disease or deterioration contended. The claimant will retain the right to return to court in the future for an assessment of damages if the defined disease or deterioration comes about.

A medical expert will need to consider the following matters:

(1) Is there a chance that at some definite or indefinite time in the future the claimant may develop some serious disease as a result of the matters arising from this exposure/incident?
(2) Is there a chance that at some definite or indefinite time in the future the claimant may suffer some serious deterioration in his physical or mental condition as a result of the matters arising from this exposure/incident?
(3) Is the chance more than a mere outside possibility?
(4) What is the percentage chance of the future occurrence?
(5) Over what period of time may the new disease or the serious deterioration take place?

15.3   ASBESTOS-RELATED DISEASE

15.3.1   Pain, suffering and disability

In asbestos-related disease cases it is important to consider whether a claim should be made for provisional damages. The *Judicial Studies Board Guidelines* (10th edn, 2004) are based on a once-and-for-all settlement, save in relation to the least serious pleural thickening cases where the guideline figures are £4,350 to £7,250. Awards of provisional damages will be significantly lower than awards made on a full and final basis, but the advantage for the claimant is that he preserves his right to claim further damages if in the future he develops one of the more serious asbestos-related conditions.

15.3.2   Mesothelioma

Mesothelioma is a condition causing painful death within 2–4 years. The *Judicial Studies Board Guidelines* suggest a bracket of £35,000–£83,750. The differentiating factors are the severity of the pain, the severity of the disablement and the length of time suffered.

Consideration of the reported cases shows that it is worth calculating the adjustments required by inflation, bearing in mind that for cases before March 2000 it will be necessary to update the award to March 2000, apply the *Heil v Rankin*[3] uplift and adjust that figure for inflation since that date. The awards in the cases reflect the differentiating factors referred to above.

The development of mesothelioma is not dose-related; it is an indivisible condition. The, apportionment of damages in respect of the exposure from two or more employers is not an issue for the claimant following the enactment of the Compensation Act 2006. The claimant is entitled to the full amount of the award; it is for the defendants to determine between themselves how they apportion it.

15.3.3   Lung cancer

This is also a fatal condition and the *Judicial Studies Board Guidelines* suggest a bracket of £51,500–£66,000.

A causation argument may arise in respect of claimants who were smokers. Consider the Causation chapter above. A smoking history will also give rise to arguments of contributory negligence. Lung cancer is an indivisible condition and the question of apportionment does not arise for the claimant.

15.3.4   Asbestosis

Asbestosis causes impairment of lung function. In the early stages the disease may be virtually symptomless. As it develops it causes increasing breathlessness, which can become severe with a consequent effect on mobility and general quality of life. The condition is usually progressive, but in a small number of cases it may remain virtually static, or progress only very slowly. The *Judicial Studies Board Guidelines* suggest a bracket of £31,500–£69,500 for a full and final settlement. A claimant who has asbestosis is also at risk of developing the separate diseases of lung cancer and mesothelioma.

The prognosis is important for asbestosis cases because it is not necessarily the case that the disease will progress at the same rate for all. Consideration must be given to how the claimant will be affected for the remainder of his life. Factors such as the age of the claimant can be important. There may be other medical conditions affecting overall disability, whether constitutional or induced by smoking. These factors have to be taken into account.

---

[3]   [2001] QB 272, [2000] 2 WLR 1173.

Awards of provisional damages in cases in the last 3 years have been around £14,000 and £21,000.

Asbestosis is dose-related and thus the issue of the apportionment of damages becomes relevant if there have been two or more employers during the relevant period.[4] The onset of asbestos disease begins many years after exposure and thus recent exposures to asbestos are not relevant. Generally, the relevant period of latency is 15 years or more. Damage will be apportioned in all of the following circumstances:

- where two or more employers exposed the claimant to asbestos;
- the exposure, although significant, is not compensationable because the tort has not been established, for example where it cannot be proved that the defendant knew or ought to have known that exposure created risk (only likely to occur where exposure was pre-1965);
- exposure occurred with one employer but also during a period of self-employment.

Where exposure at the different employments was broadly the same, apportionment will be carried out on the basis of the various periods of time of exposure. However, where there was significant difference in the degree of exposure at a particular employment or in self-employment, in principle the apportionment exercise should reflect the varying degrees of exposure (in fact, this is rarely the case).

15.3.5 Pleural thickening

Pleural thickening causes symptoms of breathlessness. The symptoms may progress to cause severe breathing difficulties and consequent disability. The prognosis for the progress of the disease and the degree of impairment likely to be suffered in the future is important in assessing the quantum of general damages. The *Judicial Studies Board Guidelines* suggest a bracket of £25,250–£51,500.

Pleural thickening is also dose-related and thus where there have been two or more employers or a period of self-employment giving rise to exposure to asbestos the damages will need to be apportioned. See **15.3.4** above in relation to asbestosis.

15.3.6 Pleural plaques

Pleural plaques are symptomless and their presence alone does not constitute damage sufficient to create a tort, and thus compensation for a civil claim no longer exists.

---

[4]   *Holtby v Brigham & Cowan (Hull) Ltd* [2000] 3 All ER 421.

15.3.7   Handicap on the labour market

The foundation for a claim for damages for handicap on the labour market is *Smith v Manchester Corporation.*[5] Such claims are thus sometimes referred to as *Smith v Manchester* claims.

Claimants who have symptomless pleural plaques are not likely to be considered as suffering any handicap on the labour market since their physical functioning is not impaired. However, the other asbestos-related conditions usually do cause impairment of physical function, with breathlessness of varying degrees, and such conditions can lead to an award of damages for handicap on the labour market. Where the claimant is close to retirement age and there is no indication that he is likely to lose his job, no award will be made under this head of damage; nor will damages be awarded where the medical condition is fairly static. The court will consider factors such as the claimant's medical condition and prognosis, his job (and whether he may need or want to change it), and his skills and experience which may enable him to find alternative, more sedentary work.

15.3.8   Loss of congenial employment

In theory a claimant may bring a claim for loss of congenial employment where the asbestos-related disease caused him to give up a job he particularly enjoyed. In practice, congenial awards in asbestos cases are rare since such awards are usually made in cases where the work included particular camaraderie, such as the fire service and police force. Work where a claimant was exposed to asbestos does not usually share the same characteristics.

15.4   ASTHMA

15.4.1   Pain, suffering and disability

The *Judicial Studies Board Guidelines* list five categories for occupational asthma claims.

The *Judicial Studies Board Guidelines* for mild asthma, bronchitis, colds and chest problems, which last only a few months, gives a bracket of up to £3,400. It is more suited to the unfit housing cases than occupational illness claims.

Where the asthma is relatively mild and (seemingly, although this is not stated) the symptoms are likely to substantially recover within a few years of exposure, the bracket of damages awards is £7,000–£12,600.

---

[5]   (1974) 17 KIR 1, CA.

Where asthma causes wheezing and affects the claimant's work and social activities, but there is a likelihood of a substantial recovery within a few years, the bracket is £12,600–£17,250.

Chronic asthma causing breathing difficulties, occasional use of an inhaler, restriction of employment and some uncertainty in prognosis, is considered by the *Judicial Studies Board Guidelines* to be in the bracket £17,250–£28,500.

The *Guidelines* suggest a bracket of £28,500–£43,000 for the most severe condition of permanent disabling asthma, which affects physical activity, causes prolonged and regular coughing and causes sleep disturbance.

15.4.2   Handicap on the labour market

The foundation for a claim for damages for handicap on the labour market is *Smith v Manchester Corporation*.[6] Such claims are thus sometimes referred to as '*Smith v Manchester*' claims.

Claimants with asthma usually suffer impairment of physical function, with breathlessness of varying degrees, and such conditions can lead to an award of damages for handicap on the labour market. See the discussion at **15.3.7** above where similar considerations apply.

15.4.3   Loss of congenial employment

See under **15.3.8** above where the same considerations apply.

15.5   HEARING LOSS

The *Judicial Studies Board Guidelines* list four categories of damages in partial hearing and tinnitus:

severe tinnitus hearing loss	£19,500–£30,000
moderate tinnitus hearing loss	£9,750–£19,500
mild tinnitus with some hearing loss	£8,250–£9,570
slight or occasional tinnitus with slight hearing loss	£4,850–£8,250

The *Guidelines* make no reference to losses at different frequencies and so damages are more difficult to assess. The reported cases show varying levels of hearing loss at the main frequencies, and whilst there is much

---

[6]   (1974) 17 KIR 1, CA.

individual variation, it is easier to make comparisons with the audiogram readings in the claim under consideration. A convenient summary is not possible here.

15.5.1   Handicap on the labour market

See generally **15.3.7** above. In hearing loss cases, some awards for damages for handicap on the labour market have been made, but perhaps surprisingly the evidence does not support the assertion that a claimant with a hearing loss is handicapped on the labour market.

15.5.2   Loss of congenial employment

See generally **15.3.8** above. Awards for loss of congenial employment in hearing cases are rare.

15.6   WORK-RELATED UPPER LIMB DISORDERS (WRULDS)

This umbrella term covers a number of distinct medical conditions and it is important not to confuse them. Whilst claimants may share general symptoms in common, such as pain on movement and swelling, the differences are important in assessing loss of function. The diagnosis of the condition will also be relevant to the prognosis of the symptoms.

Tenosynovitis is inflammation of the synovial sheaths of the tendons. De Quervains tenovaginitis is inflammation of the fibrous sheaths of the tendons of the thumb. Carpal tunnel syndrome is caused by constriction of the median nerve in the wrist because of thickening of the surrounding tissue. Epicondylitis is inflammation of the muscle attachments at the elbow.

These conditions may occur in one arm or both, there may be varying degrees of impairment to work, and the claimant may be vulnerable to recurrence or aggravation of symptoms.

Where there is complete recovery from symptoms within a short period the *Judicial Studies Board Guidelines*[7] suggest a bracket of damages awards of £1,450 to £2,300. Tenosynovitis and De Quervains tenovaginitis may cause short-lived symptoms and thus may fall into this category.

Where symptoms resolve in the course of two years the *Judicial Studies Board Guidelines* suggests a bracket of £5,700 to £6,300. This is a narrow band and it will be appreciated that there is a gap in the suggested awards

---

[7]   10th edn.

between the 'short period' of one band and this two-year period; some flexibility of approach is required; it confirms the fact that these are only guidelines.

Where continuing but fluctuating symptoms occur unilaterally the guidelines figures are £9,750 to £10,750. Once again, this is a tight band of award and there is a gap from the lesser category.

The guidelines for bilateral disability, with surgery and loss of employment, are £14,350 to £15,200.

15.6.1 Handicap in the labour market

See generally **15.3.7** above. Claimants who suffer persistent symptoms are entitled to an award of damages for handicap on the labour market. Even where the claimant has recovered he may be vulnerable to a recurrence of the symptoms if the same or similar work activity is undertaken. Thus, the claimant may be significantly restricted in the type of work that he can undertake. It is a matter of evidence in respect of the individual claimant, and the courts will consider factors such as the claimant's medical condition and prognosis, his job (and whether he may need or want to change it) and his skills and experience which may enable him to find alternative, more sedentary work.

15.6.2 Loss of congenial employment

See generally **15.3.8** above. In WRULD cases, awards for loss of congenial employment are more obvious in the case of, for example, a string player in an orchestra, and less obvious for a factory worker who carries out repetitive and mindless tasks. On the other hand, it may be that a factory worker may miss the lively social atmosphere and verbal jousting of the factory floor.

15.7 VIBRATION WHITE FINGER (VWF)

VWF symptoms can vary greatly. One or more fingers may be affected to a greater or lesser degree, and the symptoms may occur in one or both hands. The effect on a person's ability to work will vary. The tasks of ordinary living may be affected to a greater or lesser degree, and sports and recreations which involve exposure to cold, and thus may provoke symptoms, may be limited or curtailed.

The *Judicial Studies Board Guidelines* lists four categories of damages in VWF cases:

| most serious | £20,750–£25,250 |

serious	£11,000–£20,750
moderate	£5,700–£11,000
minor	£2,000–£5,700

In helping to decide into which category a claimant falls, the medical profession has developed two scales for categorising disability which provide a much more detailed assessment of the condition.

The Taylor-Pelmear table was the first to be developed and recognised by the courts. This divides the symptoms into five categories. There is no rigid division between the categories (which have been developed for convenience), and thus there is some overlap between the various stages:

- **stage 0**   intermittent tingling or intermittent numbness but causing no interference with work or social activities;
- **stage 1**   blanching of one or more of the fingertips, but causing no interference with work or social activities;
- **stage 2**   blanching of one or more fingers with numbness, usually confined to winter, causing slight interference with home and social activities, but no interference with work activities;
- **stage 3**   extensive blanching both in winter and summer causing definite interference at home with social activities and work and restriction of hobbies;
- **stage 4**   extensive blanching of most fingers with frequent episodes and requiring occupation to be changed to avoid further vibration exposure because of the severity of the signs and symptoms.

The Taylor-Pelmear scale was revised by the Stockholm Workshop scale and a different classification was produced, enabling more precise classification:

Vascular component

stage 0	no attacks	
stage 1	mild	occasional attacks affecting only the tips of one or more fingers
stage 2	moderate	occasional attacks affecting distal and middle phalanges (rarely also proximal) of one or more fingers
stage 3	severe	frequent attacks affecting all phalanges of most fingers

stage 4	very severe	as in stage 3, with trophic skin changes in the fingertips

Sensorineural component

stage 0	SN	vibration exposed but no symptoms
stage 1	SN	intermittent numbness with or without tingling
stage 2	SN	intermittent or persistent numbness reducing sensory perception
stage 3	SN	intermittent or persistent numbness, reduced tactile discrimination or manipulative dexterity

The condition of each hand is then made the subject of a notation of the scale indicating the number of affected fingers. For example 2L(2)/2R(1) indicates two left fingers at stage 2 (moderate) and two right fingers at stage 1 (mild).

Both scales are often referred to in medical reports and this can be helpful in giving a more complete understanding of the claimant's symptoms for the purpose of comparing them with previous awards of damages.

A case with 3R4/3L4 and 2SN currently attracts an award of £8,620.

15.7.1 Handicap on the labour market

See generally **15.3.7** above.

Claimants who suffer VWF to any significant degree are likely to be handicapped on the labour market. They may be limited in their use of vibrating tools and machinery, and unable to work in cold conditions, whether outside in winter or inside, for example in a cold store or food processing line. Such claimants usually have limited alternative skills to bring to the job market and so the handicap may be great.

15.7.2 Loss of congenial employment

See generally **15.3.8** above. In practice, awards in VWF cases are rare although in one case a claimant was awarded £5,600 under this head of damage.

15.8   WORK-RELATED STRESS

There is emerging medical evidence to support the view that stress can cause physical as well as psychological injury. Stress may trigger heart conditions or cause digestive problems. However, the majority of work-related stress claims are concerned with psychological or psychiatric injury. Depression is probably the most common result of work-related stress. For this reason the possible physical injuries are not considered here.

The *Judicial Studies Board Guidelines* list four categories of psychiatric damage: severe, moderately severe, moderate and minor.

Where the injured person has marked difficulties coping with life and work and there has been a significant effect on relationships with family and friends and the prognosis is very poor, the suggested bracket for awards of general damages is £36,000–£76,000.

Where the injury has affected the claimant's ability to cope with life and work, his relationships are affected and he may be vulnerable to stress in the future, but the prognosis is more optimistic, the bracket for damages is £12,500–£36,000. The Guidelines specifically state that: 'cases of work-related stress resulting in a permanent or long-standing disability preventing a return to comparable employment would appear to come within this category.'

Where moderate symptoms affect the claimant's ability to work and cope with the strains of daily existence, and there is some impairment of relationships, but there has been a marked improvement by the time of trial with a good prognosis, awards will be in the range of £3,875–£12,500.

Minor symptoms which are short-lived will only attract awards of damages of £1,000—£3,875.

15.8.1   Handicap on the labour market

See generally **15.3.7** above. A history of work-related stress will clearly be a disadvantage in seeking employment. A prospective employer will be concerned that the claimant may not be able to cope with the work. Many claimants take less stressful and demanding jobs, which will reduce their disadvantage on the labour market. For example, professional workers such as teachers can bring intelligence to a job, even though they may not be able to cope with the pressures of a higher job grade. The facts must be considered carefully in each case when preparing evidence to support a claim for damages under this heading.

15.8.2 Loss of congenial employment

See generally **15.3.8** above. Loss of congenial employment is more obvious in the case of professional workers or persons at a managerial level where the work carries its own degree of satisfaction. Less obvious is the situation where the claimant has taken a pride and satisfaction in a job which he can no longer pursue. Awards of £5,000 have been made in this type of case but awards are not made in every case.

CHAPTER 16

SPECIAL DAMAGES

16.1 LOSS OF EARNINGS

Occupational disease may lead to absence from work, for a short time whilst treatment is sought, or for longer periods. The claimant's medical evidence must support the absence from work as being reasonably required as a consequence of the occupational disease. For longer periods of absence it is important to have a prognosis.

Obtaining a prognosis is important in occupational disease cases. The claimant will make a recovery after appropriate treatment; on the other hand there may be no realistic prospect of a recovery and confirmation will be required that the claimant is no longer capable of carrying out his work, or at least not without risk of recurrence of his condition or worsening of his existing condition. The question then arises as to alternative work the claimant is fit to undertake.

The employer has a duty under employment law provisions to consider whether other work within the organisation is suitable for the claimant to undertake. Failure to consider this possibility of alternative work may give rise to an employment law remedy, which usually arises in unfair dismissal proceedings, or in discrimination proceedings, including disability discrimination proceedings. Such matters are a specialist area of law with which this book is not directly concerned. However, for these purposes, where the employer finds the claimant alternative employment at the same or increased salary there can be no claim for future loss, although there may be a claim for handicap on the labour market (see Chapter 15). Where the employer has found less well-remunerated employment the claimant will need to consider carefully whether he should take that employment and thus be seen to mitigate his loss. The difference between his previous earnings and his earnings in an alternative job will form the basis for a claim for future partial loss of earnings.

16.2 FUTURE EFFECT ON EMPLOYMENT

If the occupational disease has sensitised the claimant to something encountered in his employment, he may not be able to work in the same place because of the risk of further sensitisation. It is important to get a medical expert to consider future sensitisation. Once sensitised the claimant may need to be exposed to only a minute amount of the sensitiser to trigger the return of symptoms or an exacerbation of symptoms. In such circumstances consideration must be given to whether the claimant is likely to be similarly affected when working for other employers. Common examples are sensitivity to some metals, dusts or lubricating oils, which may dramatically reduce the claimant's opportunities for taking alternative work and cause him to spend much longer looking for work. This would give rise to a claim for loss of earnings to cover his immediate period of job search and could also give rise to a claim for damages for handicap on the labour market. The combination of medical expert evidence and, if necessary, employment expert evidence may indicate that the claimant is unlikely to find any other work for which he is suited, or alternatively that he will be limited to unskilled work.

If the claimant needs to change his employment the cost of his job search will be recoverable. Re-training costs are also recoverable if the re-training is reasonably required. However, the costs to the claimant of setting up his business will not necessarily be viewed as reasonable costs. The defendant's insurers will not be regarded as venture capitalists.

16.3   MEDICAL EXPENSES

The claimant will require medical treatment of one sort or another. Generally, treatment is available on the NHS, but there is no compulsion to use the NHS and the fact that free NHS treatment was available, or would be available in the reasonably foreseeable future, is to be disregarded under section 2(4) of the Law Reform (Personal Injuries) Act 1948, which provides:

> 'In an action for damages for personal injuries (including any such action arising out of a contract), there shall be disregarded, in determining the reasonableness of any expenses, the possibility of avoiding those expenses or part of them by taking advantage of facilities available under the National Health Services Act 1977 ....'

The cost of medicines, inhalers, creams and protective gloves are all recoverable. The test is whether the treatment is reasonably required as a consequence of the injury suffered by the claimant. Obvious costs, such as prescription medicines, do not need specific approval from a medical expert in order to be recoverable. The fact that they have been prescribed by a medical practitioner is sufficient as a matter of practice. Where treatments or medications are not obtained on prescription it will usually be necessary to produce medical evidence approving them. In this context, claimants should not expect medical doctors to approve homeopathic or herbal remedies.

Where there is prolonged use of a number of prescriptions the claimant should be advised to obtain a prescription prepayment certificate.

Specific examples of medication or treatment for which costs are recoverable include the following:

- Asbestos disease patients may require procedures to drain fluid from the lungs. Mesothelioma patients may require medical treatments including lung drainage, operations to ease pain, the cost of care whether at home or in a hospice, supplementary foods, extra laundry, extra heating and lighting, extra bathing and washing.
- Dermatitis patients may require ointments, balms and dressings. Some clothing or footwear may need to be replaced with softer materials to reduce irritation.
- Hearing loss patients may require hearing aids and tinnitus maskers, or sleep aids because of disturbance from tinnitus. In some rarer cases it will be reasonable to obtain improved means of using the telephone and hearing the door bell. Modern technology can provide headphones that allow the claimant to hear the broadcast, but which do not subject his family to excessive volume.
- Upper limb disorder sufferers may require splints and bandages. Medication may be required to reduce inflammation or to dull or remove pain.
- Vibration white finger patients suffering the most acute symptoms may require dressings for tissue necrocis.
- Work-related stress suffers may require medication, psychotherapy and/or counselling for their psychological condition, which may include a stay for a period in a residential facility.

16.4 FATAL ACCIDENTS ACT CLAIMS

Claims under the Fatal Accidents Act usually arise in asbestos-related disease cases, but may also be encountered in asthma cases.

Under the Law Reform (Personal Injuries) Act 1948 a 'lost years' claim is conventionally based on 50 per cent of the claimant's net earnings. The use of the conventional basis for Fatal Accidents Act claims limits a widow's dependency claim to 75 per cent whilst there are dependent children, and 66 per cent when the children cease to be dependent. If the widow has an income of her own then the dependency is calculated on the basis of 75 per cent of their joint income less the widow's income, or 66 per cent of their joint income, less the widow's income. The result is that if a claimant wishes to finalise a claim before his death he is likely to obtain a smaller sum of damages to leave to his widow for her support. However, for some claimants it is important that their financial matters are settled before they die. These wishes should not be ignored and their decision should be respected.

A sample Schedule is set out in Appendix 2.

CHAPTER 17

SETTLEMENT

17.1   INTRODUCTION

Most personal injury claims do not proceed to trial but are settled on terms agreed between the parties. With a more open regime of disclosure of evidence and narrowing of expert evidence by a joint statement of areas of agreement and disagreement, the scene is set for negotiation and settlement. The trial is no longer an exercise based on surprises. Pre-trial preparations progressively lay out each party's case so that it can be considered by the opposition. To the bare bones of the case set out in the particulars of claim and defence, is added the weight of the evidence. An early settlement avoids further expense but proceeds on the basis that there is imperfect assessment of all the evidence. A party can seek a settlement at any stage.

17.2   WHEN TO NEGOTIATE

There is no simple golden rule. The best time to negotiate depends upon the particular case: the issues may require the gathering of a great deal of evidence; some issues may only become clearer at a later date; or both parties may want to take their chance with an early settlement because they are uncertain how the evidence will develop. For example, in a claim for occupational asthma establishing medical causation may be difficult, despite a clear diagnosis of asthma, because pinning down one particular chemical at the workplace as the sensitiser amongst numerous others, or replicating the process which led to the exposure when this process was subsequently changed, will be practically impossible.

Negotiations often begin with the letter of claim. Basic issues are identified and the parties have some idea of the evidence that might be available to support or rebut the claim. The defendant may take the view that the chances of establishing an effective defence to the issues of liability are small; alternatively, the claimant may be tempted by an early settlement offer. Generally the value of the claim is developed over time. Defendants are therefore conscious that claims may increase as medical evidence clarifies and evidence as to employability becomes clearer, at which point the defendant may see the advantages of early settlement.

The defendant may also be aware that the claimant would be tempted to end the stress of litigation by making an early settlement.

The claimant and his legal team must consider proposals for early settlement carefully. The legal team must be careful to advise the claimant of the various possible outcomes of the litigation, explaining that the evidence might strengthen or weaken. Settlement of a case at a later stage of the litigation is more obvious. Once the evidence has been exchanged the issues are clearer. It is then easier to assess the relative risks in the litigation. The parties usually re-evaluate their strengths and weaknesses a few months before trial.

17.3   KNOW THE ISSUES

At every stage of the litigation it is important to know the issues and to make an assessment of the relative strength of the case in respect of each issue. There is no harm, and much benefit, in drawing up a list of the issues, a summary of the evidence and an assessment in one or two sentences of the strength of the evidence. It is also important to have an idea of how the other parties' evidence is developing.

Occupational illness cases consist of many, often complex issues. The task of gathering evidence can sometimes obscure the value of the evidence that has been obtained.

The preliminary work of obtaining factual and expert evidence may give a very good idea of the prospects of success. If the evidence is weak this is usually apparent at these early stages and can be borne in mind. In cases where exposure was many years ago (asbestos is the prime example) the onus will be on the defendants to gather evidence to rebut the evidence obtained on behalf of the claimant. Other factors, such as cessation of the business, will provide some indication of the difficulties likely to be experienced in obtaining evidence, and these should be borne in mind in the settlement process.

In most occupational disease cases the diagnosis and prognosis is reasonably clear from initial medical expert evidence. In such circumstances consideration can be given to settlement offers subject, of course, to the possible development of a more serious condition (for example, mesothelioma from asbestos exposure where there are only pleural plaques at present) which requires consideration of provisional damages awards.

In cases where the diagnosis is clear but the prognosis is uncertain, it may be unwise to attempt settlement at an early stage. The best example of this is in stress cases. Unlike other, more straightforward claims, it is more difficult to evaluate the strength of the claim on liability because further investigation is necessary. The prognosis for psychological injury may require the passage of some considerable time. In addition, the continuation of the litigation may exacerbate or prolong the psychological symptoms. Generally it is understood that the employee cannot return to work which has the same sorts of stress levels as before his illness.

Even in more straightforward cases a medical prognosis will be required in order to define the length of the illness and the likely length of absence from work. Some employees are able to return to work after a few months; some may never return to work with the same employer but are fit to seek alternative work; and some may remain incapable of returning to any form of work. For those who do return to work, there may be permanent limitations on the type of work that they can do.

A good strategy is to start with two calculations, a best case and a worst case calculation, and then work to see how they can be brought closer together.

17.4   PART 36 OFFERS

In considering settlement the focus is usually on settling the whole of the litigation, liability and quantum. However, it may be a good idea to settle discrete issues in the case, either by a total acceptance of one issue or a compromise expressed to be as a proportion of the damages to be awarded. Part 36 offers can be made in respect of any issue raised in the case.

17.5   PART 36 OFFERS AND LIABILITY

Part 36 can be used in respect of liability issues, in which case two aspects arise: first, the potential saving of costs if issues are identified and agreed at an early stage; and, secondly, the agreement of issues subject to a discount in the damages award. The second aspect may have greater relevance in occupational illness claims with their complex and difficult factual issues and the application of technical and medical evidence in respect of those issues. In claims of relatively modest value it is good practice to limit the cost of proving or resolving issues shrouded by the passage of time or where detail is no longer available.

17.6   PART 36 OFFERS AND QUANTUM

A Part 36 offer made on behalf of a claimant must have some attraction for the defendant if it is to be effective. Putting the Part 36 offer at the highest possible award merely encourages the defendant to litigate for a lower figure. A Part 36 offer which offers some discount is more likely to be attractive to the defendant and more likely to create a response, even if this is only a counter-offer. Of course, the discount should not be made in a cavalier fashion; any claim can be settled if the discount offered on behalf of the claimant is large enough. A realistic settlement figure should be arrived at by balancing the elements of the risks of the litigation in the particular case. A claim may be strong on foreseeability but weak on causation.

APPENDIX 1

PLEADINGS

A.1 STATEMENTS OF CASE

Asbestos

1. Asbestos exposure in a factory
2. Asbestos exposure on a construction site
3. Asbestos exposure in shipbuilding and ship-repairing
4. Asbestos exposure continuing after 1988
5. Asbestos fatal claim

Other substances hazardous to health

6. Control of Substances Hazardous to Health (COSSH) pre-2002 Regulations
7. Control of Substances Hazardous to Health (COSSH) post-2002 Regulations

Hearing loss

8. Hearing loss
9. Defence to loss claim

Work-related upper limb disorders (WRULDs)

10. WRULD

Work-related stress

11. Stress

Vibration white finger

12. VWF

1. ASBESTOS EXPOSURE IN A FACTORY

This draft pleading covers the Asbestos Industry Regulations 1931, the 1937 Factories Act, the 1961 Factories Act and the Asbestos Regulations 1969.

IN THE BABEL COUNTY COURT Claim No B

BETWEEN

DUSTY MILLER Claimant

and

ASBESTOS PRODUCTS LIMITED Defendants

Particulars of claim

Concise statement of facts
1.   The Claimant was employed by the Defendants between 1959 and 1978. The Claimant was employed as a production worker at the Defendants' premises at Canal Street, Anytown.
2.   In the course of his employment the Claimant was exposed to harmful quantities of asbestos dust and fibres which he inhaled.
3.   The Claimant worked on the production line in the main shop where asbestos products were cut, sawn, milled by machine and filed. These work processes released asbestos dust and fibres into the air where the Claimant worked.
4.   As a consequence of his exposure to asbestos the Claimant has suffered personal injury.

Legal principles relied upon
5.   The Defendants were negligent in the following respects:

(a)   the Defendants knew or should have known that the asbestos dust and fibres were liable to be injurious to the health of persons who might inhale them, but they nonetheless caused or permitted the Claimant to work in circumstances in which they knew or ought to have known that asbestos dust and fibres were given off and/or accumulated in the premises;

(b)   they failed to provide and maintain adequate ventilation or adequate exhaust appliances to collect and remove asbestos dust and fibres given off by the work processes;

(c)   they caused or permitted asbestos materials to be manhandled or worked upon by the Claimant and/or others thereby causing asbestos dust and fibres to arise in large quantities;

(d)   they failed to provide for the Claimant's use respirators which were suitable and effective in preventing the inhalation of asbestos;

(e)   they failed to give the Claimant any or any adequate warning as to the dangers of contracting disease from the inhalation of asbestos;

(f)   they failed to give any or any adequate instruction or supervision as to the steps to be taken to avoid the dangers from inhalation of asbestos;

(g)   they failed to provide and maintain a safe place of work;

(h)   they failed to devise and operate a safe system of work so as not to expose the Claimant to the dangers of the inhalation of asbestos.

6.   The Defendants were in breach of the following statutory duties:

(a)   effective and suitable provision was not made for securing and maintaining by the circulation of fresh air within the premises the adequate ventilation and for rendering harmless the dust and fibres, contrary to section 4 of the Factories Act 1937 and section 4 of the Factories Act 1961;

(b)   all practicable measures were not taken to protect the Claimant against the inhalation of asbestos dust and fibres or to prevent their accumulating in the premises, contrary to section 47 of the Factories Act 1937 and section 63 of the Factories Act 1961;

(c)   an exhaust draught effected by mechanical means which prevented the escape of asbestos dust and fibres into the air of the premises was not provided and maintained in connection with the processes and the premises, contrary to regulation 1 of the Asbestos Industry Regulations 1931;

(d)   floors and plant were not kept in a clean state and free from asbestos debris and/or suitable arrangements were not made for the storage of asbestos not immediately required for use, contrary to regulation 7 of the Asbestos Industry Regulations 1931;

(e)   no breathing apparatus by means of which a person using it breathes air free from dust was provided for the Claimant when employed in areas containing loose asbestos, contrary to regulation 10 of the Asbestos Industry Regulations 1931;

(f)   suitable overalls and head covering were not provided and maintained, contrary to regulation of 11 of the Asbestos Industry Regulations 1931;

(g)   failed to make and keep safe the Claimant's place of work contrary to section 26 of the Factories Act 1937 and section 29 of the Factories Act 1961;

(h)   failed to provide, maintain and use equipment which produced an exhaust draught which prevented the entry into the air of the workplace of asbestos dust, contrary to regulation 7 of the Asbestos Regulations 1969;

(i)   failed to provide approved respiratory protective equipment and protective clothing for the use of the Claimant contrary to regulation 8 of the Asbestos Regulations 1969;

(j)   failed to keep clean all machinery, apparatus, work benches, plant, equipment, external surfaces of exhaust ventilation equipment, floors, inside walls, ceilings, ledges and other internal surfaces, contrary to regulation 9 of the Asbestos Regulations 1969;

(k)   failed to store all loose asbestos in suitable closed receptacles when not in use, contrary to regulation 15 of the Asbestos Regulations 1969.

Particulars of damages claim

7.   The Claimant was born on 4th September 1940. The Claimant has developed an asbestos-related disease, namely pleural plaques. The Claimant suffers anxiety as to his future medical condition. A report from a medical practitioner about these personal injuries is served with these Particulars of Claim.

8.   The Claimant is at risk of developing diffuse pleural thickening, asbestosis, lung cancer and mesothelioma. The Claimant claims Provisional Damages under section 51 of the County Courts Act 1984 based on the assumption that he does not develop these conditions and seeks an Order for the future assessment of damages if he should develop one or more of these conditions.

9.   The Claimant is handicapped on the labour market.

10.   A schedule giving details of the past and future expenses and losses claimed is served with these Particulars of Claim.

Claim for interest

11.   The Claimant claims interest on damages. Interest is claimed pursuant to section 69 of the County Courts Act 1984. Interest on general damages is claimed from the date of notification of the claim until the date of settlement or Judgment at the annual rate of 2%. Interest on special damages is claimed at the full Special Account rate from the date when each loss was sustained until the date of settlement or Judgment on the grounds that the Claimant has lost the benefit of the money from that date when the loss was first sustained.

Statement of Truth

The Claimant believes that the facts stated in these Particulars of Claim are true.

2. ASBESTOS EXPOSURE ON A CONSTRUCTION SITE

As above, but substituting the Building (Safety, Health and Welfare) Regulations 1948 and the Construction (General Provisions) Regulations 1961 for the allegations under the Factories Acts and the Asbestos Industry Regulations 1931.

(a) failed to take all reasonably practicable measures to prevent inhalation of asbestos dust which was likely to be injurious, contrary to regulation 82 of the Building (Safety, Health and Welfare) Regulations 1948;
(b) failed to take all reasonably practicable measures to prevent inhalation of asbestos dust which was likely to be injurious, contrary to regulation 20 of the Construction (General Provisions) Regulations 1961.

3. ASBESTOS EXPOSURE IN SHIPBUILDING AND SHIP-REPAIRING

As above, but substituting the Shipbuilding and Ship-repairing Regulations 1960 for the allegations under the Factories Acts and the Asbestos Industry Regulations 1931.

(a) failed to take all practicable measures to protect persons employed against inhalation of asbestos dust, contrary to regulation 53(1) of the Shipbuilding and Ship-repairing Regulations 1960;
(b) failed to provide breathing apparatus of an approved type for the breaking down and removal of asbestos lagging, contrary to regulation 76 of the Shipbuilding and Ship-repairing Regulations 1960.

4. ASBESTOS EXPOSURE CONTINUING AFTER 1988

Given the long latency period between exposure and the onset of disease these cases are rather rare at the moment.

IN THE NEWTOWN COUNTY COURT Case No N

BETWEEN

HARDAV SINGH Claimant

and

CLOAK INSULATIONS PRODUCTS LTD Defendants

Particulars of claim

Concise statement of facts

1.   The Claimant was employed by the Defendants between 1986 and 1998. The Claimant was employed as an assembler in the Defendants' premises on the Willows Factory Estate.
2.   In the course of his employment the Claimant was exposed to harmful quantities of asbestos dust and fibres which he inhaled.
3.   The Claimant worked repairing ovens and boilers. He took out the old insulation and replaced it with new insulation. The old insulation was made from asbestos. The old insulation was thrown into open bins.
4.   The pillars holding the roof in the main workshop were covered with a thick layer of asbestos lagging. The lagging was old and parts crumbled and fell to the floor. The asbestos debris was further broken down and spread about by the wheels of fork-lift trucks. The asbestos lagging on the pillars was also damaged when fork-lift trucks knocked into them.

Legal principles relied upon

5.   The Defendants were negligent in the following respects:

   (a)   the Defendants knew or should have known that the asbestos dust and fibres were liable to be injurious to the health of persons who might inhale them, but they nonetheless caused or permitted the Claimant to work in circumstances in which they knew or ought to have known that asbestos dust and fibres were given off and/or accumulated in the premises;
   (b)   they failed to provide and maintain adequate ventilation or adequate exhaust appliances to collect and remove asbestos dust and fibres given off by the work processes;
   (c)   they caused or permitted asbestos materials to be manhandled or worked upon by the Claimant and/or others thereby causing asbestos dust and fibres to arise in large quantities;
   (d)   they failed to provide for the Claimant's use respirators which were suitable and effective in preventing the inhalation of asbestos;
   (e)   they failed to give the Claimant any or any adequate warning as to the dangers of contracting disease from the inhalation of asbestos;
   (f)   they failed to give any or any adequate instruction or supervision as to the steps to be taken to avoid the dangers from inhalation of asbestos;
   (g)   they failed to remove the asbestos lagging from the roof pillars;
   (h)   they failed to provide and maintain a safe place of work;.
   (i)   they failed to devise and operate a safe system of work so as not to expose the Claimant to the dangers of the inhalation of asbestos.

6. The Defendants were in breach of the following statutory duties:

   (a) effective and suitable provision was not made for securing and maintaining by the circulation of fresh air within the premises the adequate ventilation and for rendering harmless the dust and fibres, contrary to section 4 of the Factories Act 1961;

   (b) all practicable measures were not taken to protect the Claimant against the inhalation of asbestos dust and fibres or to prevent their accumulating in the premises, contrary to section 63 of the Factories Act 1961;

   (c) failed to make and keep safe the Claimant's place of work contrary to section 29 of the Factories Act 1961;

   (d) failed to provide, maintain and use equipment which produced an exhaust draught which prevented the entry into the air of the workplace of asbestos dust, contrary to regulation 7 of the Asbestos Regulations 1969;

   (e) failed to provide approved respiratory protective equipment and protective clothing for the use of the Claimant contrary to regulation 8 of the Asbestos Regulations 1969;

   (f) failed to keep clean all machinery, apparatus, work benches, plant, equipment, external surfaces of exhaust ventilation equipment, floors, inside walls, ceilings, ledges and other internal surfaces, contrary to regulation 9 of the Asbestos Regulations 1969;

   (g) failed to store all loose asbestos in suitable closed receptacles when not in use, contrary to regulation 15 of the Asbestos Regulations 1969;

   (h) carried out work which exposed or was liable to expose persons to asbestos without having made an adequate assessment of the exposure, contrary to regulation 5 of the Control of Asbestos at Work Regulations 1987;

   (i) failed to ensure that adequate information, instruction and training was given to employees so that they were aware of the risks from asbestos and the precautions which should be observed, contrary to regulation 7 of the Control of Asbestos at Work Regulations 1987;

   (j) failed to prevent the exposure of the Claimant to asbestos, contrary to regulation 8(1)(a) of the Control of Asbestos at Work Regulations 1987;

   (k) failed to reduce the asbestos exposure of the Claimant to the lowest extent reasonably practicable, contrary to regulation 8(1)(b) of the Control of Asbestos at Work Regulations 1987;

   (l) failed to provide suitable respiratory equipment for the Claimant, contrary to regulation 8(2) of the Control of Asbestos at Work Regulations 1987;

(m) failed to provide adequate and suitable protective clothing for the Claimant, contrary to regulation 11(1) of the Control of Asbestos at Work Regulations 1987;

(n) failed to prevent or to reduce to the lowest level reasonably practicable the spread of asbestos, contrary to regulation 5 of the Control of Asbestos at Work Regulations 1987;

(o) failed to ensure that the premises were kept in a clean state and were throughly cleaned, contrary to regulation 13 of the Control of Asbestos at Work Regulations 1987;

(p) failed to take adequate steps to monitor the exposure of employees to asbestos, contrary to regulation 15 of the Control of Asbestos at Work Regulations 1987;

(q) failed to ensure that the Claimant was under adequate medical surveillance, contrary to regulation 16(2) of the Control of Asbestos at Work Regulations 1987;

(r) failed to provide adequate and suitable washing and changing facilities or facilities for the storage of clothing and respiratory equipment, contrary to regulation 17 of the Control of Asbestos at Work Regulations 1987;

(s) contrary to regulation 5 of the Workplace (Health, Safety and Welfare) Regulations 1992, failed to maintain the workplace and the equipment, devices and systems in an efficient state, in efficient working order and in good repair;

(t) contrary to regulation 6(1) of the Workplace (Health, Safety and Welfare) Regulations 1992, failed to ensure that effective and suitable provision was made to ensure that every closed workplace was ventilated by a sufficient quantity of fresh or purified air;

(u) contrary to regulation 9(1) of the Workplace (Health, Safety and Welfare) Regulations 1992, failed to keep the workplace, furniture, furnishings and fittings sufficiently clean;

(v) contrary to regulation 9(3) of the Workplace (Health, Safety and Welfare) Regulations 1992, allowed waste materials to accumulate in the workplace outside suitable materials;

(w) contrary to regulation 4(1) of the Provision and Use of Work Equipment Regulations 1998 failed to ensure that work equipment was so constructed or adapted as to be suitable for the purpose for which it was used or provided;

(x) contrary to regulation 4(2) of the Provision and Use of Work Equipment Regulations 1998 in selecting work equipment failed to have regard to the working conditions and to the risks to health and safety of persons which existed in their premises or undertaking in which that work equipment was used and any additional risk posed by the use of that work equipment.

Particulars of damages claim

7. The Claimant was born on 27th August 1951.

8. The Claimant has developed an asbestos-related disease, namely asbestosis. The Claimant was first aware of this condition in about 2003. He suffers episodes of breathlessness. His condition is progressive. A report from a medical practitioner about these personal injuries is served with these Particulars of Claim.
9. The Claimant is handicapped on the labour market.
10. The Claimant is at risk of developing lung cancer and mesothelioma. The Claimant claims Provisional Damages under section 51 of the County Courts Act 1984 based on the assumption that he does not develop these conditions and seeks an Order for the future assessment of damages if he should develop one or more of these conditions.
11. A schedule giving details of the past and future expenses and losses claimed is served with these Particulars of Claim.

Claim for interest
12. The Claimant claims interest on damages. Interest is claimed pursuant to section 69 of the County Courts Act 1984. Interest on general damages is claimed from the date of notification of the claim until the date of settlement or Judgment at the annual rate of 2%. Interest on special damages is claimed at the full Special Account rate from the date when each loss was sustained until the date of settlement or Judgment on the grounds that the Claimant has lost the benefit of the money from that date when the loss was first sustained.

Statement of Truth

The Claimant believes that the facts stated in these Particulars of Claim are true.

5. ASBESTOS FATAL CLAIM

IN THE CHURCHTOWN COUNTY COURT Case No C

BETWEEN

MARY MARSHALL

(Widow and Executrix) Claimant

and

GEARSONS INSULATIONS CONTRACTORS LIMITED

Defendants

Particulars of claim

Concise statement of facts

1. The Claimant is the Administratrix of the Estate of Thomas Marshall, deceased. Letters of Administration were granted on 8th June 2010 by the Churchtown District Registry. The Claimant brings this action on behalf of the Estate under the Law Reform (Miscellaneous Provisions) Act 1934, and under the Fatal Accidents Act 1976 on behalf of herself and all other dependants.
2. The deceased was employed by the Defendants between 1958 and 1991. The deceased was employed as an insulation installer and worked at the premises of third parties.
3. In the course of his employment the deceased was exposed to harmful quantities of asbestos dust and fibres which he inhaled.
4. The deceased was required to hack off the old asbestos lagging and to dry sweep it into hessian sacks. At the end of the day he had to carry the sacks to the lorry and throw it into the back of the lorry. The deceased had to mix new asbestos lagging material and apply it to pipes and boilers.

Legal principles relied upon

5. The Defendants were negligent in the following respects:

   (a) the Defendants knew or should have known that the asbestos dust and fibres were liable to be injurious to the health of persons who might inhale them, but they nonetheless caused or permitted the deceased to work in circumstances in which they knew or ought to have known that asbestos dust and fibres were given off and/or accumulated in the premises;
   (b) they failed to provide and maintain adequate ventilation or adequate exhaust appliances to collect and remove asbestos dust and fibres given off by the work processes;
   (c) they caused or permitted asbestos materials to be manhandled or worked upon by the deceased and/or others thereby causing asbestos dust and fibres to arise in large quantities;
   (d) they failed to provide for the deceased's use respirators which were suitable and effective in preventing the inhalation of asbestos;
   (e) they failed to give the deceased any or any adequate warning as to the dangers of contracting disease from the inhalation of asbestos;
   (f) they failed to give any or any adequate instruction or supervision as to the steps to be taken to avoid the dangers from inhalation of asbestos;
   (g) they failed to provide and maintain a safe place of work;
   (h) they failed to devise and operate a safe system of work so as not to expose the deceased to the dangers of the inhalation of asbestos.

6. The Defendants were in breach of the following statutory duties:

(a) failed to take all reasonably practicable measures to prevent inhalation of asbestos dust which was likely to be injurious, contrary to regulation 82 of the Building (Safety, Health and Welfare) Regulations 1948;

(b) failed to take all reasonably practicable measures to prevent inhalation of asbestos dust which was likely to be injurious, contrary to regulation 20 of the Construction (General Provisions) Regulations 1961;

(c) to provide, maintain and use equipment which produced an exhaust draught which prevented the entry into the air of the workplace of asbestos dust, contrary to regulation 7 of the Asbestos Regulations 1969;

(d) failed to provide approved respiratory protective equipment and protective clothing for the use of the deceased contrary to regulation 8 of the Asbestos Regulations 1969;

(e) failed to keep clean all machinery, apparatus, work benches, plant, equipment, external surfaces of exhaust ventilation equipment, floors, inside walls, ceilings, ledges and other internal surfaces, contrary to regulation 9 of the Asbestos Regulations 1969;

(f) failed to store all loose asbestos in suitable closed receptacles when not in use, contrary to regulation 15 of the Asbestos Regulations 1969;

(g) carried out work which exposed or was liable to expose persons to asbestos without having made an adequate assessment of the exposure, contrary to regulation 5 of the Control of Asbestos at Work Regulations 1987;

(h) failed to ensure that adequate information, instruction and training was given to employees so that they were aware of the risks from asbestos and the precautions which should be observed, contrary to regulation 7 of the Control of Asbestos at Work Regulations 1987;

(i) failed to prevent the exposure of the deceased to asbestos, contrary to regulation 8(1)(a) of the Control of Asbestos at Work Regulations 1987;

(j) failed to reduce the asbestos exposure of the deceased to the lowest extent reasonably practicable, contrary to regulation 8(1)(b) of the Control of Asbestos at Work Regulations 1987;

(k) failed to provide suitable respiratory equipment for the deceased, contrary to regulation 8(2) of the Control of Asbestos at Work Regulations 1987;

(l) failed to provide adequate and suitable protective clothing for the deceased, contrary to regulation 11(1) of the Control of Asbestos at Work Regulations 1987;

    (m) failed to prevent or to reduce to the lowest level reasonably practicable the spread of asbestos, contrary to regulation 5 of the Control of Asbestos at Work Regulations 1987;

    (n) failed to ensure that the premises were kept in a clean state and were throughly cleaned, contrary to regulation 13 of the Control of Asbestos at Work Regulations 1987;

    (o) failed to take adequate steps to monitor the exposure of employees to asbestos, contrary to regulation 15 of the Control of Asbestos at Work Regulations 1987;

    (p) failed to ensure that the deceased was under adequate medical surveillance, contrary to regulation 16(2) of the Control of Asbestos at Work Regulations 1987;

    (q) failed to provide adequate and suitable washing and changing facilities or facilities for the storage of clothing and respiratory equipment, contrary to regulation 17 of the Control of Asbestos at Work Regulations 1987;

    (r) failed to take all reasonably practicable measures to prevent inhalation of asbestos dust which was likely to be injurious, contrary to regulation 82 of the Building (Safety, Health and Welfare) Regulations 1948;

    (s) failed to take all reasonably practicable measures to prevent inhalation of asbestos dust which was likely to be injurious, contrary to regulation 20 of the Construction (General Provisions) Regulations 1961.

Particulars of damages claim

7.   The Claimant was born on 14th June 1959.

8.   The other dependants for whom a claim is brought under the Fatal Accidents Acts are Veronica, Thomas, Edward, Margaret and Harold. A Schedule of Special Damage and Dependancy is served with these Particulars of Claim.

9.   The deceased contracted malignant mesothelioma from which he died on 13th February 2010. The deceased was born on 5th September 1949. The deceased first experienced symptoms in April 2009 with breathlessness and discomfort. He experienced increasing pain and disability. In the final months he required constant nursing care. A report from a medical practitioner about the deceased's personal injuries is served with these Particulars of Claim.

10.   There is a claim for Bereavement damages.

Claim for interest

11.   The Claimant claims interest on damages. Interest is claimed pursuant to section 69 of the County Courts Act 1984. Interest on general damages is claimed from the date of notification of the claim until the date of settlement or Judgment at the annual rate of 2%. Interest on special damages is claimed at the full Special Account rate from the date when each loss was sustained until the date of

settlement or Judgment on the grounds that the Claimant has lost the benefit of the money from that date when the loss was first sustained.

Statement of truth

The Claimant believes that the facts stated in the Particulars of Claim are true.

6. CONTROL OF SUBSTANCES HAZARDOUS TO HEALTH – COSSH – PRE-2002 REGULATIONS

IN THE POLLUTON COUNTY COURT Case No

BETWEEN

WILLIAM CLINTON Claimant

and

THE CARBOLIC SMOKEBALL CO LTD Defendants

Particulars of claim

Concise statement of facts

1. At all material times between 1963 and October 2002 the Claimant was employed by the Defendants as a production operative at their premises at Canal Street, Polluton.
2. The Claimant worked on the main production line and was there exposed to Nastychem in the course of his work.
3. Until about 1996 the Claimant was not provided with a mask.
4. As a consequence of his exposure to Nastychem the Claimant suffered personal injury.

Legal principles relied upon

5. The Defendants were negligent in the following respects:

   (a) the Defendants knew or should have known that Nastychem created a risk to the Claimant's health, but they nonetheless caused or permitted the Claimant to work in circumstances in which they knew or ought to have known that such a risk was created;

   (b) failed to heed the data sheets provided by the manufacturers of Nastychem which warned against inhalation of the fume or ingestion of the liquid;

(c)   failed to make any or any sufficient assessment of the risk of injury from exposure to Nastychem which was caused by the work processes carried on at their premises;

(d)   failed to control the release of fumes of Nastychem;

(e)   failed to provide an or any adequate respiratory equipment for the Claimant's use;

(f)   failed to instruct the Claimant as to the means of fitting and wearing the respiratory equipment that was available;

(g)   failed to instruct and warn the Claimant to wear the respiratory equipment that was available at all times when working with Nastychem;

(h)   failed to maintain and keep in proper working order the respiratory equipment that was available;

(i)   failed to heed that the Claimant wore spectacles and that the arms of the spectacles interfered with the proper fit of respiratory equipment;

(j)   failed to supervise and enforce the wearing of respiratory equipment;

(k)   failed to provide suitable and effective fume extraction equipment; the extraction did not work when the wind blew from the west;

(l)   failed adequately or at all to monitor the Claimant's exposure to Nastychem;

(m) failed to provide an adequate system of health surveillance;

(n)   failed to provide the Claimant with any or any adequate information concerning the risks of exposure to Nastychem;

(o)   failed to instruct and warn the Claimant to seek immediate medical advice if he began to suffer symptoms of breathlessness or wheeze;

(p)   failed to heed complaints made to the various foremen to the effect that fumes of Nastychem could be smelt when the mixing machine was operating;

(q)   failed to heed complaints made through the Health and Safety Committee that the extraction fans were often switched off by the foreman in order to reduce the noise levels;

(r)   failed to provide and maintain a safe place of work;

(s)   failed to devise and operate a safe system of work so as not to subject the Claimant to the risks of exposure.

6.   The Defendants were in breach of the following statutory duties:

(a)   effective and suitable provision was not made for securing and maintaining by the circulation of fresh air within the premises the adequate ventilation and for rendering harmless the identified substances, contrary to section 4 of the Factories Act 1961;

(b)   all practicable measures were not taken to protect the Claimant against the inhalation of the fumes of Nastychem nor to prevent them accumulating in the premises, contrary to section 63 of the Factories Act 1961;

(c) contrary to regulation 6(1) of the Control of Substances Hazardous to Health Regulations 1988, 1994 and 1999, failed to make a suitable and sufficient assessment of the risks to the Claimant's health created by the Claimant's work and an assessment of the steps that need to be taken to meet the requirements of these Regulations;

(d) contrary to regulation 6(2) of the Control of Substances Hazardous to Health Regulations 1988, 1994 and 1999, failed to review the assessment of the risks to the Claimant's health created by the work and an assessment of the steps that need to be taken to meet the requirements of these Regulations;

(e) contrary to regulation 7(1) of the Control of Substances Hazardous to Health Regulations 1988, 1994 and 1999, failed to ensure that the Claimant's exposure to substances hazardous to health was either prevented or adequately controlled;

(f) contrary to regulation 7(3) of the Control of Substances Hazardous to Health Regulations 1988 and regulation 7(4) of the Control of Substances Hazardous to Health Regulations 1994 and 1999, failed to provide the Claimant with suitable personal protective equipment that would control exposure to substances hazardous to health;

(g) contrary to regulation 8(1) of the Control of Substances Hazardous to Health Regulations 1988, 1994 and 1999, failed to ensure that all control measures, personal protective equipment, facilities or thing provided were properly used and applied;

(h) contrary to regulation 9(1) of the Control of Substances Hazardous to Health Regulations 1988 and 1994, failed to ensure that all control measures were maintained in an efficient state, in efficient working order and in good repair;

(i) contrary to regulation 9(2) of the Control of Substances Hazardous to Health Regulations 1988, 1995 and 1999, failed to ensure that thorough examinations and tests of engineering controls were carried out at the specified intervals;

(j) contrary to regulation 9(3) of the Control of Substances Hazardous to Health Regulations 1988, 1994 and 1999, failed to ensure that at suitable intervals thorough examinations and tests of respiratory equipment were carried out;

(k) contrary to regulation 10(1) of the Control of Substances Hazardous to Health Regulations 1988, 1994 and 1999, failed to ensure that the Claimant's exposure to substances hazardous to health were monitored;

(l) contrary to regulation 11(1) of the Control of Substances Hazardous to Health Regulations 1988, 1994 and 1999, failed to ensure that the Claimant was under suitable health surveillance;

(m) contrary to regulation 12(1) of the Control of Substances Hazardous to Health Regulations 1988, 1994 and 1999, failed to provide the Claimant with such information, instruction and training as was suitable and sufficient for the Claimant to know the risks to health created by exposure to Nastychem and the precautions which should be taken.

Particulars of damages claim

7. The Claimant was born on 27th August 1958.
8. The Claimant suffered shortness of breath and consequent limitation in his activities. His sleep was disturbed. He became sensitive to atmospheres containing smoke and could not follow his recreations of darts and pool. He became sensitive to the fumes from paint and could not carry out DIY. The prognosis is uncertain. A report from a medical practitioner about these personal injuries is served with these Particulars of Claim.
9. The Claimant is handicapped on the labour market.
10. A schedule giving details of the past and future expenses and losses claimed is served with these Particulars of Claim.

Claim for Interest

11. The Claimant claims interest on damages. Interest is claimed pursuant to section 69 of the County Courts Act 1984. Interest on general damages is claimed from the date of notification of the claim until the date of settlement or Judgment at the annual rate of 2%. Interest on special damages is claimed at the full Special Account rate from the date when each loss was sustained until the date of settlement or Judgment on the grounds that the Claimant has lost the benefit of the money from that date when the loss was first sustained.

Statement of Truth

The Claimant believes that the facts stated in the Particulars of Claim are true.

7. CONTROL OF SUBSTANCES HAZARDOUS TO HEALTH – COSSH – POST-2002 REGULATIONS

IN THE POLLUTON COUNTY COURT Case No

BETWEEN

GEORGE HACKENBUSH Claimant

and

THE CARBOLIC SMOKEBALL CO LTD Defendants

Particulars of claim

Concise statement of facts

1. At all material times between December 2002 and July 2010 the Claimant was employed by the Defendants as a production operative at their premises at Canal Street, Polluton.
2. The Claimant worked on the main production line and was there exposed to Nastychem in the course of his work.
3. Until about January 2008 the Claimant was not provided with a mask.
4. As a consequence of his exposure to Nastychem the Claimant suffered personal injury.

Legal principles relied upon

5. The Defendants were negligent in the following respects:

   (a) the Defendants knew or should have known that Nastychem created a risk to the Claimant's health, but they nonetheless caused or permitted the Claimant to work in circumstances in which they knew or ought to have known that such a risk was created;

   (b) failed to heed the data sheets provided by the manufacturers of Nastychem which warned against inhalation of the fume or ingestion of the liquid;

   (c) failed to make any or any sufficient assessment of the risk of injury from exposure to Nastychem which was caused by the work processes carried on at their premises;

   (d) failed to control the release of fumes of Nastychem;

   (e) failed to provide an or any adequate respiratory equipment for the Claimant's use;

   (f) failed to instruct the Claimant as to the means of fitting and wearing the respiratory equipment that was available;

   (g) failed to instruct and warn the Claimant to wear the respiratory equipment that was available at all times when working with Nastychem;

   (h) failed to maintain and keep in proper working order the respiratory equipment that was available;

   (i) failed to heed that the Claimant wore spectacles and that the arms of the spectacles interfered with the proper fit of respiratory equipment;

   (j) failed to supervise and enforce the wearing of respiratory equipment;

   (k) failed to provide suitable and effective fume extraction equipment; the extraction did not work when the wind blew from the west;

(l)   failed adequately or at all to monitor the Claimant's exposure to Nastychem;

(m) failed to provide an adequate system of health surveillance;

(n) having found as a result of health surveillance an identifiable disease or adverse health effect failed to inform the Claimant and failed to provide information and advice regarding further health surveillance;

(o) failed to provide the Claimant with any or any adequate information concerning the risks of exposure to Nastychem;

(p) failed to instruct and warn the Claimant to seek immediate medical advice if he began to suffer symptoms of breathlessness or wheeze;

(q) failed to heed complaints made to the various foremen to the effect that fumes of Nastychem could be smelt when the mixing machine was operating;

(r) failed to heed complaints made through the Health and Safety Committee that the extraction fans were often switched off by the foreman in order to reduce the noise levels;

(s) failed to provide and maintain a safe place of work;

(t) failed to devise and operate a safe system of work so as not to subject the Claimant to the risks of exposure.

6.   The Defendants were in breach of the following statutory duties:

(a) contrary to regulation 6(1) and (2) of the Control of Substances Hazardous to Health Regulations 2002, failed to make a suitable and sufficient assessment of the risks to the Claimant's health created by the Claimant's work and an assessment of the steps that need to be taken to meet the requirements of these Regulations;

(b) contrary to regulation 6(3) of the Control of Substances Hazardous to Health Regulations 2002, failed to review the assessment of the risks to the Claimant's health created by the work and an assessment of the steps that need to be taken to meet the requirements of these Regulations;

(c) contrary to regulation 7(1) of the Control of Substances Hazardous to Health Regulations 2002, failed to ensure that the Claimant's exposure to substances hazardous to health was either prevented or adequately controlled;

(d) contrary to regulation 7(3) of the Control of Substances Hazardous to Health Regulations 2002, failed to apply appropriate protection measures;

(e) contrary to regulation 7(3)(c) of the Control of Substances Hazardous to Health Regulations 2002 failed to provide the Claimant with suitable personal protective equipment that would control exposure to substances hazardous to health;

(f) contrary to regulation 8(1) of the Control of Substances Hazardous to Health Regulations 2002, failed to ensure that all control measures, other things or facilities or thing provided were properly used and applied;

(g) contrary to regulation 9(1) of the Control of Substances Hazardous to Health Regulations 2002, failed to ensure that all control measures were maintained in an efficient state, in efficient working order and in good repair;

(h) contrary to regulation 9(2) of the Control of Substances Hazardous to Health Regulations 2002, failed to ensure that thorough examinations and tests of engineering controls were carried out at the specified intervals;

(i) contrary to regulation 9(3) of the Control of Substances Hazardous to Health Regulations 2002, failed to ensure that at suitable intervals thorough examinations and tests of respiratory equipment were carried out;

(j) contrary to regulation 10(1) of the Control of Substances Hazardous to Health Regulations 2002, failed to ensure that the Claimant's exposure to substances hazardous to health were monitored;

(k) contrary to regulation 11(1) of the Control of Substances Hazardous to Health Regulations 2002, failed to ensure that the Claimant was under suitable health surveillance;

(l) contrary to regulation 11(9) of the Control of Substances Hazardous to Health Regulations 2002, having found as a result of health surveillance an identifiable disease or adverse health effect failed to inform the Claimant and failed to provide information and advice regarding further health surveillance;

(m) contrary to regulation 12(1) of the Control of Substances Hazardous to Health Regulations 2002, failed to provide the Claimant with such information, instruction and training as was suitable and sufficient for the Claimant to know the risks to health created by exposure to Nastychem and the precautions which should be taken.

Particulars of damages claim

(to be completed as appropriate).

8. HEARING LOSS

Pre Control of Noise at Work Regulations 2005

IN THE LOUDTOWN COUNTY COURT Case No

BETWEEN

LUDWIG BEETHOVEN Claimant

and

METALLICA (a partnership) Defendants

Particulars of claim

Concise statement of facts

1. Between 1965 and 1973 and between 1981 and 2002 the Claimant was employed by the Defendants as a production operative at their premises in Saint Anger Way, Loudtown.
2. During the course of his employment the Claimant was regularly and persistently exposed to excessive and damaging noise in excess of 90 dBA which was created by the processes carried on and the machinery, tools and equipment used.
3. The Claimant operated a metal sawing machine for 7 hours during a working shift.
4. The Claimant worked in close proximity to 3 lathes, 2 vertical boring machines and a pedestal drill. These machines were used throughout the Claimant's working shift of 8 hours.
5. As a result of his exposure to the excessive noise the Claimant has suffered injury and damage to his ears and has experienced a diminution in his hearing ability.

Legal principles relied upon

6. The Defendants were negligent in the following respects:

    (a) caused or permitted the Claimant to work in conditions in which he was exposed to excessive and damaging levels of noise;
    (b) failed to devise and operate processes and to provide machinery, tools and equipment which did not produce excessive and damaging levels of noise;
    (c) failed to maintain and keep in repair the machinery, tools and equipment used so that the noise levels created were less than 90 dBA;
    (d) failed to provide baffles, screens or other means of containing the noise created by the processes, machinery, tools and equipment;
    (e) failed to limit the period or periods during which the Claimant was exposed to noise levels in excess of 90 dBA so as to reduce his total noise-dose to a level that was reasonably safe;
    (f) failed to instruct or warn the Claimant that there was a risk of permanent damage to his ears and his hearing from continued exposure to excessive noise;
    (g) failed to instruct or advise the Claimant to wear properly fitted and adjusted ear protection at all times when his work exposed

him to excessive noise levels and failed to instruct or advise him that failure so to do could result in permanent damage to his ears and hearing ability;

(h) failed to supervise the wearing of the ear protection;

(i) failed to provide repeat warnings about the need to wear ear protection;

(j) failed to provide repeat instructions as to the proper fitting and adjustment of the ear protection;

(k) failed to provide hearing protection for the Claimant's use until about 1997;

(l) failed to carry out annual or six-monthly medical examinations and testing of the Claimant's ears and hearing ability. Such examinations and testing would have detected the early onset of damage and loss of hearing and would have enabled the claimant to take protective or avoidance measures against exposure to excessive noise;

(m) failed to monitor and record the levels of noise produced by the processes carried on and the machinery, tools and equipment used. Such monitoring would have alerted the Defendants to the risk of damage to the ears and hearing ability of those employees who were exposed to excessive noise;

(n) failed to seek advice from acoustic engineers or persons experienced in matters of industrial health and safety;

(o) failed to make a suitable and/or sufficient assessment of the risks to the health and safety of their employees to which they were exposed whilst at work;

(p) in all the circumstances, failed to devise and operate a safe system of work.

7. The Defendants were in breach of the following statutory duties:

(a) failed to make and keep safe the Claimant's place of work contrary to section 26 of the Factories Act 1937 as amended by section 5 of the Factories Act 1959 and contrary to section 29(1) of the Factories Act 1961. The Claimant will rely upon the facts and matters set out in these Particulars of Claim;

(b) contrary to regulation 4(1) of the Noise at Work Regulations 1989 failed to ensure that a competent person made an adequate noise assessment. No noise assessment was made until October 2001; no admission is made as to its adequacy;

(c) contrary to regulation 6 of the Noise at Work Regulations 1989 failed to reduce the risk of damage to the hearing of employees from exposure to noise to the lowest level reasonably practicable;

(d) contrary to regulation 7 of the Noise at Work Regulations 1989 failed to reduce the Claimant's exposure to noise;

(e) contrary to regulation 8(1) of the Noise at Work Regulations 1989 failed to provide suitable and efficient personal ear protectors. Ear protection was not provided until about 1997. No admission is made as to its suitability or efficiency;

(f) contrary to regulation 9(1) of the Noise at Work Regulations 1989 failed to demarcate and identify by means of a sign each ear protection zone;

(g) contrary to regulation 11 of the Noise at Work Regulations 1989 failed to provide any or any adequate information, instruction or training on the risk of damage to hearing from exposure to noise at work, the steps the claimant could take to minimise that risk, the steps that the Claimant must take in order to obtain personal ear protectors and the Claimant's obligations under the Regulations.

Particulars of damages claim

8. The Claimant was born on 16th December 1950.
9. The Claimant suffered bilateral noise-induced hearing loss. He is handicapped socially. His enjoyment of concerts has been reduced. He requires the volume of his Hi-Fi to be turned up louder. He suffers intermittent tinnitus, which occasionally disturbs his sleep. A report from a medical practitioner about these personal injuries is served with these Particulars of Claim.
10. The Claimant is handicapped on the labour market.
11. A schedule giving details of the past and future expenses and losses claimed is served with these Particulars of Claim.

Claim for Interest

12. The Claimant claims interest on damages. Interest is claimed pursuant to section 69 of the County Courts Act 1984. Interest on general damages is claimed from the date of notification of the claim until the date of settlement or Judgment at the annual rate of 2%. Interest on special damages is claimed at the full Special Account rate from the date when each loss was sustained until the date of settlement or Judgment on the grounds that the Claimant has lost the benefit of the money from that date when the loss was first sustained.

Statement of Truth

The Claimant believes that the facts stated in the Particulars of Claim are true.

9. DEFENCE TO NOISE CLAIM

IN THE LOUDTOWN COUNTY COURT Case No

BETWEEN

LUDWIG BEETHOVEN Claimant

and

METALLICA (a partnership) Defendants

Defence

1. It is admitted that between 1965 and 2002 the Defendants had factory premises in St Anger Way, Loudtown. No admissions are made as the alleged periods of the claimant's employment. The Defendants lost their employment records in a fire on 29th February 2003. Following the destruction of the factory by fire the workforce were made redundant and have dispersed. In the circumstances the Defendants are are present unable to plead a more detailed case as to the employment.

2. It is denied that during the course of his employment the Claimant was regularly and persistently exposed to excessive and damaging noise in excess of 90 dBA whether created by the processes carried on and the machinery, tools and equipment used or from other sources.

3. If, which is denied, the Claimant worked in conditions where the noise levels were in excess of 90 dBA he worked there for no more than 20 minutes per day.

4. The Claimant was provided with ear protection from 1992. The Claimant attended a talk on the use and fitting of ear protection on 17th April 1993.

5. It is not admitted that the Claimant has suffered injury or damage to his ears and hearing ability. The Defendants cannot deal adequately with this issue until they have had the Claimant examined by a medical expert.

6. Such damages as may have been sustained by the Claimant's hearing was caused wholly or in part by the negligence of the Claimant:

    (a) failed to wear the hearing protection with which he was provided;

    (b) failed to replace his hearing protection when it became worn;

    (c) failed to heed the instruction that he was given about wearing hearing protection;

    (d) failed to heed the warnings that he was given about the risks of hearing loss from exposure to loud noise;

(e)   the Claimant had a part-time evening job in the Hellraisers Disco and it is contended that any damage to his hearing was caused by that employment;

(f)   failed to report the onset of symptoms of hearing loss to the Defendants' medical centre staff;

(g)   failed to report the onset of symptoms of hearing loss to his GP.

Statement of Truth

The Defendants believe that the facts stated in the Defence are true.

Post Control of Noise at Work Regulations 2005

IN THE LOUDTOWN COUNTY COURT Case No

BETWEEN

LUDWIG BEETHOVEN Claimant

and

METALLICA (a partnership) Defendants

Particulars of claim

Concise statement of facts

7.   Between about 2005 and December 2010 the Claimant was employed by the Defendants as a production operative at their premises in Saint Anger Way, Loudtown.

(complete as necessary based on earlier precedent)

8.   The Defendants were in breach of the following statutory duties:

(a)   contrary to regulation 5 of the Control of Noise at Work Regulations 2005 failed to make a suitable and sufficient assessment of the risk from noise to the health and safety of the Claimant;

(b)   contrary to regulation 6 of the Control of Noise at Work Regulations 2005 failed to ensure that risk from exposure of the Claimant to noise was either eliminated at source or where not reasonably practicable, reduced to as low a level as was reasonably practicable;

(c)   contrary to regulation 7(1) of the Control of Noise at Work Regulations 2005 failed to make available personal hearing protection so as to eliminate the risk to hearing or to reduce the risk to as low a level as was reasonably practicable;

(d) contrary to regulation 8(1)(a) of the Control of Noise at Work Regulations 2005 failed to ensure that means of eliminating or reducing noise was fully and properly used;

(e) contrary to regulation 8(1)(b) of the Control of Noise at Work Regulations 2005 failed to ensure that anything provided in compliance with the Regulations was maintained in an efficient state, in efficient working order and in good repair;

(f) contrary to regulation 9(1) of the Control of Noise at Work Regulations 2005 failed to ensure that the Claimant was placed under suitable health surveillance, including testing of his hearing;

(g) contrary to regulation 5 of the Control of Noise at Work Regulations 2005 failed to provide suitable and sufficient information, instruction and training.

10. WORK-RELATED UPPER LIMB DISORDERS (WRULDS)

IN THE SOUTHFOLK COUNTY COURT Case No

BETWEEN

DEIDRE FENMAN Claimant

and

THE REAL GAME CO LTD Defendants

Particulars of claim

Concise statement of facts

1. At all material times the Claimant was employed as a game plucker and eviscerator by the Defendants at the Fenland Industrial Park, Datt, Southfolk

2. In about April 2003 the Defendants changed the method of working and the Claimant was required to work all of her working shift of 8 hours on the pheasant eviscerating line. The Claimant was required to grasp the innards pull and twist to remove them. She held the pheasant in her left hand and used her right hand to grasp and remove the innards.

3. The Defendants operated a bonus scheme, awarding extra pay for eviscarators who exceeded the target of 250 pheasants a day. The Claimant regularly exceeded the target.

4. As a consequence of the work carried out by the Claimant she developed tenosynovitis of the right wrist.

Legal principles relied upon

5.   The Defendants were negligent in the following respects:

(a)   failed to heed the risks of tenosynovitis and carpal tunnel syndrome from the work at their premises; these were risks which they knew or ought to have known;

(b)   failed to obtain or act upon medical advice or ergonomic advice as to the risk of injury from the work carried out;

(c)   caused, permitted or suffered the Claimant to undertake the work pleaded;

(d)   failed to operate a system of work in which jobs were rotated at sufficiently regular intervals to minimise or eliminate the risk of tenosynovitis;

(e)   failed to slow the work rate so as to minimise or eliminate the risk of injury from the work;

(f)   caused, permitted or suffered the Claimant to carry out the work without adequate intervals and/or breaks;

(g)   failed to warn the Claimant of the risk of contracting the condition by reason of the work; they failed to warn the Claimant to be alert for the first signs and symptoms of the condition; they failed to warn the Claimant of the need to obtain immediate medical advice as and when the first signs and symptoms occurred and of the need to report the first signs and symptoms to the Defendants;

(h)   failed adequately or at all to supervise the Claimant and the work and working conditions;

(i)   failed to instruct and/or warn the Claimant how to perform the work safely;

(j)   failed properly or at all to heed previous cases of similar injuries in persons carrying out similar work;

(k)   failed to carry out a suitable and sufficient assessment of the risks to the health and safety of their employees to which they were exposed whilst working; the Defendants had a duty to carry out an assessment under Regulation 3 of the Management of Health and Safety at Work Regulations 1999;

(l)   failed to implement preventive and protective measures on the basis of the principles specified in Schedule 1 to the Management of Health and Safety at Work Regulations 1999;

(m)   failed to make and give effect to such arrangements as were appropriate, having regard to the nature of the activities and the size of the undertaking, for the effective planning, organisation, control, monitoring and review of the preventive and protective measures required by the Regulations, contrary to Regulation 5 of the Management of Health and Safety at Work Regulations 1999;

(n)   operated an unsafe system of working. A safe system of working would have avoided injury from repetitive actions.

6.   The Defendants were in breach of the following statutory duties:

    (a)   failed to avoid the need for the Claimant to undertake a manual handling operation at work which involved a risk of being injured contrary to regulation 4(1)(a) of the Manual Handling Operations Regulations 1992;

    (b)   failed to make a suitable and sufficient assessment of the manual handling operation having regard to the factors set out in the Schedule to the Regulations contrary to regulation 4(1)(b)(i) of the Manual Handling Operations Regulations 1992;

    (c)   failed to take appropriate steps to reduce the risk of injury to those employees undertaking manual handling operations to the lowest level reasonably practicable contrary to regulation 4(1)(b)(ii) of the Manual Handling Operations Regulations 1992.

Particulars of damages claim

7.   The Claimant was born on 5th June 1981.

8.   The Claimant suffered tenosynovitis of the right wrist. She suffered pain and limitation of movement. Her ability to perform standard domestic tasks was impaired. Her sleep was disturbed by pain. A report from a medical practitioner about these personal injuries is served with these Particulars of Claim.

9.   The Claimant is handicapped on the labour market.

10.   A schedule giving details of the past and future expenses and losses claimed is served with these Particulars of Claim.

Claim for Interest

11.   The Claimant claims interest on damages. Interest is claimed pursuant to section 69 of the County Courts Act 1984. Interest on general damages is claimed from the date of notification of the claim until the date of settlement or Judgment at the annual rate of 2%. Interest on special damages is claimed at the full Special Account rate from the date when each loss was sustained until the date of settlement or Judgment on the grounds that the Claimant has lost the benefit of the money from that date when the loss was first sustained.

Statement of Truth

The Claimant believes that the facts stated in the Particulars of Claim are true.

11. WORK-RELATED STRESS

IN THE NEW LONDON COUNTY COURT Case No

BETWEEN

SHERMAN CHALLENGER Claimant

and

THE BIG BANKING COMPANY Defendants

Particulars of claim

Concise statement of facts

1. At all material times the Claimant was employed by the Defendants as a dealer in guano futures and was based at the Defendants' premises at Budgerigar Dock, Eastern Mud Flats, New London.
2. The Claimant was required to work from 7am to 7pm 5 days a week. Refreshment breaks were taken at the desk. The Claimant did not take a lunch break as the culture at the Defendants dealing floor was not to take food breaks, as lunch was for wimps.
3. The Claimant handled a large number of trades each day and had an assistant who kept the computer records of the trades and the details of the contacts.
4. Pursuant to a re-evaluation of working practices, called "Back to Basics – the Core Needs" from 1st April 2004 the Defendants made the assistant redundant. The Claimant was required to carry out the same number of trades, but was also required to carry out the tasks of entering data into the computer and keeping contacts details.
5. From the same date the Claimant was required to carry out world-wide trades in coconut futures, a business with which he was not familiar.
6. From the same date the management structure was changed and the Claimant was required to report to the Director in Charge of Everything Else, who was based at West Middlesex House, the Golf Links Estate, Greenville.
7. The Claimant was unable to keep up with the pace of the work. He was unable to obtain support and advice from his manager. He made complaints by e-mail but never received any reply.
8. As a consequence of these excessive demands made upon him and as a consequence of his feelings of helplessness and lack of control, the Claimant suffered mental illness.

Legal principles relied upon

9. The Defendants were negligent in the following respects:

(a) failed to carry out a suitable and sufficient assessment of the risks to the health and safety of their employees to which they were exposed whilst at work;

(b) failed to make and give effect to appropriate arrangements for the effective planning, organisation, control, monitoring and review of the preventive and protective measures required to ensure the health and safety of their employees;

(c) failed to carry out a suitable and sufficient re-assessment of the risks to the health and safety of their employees to which they were exposed whilst at work following the re-evaluation of working practices, "Back to Basics – the Core Needs";

(d) failed to heed the long hours worked by the Claimant;

(e) failed to heed the effect of the withdrawal of the Claimant's assistant and the consequent increase in the Claimant's duties;

(f) failed to heed the impact of the other trading duties transferred to the Claimant;

(g) failed to heed the Claimant's e-mails in which he complained that the work was making him ill;

(h) failed to provide appropriate health surveillance in respect of the risks to health and safety of their employees;

(i) failed to provide the Claimant with information on the risks to his health and safety identified by any risk assessment and the preventive and protective measures that were to be given effect;

(j) in entrusting tasks to the Claimant, failed to take into account his capabilities as regards health and safety;

(k) failed to observe or heed that the Claimant was increasingly tired, irritable and more withdrawn;

(l) failed to heed the Claimant's complaints of an excessive workload;

(m) failed to provide effective management;

(n) failed to provide the Claimant with help from the Occupational Health Department or other similar organisation.

10. The Defendants were in breach of the following statutory duties:

(a) contrary to regulation 3 of the Management of Health and Safety at Work Regulations 1999, failed after 28th October 2003 to carry out a suitable and sufficient assessment of the risks to the health and safety of their employees to which they were exposed whilst at work;

(b) contrary to regulation 3 of the Management of Health and Safety at Work Regulations 1999, failed after 1st April 2004 to carry out a suitable and sufficient re-assessment of the risks to the health and safety of their employees to which they were exposed whilst at work, following the changes to the Claimant's work;

(c) contrary to regulation 4 of the Management of Health and Safety at Work Regulations 1999, failed to implement preventive and protective measures on the basis of the principles specified in Schedule 1 to the Regulations;

(d)   contrary to regulation 5 of the Management of Health and Safety at Work Regulations 1999, failed to make and give effect to appropriate arrangements for the effective planning, organisation, control, monitoring and review of the preventive and protective measures required to ensure the health and safety of their employees;

(e)   contrary to regulation 6 of the Management of Health and Safety at Work Regulations 1992, failed to provide appropriate health surveillance in respect of the risks to health and safety of their employees;

(f)   contrary to regulation 10 of the Management of Health and Safety at Work Regulations 1999, the Defendants failed to provide the Claimant with information on the risks to his health and safety identified by their risk assessment and the preventive and protective measures that were to be given effect;

(g)   contrary to regulation 13 of the Management of Health and Safety at Work Regulations 1992 in entrusting tasks to the Claimant, failed to take into account his capabilities as regards health and safety.

Particulars of damages claim
11.   (As above)

12. VIBRATION WHITE FINGER (VWF)

IN THE SHAKERTOUN COUNTY COURT Case No

BETWEEN

BUFFY GLEAMER Claimant

and

STEEL VESSELS (2001) LTD Defendants

Particulars of claim

Concise statement of facts
1.   The Claimant was employed as a metal grinder and polisher by the Defendants, and their predecessors in title for whose torts they are liable, from 1989 to September 2010 at their premises at Cherry Tree Lane, Shakertoun.

2. During the course of his employment the Claimant was required to work regularly with vibrating tools including compressed air powered needle guns, de-scalers, grinders and hand-held polishing machines.
3. The Claimant used these tools for 6 hours during each 8-hour shift. The only periods during which the Claimant was not using these tools was when the steel vessels were re-positioned at his workstation so that he could work on another section.
4. As a consequence of the Claimant's work with these tools he has contracted Vibration White Finger.

Legal principles relied upon

5. The Defendants were negligent in the following respects:

    (a) caused or permitted the Claimant to use tools and machinery whereby he was exposed to excessive levels of vibration;

    (b) caused or permitted the Claimant to operate tools and machinery which produced vibration above acceptable limits;

    (c) failed to provide tools and machinery which had been designed and adapted to reduce harmful vibrations. In particular, the speed and amplitude produced by the tools should have been changed and/or the handles should have been dampened, or some other suitable device should have been provided and used;

    (d) failed to provide for the Claimant's use specially padded and, if necessary, specially made gloves so as to reduce the effects of vibration upon the hands and arms;

    (e) failed to provide a suitable working temperature but caused or permitted the Claimant to work in cold and/or low working temperatures whereby, as they knew or should have known, the risks of circulatory diseases such as vibration white finger were increased;

    (f) caused required or permitted the Claimant to work for prolonged and unbroken periods with the tools and machines. The Claimant should have been permitted to work only intermittently with tools and machines producing high levels of vibration;

    (g) failed to enforce a system of frequent rest periods and to instruct the Claimant and to warn him of provision existing for such rest periods, and that such rest periods were or should have been designed to reduce the risk of vibration and/or that the same were necessary to secure and maintain good health;

    (h) failed to instruct and/or warn the Claimant how to perform his work safely and/or failed to instruct and/or warn the Claimant to protect his hands. In particular they failed to instruct and/or warn the Claimant as to the risk of contracting the condition and as to the measures to be taken to reduce or avoid the risk;

    (i) failed adequately or at all to supervise the Claimant and his work and working conditions;

(j) failed to make and keep safe the Claimant's place of work;

(k) operated an unsafe system of working. A safe system of working would have avoided injury from vibration;

(l) failed to have the Claimant medically examined, either regularly, adequately or at all;

(m) failed to heed the fact that other employees had suffered from the same or similar condition as a consequence of their employment with the Defendants;

(n) failed to warn the Claimant of the risk of contracting the condition by reason of his work and the tools and machinery used; they failed to warn the Claimant to be alert for the first signs and symptoms of the condition; they failed to warn the Claimant of the need to obtain immediate medical advice as and when the first signs and symptoms occurred and of the need to report the first signs and symptoms to the Defendants;

(o) failed to carry out a suitable and sufficient assessment of the risks to the health and safety of their employees to check they were exposed whilst working; the Defendants had a duty to carry out an assessment under regulation 3 of the Management of Health and Safety at Work Regulations 1992 and 1999;

(p) failed to make and give effect to appropriate arrangements for the effective planning, organisation, control, monitoring and review of the preventive and protective measures required to ensure the health and safety of their employees; the Defendants had a duty to take such steps under regulation 4 of the Management of Health and Safety at Work Regulations 1992 and Regulation 5 of the 1999 Regulations.

6. The Defendants were in breach of the following statutory duties:

(a) failed to provide suitable work equipment contrary to regulation 5 of the Provision and Use of Work Equipment Regulations 1992;

(b) failed to ensure that the work equipment was maintained in an efficient state, in efficient working order and in good repair so as to prevent excessive vibration and force being transmitted to the claimant's hands, contrary to regulation 6 of the Provision and Use of Work Equipment Regulations 1992;

(c) failed to make available adequate health and safety information pertaining to the use of the work equipment, contrary to regulation 8(1) of the Provision and Use of Work Equipment Regulations 1992;

(d) failed to make available to supervisory staff adequate health and safety information pertaining to the use of the work equipment, contrary to regulation 8(2) of the Provision and Use of Work Equipment Regulations 1992;

(e) failed to provide adequate training for purposes of health and safety, contrary to regulation 9 of the Provision and Use of Work Equipment Regulations 1992;

(f) contrary to regulation 5(1) of the Control of Vibration at Work Regulations 2005 failed to make a suitable and sufficient risk assessment of the risk created by the work to the health and safety of employees and to identify the measures that needed to be taken to meet the requirement of the Regulations;

(g) contrary to regulation 6(1) of the Control of Vibration at Work Regulations 2005 failed to ensure that risk from the exposure to vibration was either eliminated at source or reduced to as low a level as is reasonably practicable;

(h) contrary to regulation 6(2) of the Control of Vibration at Work Regulations 2005 failed to reduce exposure to as low a level as is reasonably practicable by establishing and implementing a programme of organisational and technical measures which was appropriate to the activity;

(i) contrary to regulation 7(1) of the Control of Vibration at Work Regulations 2005 failed to ensure that employees and in particular the Claimant were placed under suitable health surveillance;

(j) contrary to regulation 8(1) of the Control of Vibration at Work Regulations 2005 failed to provide employees and in particular the Claimant with suitable and sufficient information, instruction and training.

Particulars of damages claim
7. (As above).

APPENDIX 2

SAMPLE SCHEDULE

A.2   SCHEDULE IN ASBESTOS FATAL CLAIM

IN THE EASTFORD COUNTY COURT Case No

BETWEEN

ANTHONY GEORGE FLETCHER

(Personal Representative of the Estate of

Norman Stanley Fletcher, deceased) Claimant

and

BRUNEL SHIPBUILDERS (THAMES) LIMITED Defendants

SCHEDULE OF LOSS

Date of Schedule	1 December 2011
Deceased's date of birth	13 June 1937
Deceased's date of death	2 November 2007
Age at death	70 years
Normal life expectancy	10.5 years
Claimant's date of birth	5 December 1947
Age at date of Schedule	a few days short of 64 years of age
Bereavement damages	£10,000.00
Interest 2 November 2007 to 1 December 2011 = 4 years 1 month	£983.00

Care		£12,500.00
Interest, assessed for 4 years 1 month		1,228.75
Claimant's loss of earnings		
Losses 2 July 2007 to 24 January 2008		£2,816.43
Interest at full rate from mid-point 13 October 2007		£286.15
Cost of travel for medical treatment		£400.00
Interest		£61.40
Cost of additional food, electricity, heating and laundry		
Additional dietary supplements, £10 pw		
Additional heating, lighting and laundry, estimated at £15 pw		
Claim from August 2005 to end October 2007		
117 weeks x £25 pw		£2,925.00
Interest		£448.99
Funeral expenses		£3,348.65
Interest from 28 November 2007		£314.77
Past loss of Dependency		
Deceased's UK State Pension	£87.02 pw	£4,525.04 pa
Deceased's G pension	£60.00 pw	£3,120.00 pa
Deceased's D pension	£170.15 pm	£2,041.80 pa
Deceased's T pension	£598.72 pm	£7,184.64 pa
		£16,871.48 pa
Claimant's S pension	£255.24 pm	£3,062.88 pa
Claimant's earnings		£12,004.11 pa
		£15,066.99 pa
Joint Income	£16,871.48 + £15,066.99 =	£31,938.47 pa
	66% =	£21,079.39 pa

	less Claimant's income	£15,066.99 pa
Annual dependency		£6,012.40 pa
Past loss of dependency	£6,012.40 x 4 yrs, 1 month =	£24,550.63
Interest at half rate		£2,413.32

Past loss of services dependency

The deceased worked in the garden and performed DIY

Claimed at £1,000 pa for 2 years		£2,000.00

FUTURE LOSSES

Loss of future dependency

The Claimant would have continued working to age 65 on 5 December 2012

Joint Income	£16,871.48 + £15,066.99 =	£31,938.47 pa
	66% =	£21,079.39 pa
	less Claimant's income	£15,066.99 pa
		£6,012.40 pa

Loss of dependency from 1 December 2011 to 5 December 2012

Say multiplier of 1 x £6,012.40 = £6,012.40

Loss from 6 December 2012

Deceased's UK State Pension	£87.02 pw	£4,525.04 pa
Deceased's G pension	£60.00 pw	£3,120.00 pa
Deceased's D pension	£170.15 pm	£2,041.80 pa
Deceased's T pension	£598.72 pm	£7,184.64 pa
		£16,871.48 pa
Claimant's UK State Pension	£117.43 pw	£6,106.36 pa
Claimant's T pension	£255.24 pm	£3,062.88 pa
		£9,169.24 pa

Joint Income	£16,871.48 + £9,169.24 =	£26,040.72 pa
	66% =	£17,186.88 pa
	less Claimant's income	£9,169.24 pa
Annual dependency		£8,017.64 pa
Multiplier on life expectancy of 10.5 years	Table 28 at 2.5% = 9.25	no further discount on assessed life expectancy
Multiplier 9.25 less 4 yr, 1 month to Schedule less 1 =		4.17
Loss of remainder of dependency	£8,017.64 x 4.17 =	£33,433.56

Future cost of dependency on services

The claim is limited to 5 years, £5,000.00

Statement of Truth

The Claimant believes that the facts stated in the Schedule are true.

APPENDIX 3

RESTORING A COMPANY TO THE REGISTER

A.3   WITNESS STATEMENT FOR RESTORING A COMPANY

IN THE COURT Case No

IN THE MATTER OF LIMITED AND IN THE MATTER OF THE COMPANIES ACT 2006

Claimant/Applicant

and

(Liquidator [if any])

(Insurance company) Respondents

WITNESS STATEMENT IN SUPPORT

I, solicitor of state as follows:

1.   I am a solicitor in the firm of and I have conduct of this matter. I make this witness statement in support of an application on behalf of the Claimant for the restoration to the register of Limited and a declaration that the dissolution of the company is void. I am duly authorised to make this witness statement on behalf of the Claimant. Save where it otherwise appears, the matters stated in this witness statement are within my own knowledge and they are true. Where any matters are not within my own knowledge then I state the source of my information and belief.

2.   This Application is made in order that the company may be made Defendant to proceedings to be brought by the Claimant for damages for personal injuries sustained by the claimant in the course of his employment with the company.

3.   The Claimant was employed by the company between 19 and 19 . The claimant suffered injury when .

4.   From what the Claimant has told me and from my conduct of the case I believe that the Claimant has a good cause of action in respect

of his injuries. There is now shown to me marked a copy of the draft Particulars of Claim in the intended personal injury action.

5.   The company Limited was dissolved on .

6.   It will be contended that the primary limitation period under sections 11 and 14 of the Limitation Act 1980 has not yet expired. It is contended that the Claimant's date of knowledge for the purpose of those provisions did not arise more than 3 years ago. The Claimant did not know that he had suffered significant injury within the meaning of section 14 because he was unaware that he had (asbestos related disease) until . When he was told the results of a medical examination undergone on .

7.   If the primary limitation period has expired it is submitted that this is an appropriate case for the Court to exercise its discretion under section 33 of the Limitation Act 1980. The Claimant was not aware until that he might have (asbestos related disease). The Claimant was not aware that his injury was referable to the acts or defaults of the company until about . The Claimant first consulted solicitors on about and since then the action has been diligently pursued. The evidence likely to be adduced by the claimant and by the company as Defendants relates to periods of work lasting days and weeks and relates to the system of work and thus is not likely to be less cogent than if the action had been brought earlier. Evidence is available from publications and other documents and expert evidence is currently available as to the date or dates when it should have been known that exposure to (asbestos) created a risk of significant injury. The claimant has a permanent condition and evidence as to his condition and prognosis is readily obtainable.

8.   The Liquidator of the company (name and address) has been notified of this application and in particular of the Order sought re-appointing him as Liquidator. He has indicated that he does not object. True copies of the correspondence are now shown to me marked . Although it appears that the company has no assets the company was insured in respect of personal injury claims by its employees with and the Claimant will rely upon his rights under the Third Parties (Rights Against Insurers) Act 1930.

9.   In the circumstances I ask the Court to make the Orders in the terms sought.

Statement of truth

I believe that the facts stated in this Witness Statement are true.

Signed

Dated

APPENDIX 4

CHECKLISTS

Some of the lists annexed to the Personal Injury Protocol are of assistance in this context and are set out here (they are numbered here slightly differently).

A.4 GENERAL WORKPLACE DOCUMENTS
(i)   Accident book entry.
(ii)   First aider report.
(iii)   Surgery record.
(iv)   Foreman/supervisor accident report.
(v)   Safety representative's accident report.
(vi)   RIDDOR report to HSE.
(vii)   Other communications between defendants and HSE.
(viii)   Minutes of Health and Safety Committee meeting(s) where accident/matter considered.
(ix)   Report to DSS.
(x)   Documents listed above relative to any previous accident/matter identified by the claimant and relied upon as proof of negligence.
(xi)   Earnings information where defendant is employer.
(xii)   Pre-accident Risk Assessment required by regulation 3 of the Management of Health and Safety at Work Regulations 1992 and 1999.
(xiii)   Post-accident Re-Assessment required by regulation 3.
(xiv)   Accident Investigation Report prepared in implementing the requirements of the Management of Health and Safety at Work Regulations 1992.
(xv)   Health Surveillance Records in appropriate cases.
(xvi)   Information provided to employees.
(xvii)   Documents relating to the employees health and safety training required by the Management of Health and Safety at Work Regulations 1992 and 1999.

WORKPLACE (HEALTH SAFETY AND WELFARE) REGULATIONS 1992
(i)   Repair and maintenance records required by Regulation 5.
(ii)   Housekeeping records to comply with the requirements of Regulation 9.

PROVISION AND USE OF WORK EQUIPMENT REGULATIONS 1992 AND 1998

(i)   Manufacturers' specifications and instructions in respect of relevant work equipment establishing its suitability to comply with Regulation 5.

(ii) Maintenance log/maintenance records required to comply with Regulation 6.

(iii) Documents providing information and instructions to employees to comply with Regulation 8.

(iv) Documents provided to the employee in respect of training for use to comply with Regulation 9.

(v)   Any notice, sign or document relied upon as a defence to alleged breaches of Regulations 14 to 18 dealing with controls and control systems.

(vi) Instruction/training documents issued to comply with the requirements of Regulation 22 insofar as it deals with maintenance operations where the machinery is not shut down.

(vii) Copies of markings required to comply with Regulation 23.

(viii) Copies of warnings required to comply with Regulation 24.

PERSONAL PROTECTIVE EQUIPMENT AT WORK REGULATIONS 1992

(i)   Documents relating to the assessment of the Personal Protective Equipment to comply with Regulation 6.

(ii) Documents relating to the maintenance and replacement of Personal Protective Equipment to comply with Regulation 7.

(iii) Record of maintenance procedures for Personal Protective Equipment to comply with Regulation 7.

(iv) Records of tests and examinations of Personal Protective Equipment to comply with Regulation 7.

(v)   Documents providing information, instruction and training in relation to the Personal Protective Equipment to comply with Regulation 9.

(vi) Instructions for use of Personal Protective Equipment to include the manufacturers' instructions to comply with Regulation 10.

HEALTH AND SAFETY (DISPLAY SCREEN EQUIPMENT) REGULATIONS 1992

(i)   Analysis of work stations to assess and reduce risks carried out to comply with the requirements of Regulation 2.

(ii) Re-assessment of analysis of work stations to assess and reduce risks following development of symptoms by the claimant.

(iii) Documents detailing the provision of training including training records to comply with the requirements of Regulation 6.

(iv) Documents providing information to employees to comply with the requirements of Regulation 7.

CONTROL OF SUBSTANCES HAZARDOUS TO HEALTH REGULATIONS

(i)   Risk assessment carried out to comply with the requirements of the regulations.

(ii)   Reviewed risk assessment carried out.

(iii)   Copy labels from containers used for storage handling and disposal of carcinogens to comply with the regulations.

(iv)   Warning signs identifying designation of areas and installations which may be contaminated by carcinogens.

(v)   Documents relating to the assessment of the Personal Protective Equipment.

(vi)   Documents relating to the maintenance and replacement of Personal Protective Equipment to comply with the regulations.

(vii)   Record of maintenance procedures for Personal Protective Equipment.

(viii) Records of tests and examinations of Personal Protective Equipment to comply with the regulations.

(ix)   Documents providing information, instruction and training in relation to the Personal Protective Equipment.

(x)   Instructions for use of Personal Protective Equipment to include the manufacturers' instructions.

(xi)   Air monitoring records for substances assigned a maximum exposure limit or occupational exposure standard to comply with the regulations.

(xii)   Maintenance examination and test of control measures records.

(xiii) Monitoring records.

(xiv)   Health surveillance.

(xv)   Documents detailing information, instruction and training including training records for employees.

(xvi)   Labels and Health and Safety data sheets supplied to the employers to comply with the CHIP Regulations.

THE NOISE AT WORK REGULATIONS 1989

(i)   Any risk assessment records required to comply with the requirements of Regulations 4 and 5.

(ii)   Manufacturers' literature in respect of all ear protection made available to claimant to comply with the requirements of Regulation 8.

(iii)   All documents provided to the employee for the provision of information to comply with Regulation 11.

APPENDIX 5

PRE-ACTION PROTOCOL FOR DISEASE AND ILLNESS CLAIMS

CONTENTS

A.5 1 Introduction

1.1 Lord Woolf in his final Access to Justice Report of July 1996 recommended the development of protocols: 'To build on and increase the benefits of early but well informed settlements which genuinely satisfy both parties to a dispute.'

1.2 The aims of these protocols are:

- more contact between the parties
- better and earlier exchange of information
- better investigation by both sides
- to put the parties in a position where they may be able to settle cases fairly and early without litigation
- to enable proceedings to run to the court's timetable and efficiently, if litigation does become necessary.

1.3 The concept of protocols is relevant to a range of initiatives for good claims practice, especially:

- predictability in the time needed for steps to be taken
- standardisation of relevant information, including documents to be disclosed.

1.4 The Courts will be able to treat the standards set in protocols as the normal reasonable approach. If proceedings are issued, it will be for the court to decide whether non-compliance with a protocol should merit adverse consequences. Guidance on the court's likely approach will be given from time to time in practice directions.

1.5 If the court has to consider the question of compliance after proceedings have begun, it will not be concerned with minor infringements, eg failure by a short period to provide relevant information. One minor breach will not exempt the 'innocent' party from following the protocol. The court will look at the effect of non-compliance on the other party when deciding whether to impose sanctions.

2 Notes of Guidance

Scope of the Protocol

2.1 This protocol is intended to apply to all personal injury claims where the injury is not as the result of an accident but takes the form of an illness or disease.

2.2 This protocol covers disease claims which are likely to be complex and frequently not suitable for fast-track procedures even though they may fall within fast track limits. Disease for the purpose of this protocol primarily covers any illness physical or psychological, any disorder, ailment, affliction, complaint, malady, or derangement other than a physical or psychological injury solely caused by an accident or other similar single event.

2.3 In appropriate cases it may be agreed between the parties that this protocol can be applied rather than the Pre-Action Protocol for Personal Injury Claims where a single event occurs but causes a disease or illness.

2.4 This protocol is not limited to diseases occurring in the workplace but will embrace diseases occurring in other situations for example through occupation of premises or the use of products. It is not intended to cover those cases, which are dealt with as a 'group' or 'class' action.

2.5 The 'cards on the table' approach advocated by the personal injury protocol is equally appropriate to disease claims. The spirit of that protocol, and of the clinical negligence protocol is followed here, in accordance with the sense of the civil justice reforms.

2.6 The timetable and the arrangements for disclosing documents and obtaining expert evidence may need to be varied to suit the circumstances of the case. If a party considers the detail of the protocol to be inappropriate they should communicate their reasons to all of the parties at that stage. If proceedings are subsequently issued, the court will expect an explanation as to why the protocol has not been followed, or has been varied.

2.7 In a terminal disease claim with short life expectancy, for instance where a claimant has a disease such as mesothelioma, the time scale of the protocol is likely to be too long. In such a claim, the claimant may not be able to follow the protocol and the defendant would be expected to treat the claim with urgency including any request for an interim payment.

2.8 In a claim for mesothelioma, additional provisions apply, which are set out in Annex C of this protocol.

2A Alternative Dispute Resolution

2A.1 The parties should consider whether some form of alternative dispute resolution procedure would be more suitable than litigation, and if so, endeavour to agree which form to adopt. Both the Claimant and

Defendant may be required by the Court to provide evidence that alternative means of resolving their dispute were considered. The Courts take the view that litigation should be a last resort, and that claims should not be issued prematurely when a settlement is still actively being explored. Parties are warned that if the protocol is not followed (including this paragraph) then the Court must have regard to such conduct when determining costs.

2A.2 It is not practicable in this protocol to address in detail how the parties might decide which method to adopt to resolve their particular dispute. However, summarised below are some of the options for resolving disputes without litigation:

- Discussion and negotiation.
- Early neutral evaluation by an independent third party (for example, a lawyer experienced in the field of disease or illness, or an individual experienced in the subject matter of the claim).
- Mediation – a form of facilitated negotiation assisted by an independent neutral party; and
- Arbitration (where an independent person or body makes a binding decision).

2A.3 The Legal Services Commission has published a booklet on 'Alternatives to Court', CLS Direct Information Leaflet 23 (http://www.communitylegaladvice.org.uk/media/808/FD/leaflet23e.pdf), which lists a number of organisations that provide alternative dispute resolution services.

2A.4 It is expressly recognised that no party can or should be forced to mediate or enter into any form of ADR, but the parties should continue to consider the possibility of reaching a settlement at all times.

3 The Aims of the Protocol

3.1 The *general* aims of the protocol are –

- to resolve as many disputes as possible without litigation;
- where a claim cannot be resolved to identify the relevant issues which remain in dispute.

3.2 The *specific* objectives are –

Openness

- to encourage early communication of the perceived problem between the parties or their insurers;
- to encourage employees to voice any concerns or worries about possible work-related illness as soon as practicable;
- to encourage employers to develop systems of early reporting and investigation of suspected occupational health problems and to provide full and prompt explanations to concerned employees or former employees;

- to apply such principles to perceived problems outside the employer/employee relationship, for example occupiers of premises or land and producers of products;
- to ensure that sufficient information is disclosed by both parties to enable each to understand the other's perspective and case, and to encourage early resolution;

Timeliness

- to provide an early opportunity for employers (past or present) or their insurers to identify cases where an investigation is required and to carry out that investigation promptly;
- to encourage employers (past or present) or other defendants to involve and identify their insurers at an early stage;
- to ensure that all relevant records including health and personnel records are provided to employees (past or present) or their appointed representatives promptly on request, by any employer (past or present) or their insurers. This should be complied with to a realistic timetable;
- to ensure that relevant records which are in the claimant's possession including where appropriate GP and hospital records are made available to the defendant or to the nominated insurance manager or solicitor representing the defendant by claimants or their advisers at an appropriate stage;
- to proceed on a reasonable timetable where a resolution is not achievable to lay the ground to enable litigation to proceed at a reasonable and proportionate cost, and to limit the matters in contention;
- to communicate promptly where any of the requested information is not available or does not exist;
- to discourage the prolonged pursuit of unmeritorious claims and the prolonged defence of meritorious claims;
- to encourage all parties, at the earliest possible stage, to disclose voluntarily any additional documents which will assist in resolving any issue;
- to promote the provision of medical or rehabilitation treatment in appropriate cases to address the needs of the claimant.

4 The Protocol

This protocol is not a comprehensive code governing all the steps in disease claims. Rather it attempts to set out **a code of good practice** which parties should follow.

This protocol must be read in conjunction with the Practice Direction on Pre-Action Conduct.

Obtaining Occupational Records Including Health Records

4.1 In appropriate cases, a **potential claimant** may request Occupational Records including Health Records and Personnel Records before sending a Letter of Claim.

4.2 Any request for records by the **potential claimant** or his adviser should **provide sufficient information** to alert the **potential defendant** or his insurer where a possible disease claim is being investigated; Annex A1 provides a suggested form for this purpose for use in cases arising from employment. Similar forms can be prepared and used in other situations.

4.3 The copy records should be provided **within a maximum of 40 days** of the request at no cost. Although these will primarily be occupational records, it will be good practice for a **potential defendant** to disclose product data documents identified by a **potential claimant** at this stage which may resolve a causation issue.

4.4 Where the **potential defendant** or his insurer has difficulty in providing information quickly (in particular where the information is, or may be, held by someone else such as the Health and Safety Executive) details should be provided of steps being taken to resolve this problem together with a reasonable time estimate for doing so.

4.5 If the **potential defendant** or his insurer fails to provide the records including health records within 40 days and fails to comply with paragraph 4.4 above, the **potential claimant** or his adviser may then apply to the court for an **order for pre-action disclosure**. The Civil Procedure Rules make pre-action applications to the court easier. The court also has the power to impose costs sanctions for unreasonable delay in providing records.

5 Communication

5.1 If either the **potential claimant** or his adviser considers **additional records are required from a third party**, such as records from previous employers or GP and hospital records, in the first instance these should be requested by the **potential claimant** or their advisers. Third party record holders would be expected to co-operate. The Civil Procedure Rules enable parties to apply to the court for pre-action disclosure by third parties.

5.2 As soon as the records have been received and analysed, the **potential claimant** or his adviser should consider whether a claim should be made. GP and hospital records will normally be obtained before a decision is reached.

5.3 If a decision is made not to proceed further at this stage against a party identified as a **potential defendant**, the **potential claimant** or his adviser should notify that **potential defendant** in writing as soon as practicable.

6 Letter of Claim

6.1 Where a decision is made to make a claim, the claimant shall send to the proposed defendant two copies of a letter of claim, as soon as sufficient information is available to substantiate a realistic claim and before issues of quantum are addressed in detail. One copy is for the defendants, the second for passing on to his insurers.

6.2 This letter shall contain a **clear summary of the facts** on which the claim is based, including details of the illness or disease alleged, and the **main allegations of fault**. It shall also give details of present condition and prognosis. The **financial loss** incurred by the claimant should be outlined. Where the case is funded by a conditional fee agreement, notification should be given of the existence of the agreement and where appropriate, that there is a success fee and insurance premium, although not the level of the success fee or premium.

6.3 Where the funding arrangement is an insurance policy the party must state –

(1) the name and address of the insurer;
(2) the policy number;
(3) the date of the policy;
(4) the claim or claims to which it relates (including Part 20 claims if any);
(5) the level of cover; and
(6) whether the premiums are staged and if so the points at which the increased premiums are payable.

6.4 Solicitors are recommended to use a **standard format** for such a letter – an example is at Annex B: this can be amended to suit the particular case, for example, if the client has rehabilitation needs these can also be detailed in the letter.

6.5 A **chronology** of the relevant events (eg dates or periods of exposure) should be provided (with a work history from HM Revenue and Customs. In the case of alleged occupational disease an appropriate employment history should also be provided, particularly if the claimant has been employed by a number of different employers and the illness in question has a long latency period. Where there is more than one employer the chronology should state if there was any relevant exposure during each of those different periods of employment. Details should also be given about any periods of self-employment during which there was any relevant exposure and whether any claims have been made and payments received under the Pneumoconiosis etc (Workers' Compensation) Act 1979.

6.6 The letter of claim should identify any **relevant documents**, including health records not already in the defendant's possession eg any relevant GP and hospital records. These will need to be disclosed in confidence to the nominated insurance manager or solicitor representing the defendant following receipt of their letter of acknowledgement. Where the action is brought under the Law Reform Act 1934 or the Fatal Accidents Act 1976 then **relevant documents** will normally include copies of the death certificate, the post mortem report, the inquest depositions and if obtained by that date the grant of probate or letters of administration.

6.7 The letter of claim should indicate whether a claim is also being made against any **other potential defendant** and identify any known insurer involved. Copies of any relevant result from the Association of British Insurers Employers' Liability Tracing Service, both positive and negative, should be attached to the letter of claim. If the claimant receives any insurance database results after sending the letter of claim those results should be forwarded to the defendant as soon as is reasonably practicable.

6.8 Sufficient information should be given to enable the defendant's insurer/solicitor to commence **investigations** and at least to put a broad valuation on the 'risk'.

6.9 It is not a requirement for the claimant to provide **medical evidence** with the letter of claim, but the claimant may choose to do so in very many cases.

6.10 **Letters of claim and response** are not intended to have the same **status** as a statement of case in proceedings. Matters may come to light as a result of investigation after the letter of claim has been sent, or after the defendant has responded, particularly if disclosure of documents takes place outside the recommended 90 day period. These circumstances could mean that the 'pleaded' case of one or both parties is presented slightly differently than in the letter of claim or response. It would not be consistent with the spirit of the protocol for a party to 'take a point' on this in the proceedings, provided that there was no obvious intention by the party who changed their position to mislead the other party.

6.11 **Proceedings should not be issued until after 90 days from the date of acknowledgement** (see paragraph 7), unless there is a limitation problem and/or the claimant's position needs to be protected by early issue. (See paragraphs 2.6 and 2.7)

7 The Response

7.1 The defendant should **send an acknowledgement within 21 days** of the date of posting of the letter of claim, identifying the liability insurer (if any) who will be dealing with the matter and, if necessary, identifying specifically any significant omissions from the Letter of Claim. If there has been no acknowledgement by the defendant or insurer within 21 days, the claimant will be entitled to issue proceedings.

7.2 The identity of all relevant insurers, if more than one, should be notified to the claimant by the insurer identified in the acknowledgement letter, within 30 days of the date of that acknowledgement. For claims with a long latency period it is recognised that it may not be possible to identify the full insurance history within 30 days. In these circumstances the insurer or defendant should notify the claimant in writing as soon as possible. In any event, within 30 days the insurer or the defendant should state which other insurers have been identified. Where insurers have not been identified the defendant or insurer should state what steps have been taken to determine this information.

7.3 The defendant or his representative should, **within 90 days of the date of the acknowledgement letter**, provide a **reasoned answer**: –

- if the **claim is admitted**, they should say so in clear terms;
- if only **part of the claim is admitted** they should make clear which issues of fault and/or causation and/or limitation are admitted and which remain in issue and why;
- if the **claim is not admitted in full**, they should explain why and should, **for example**, include comments on the employment status of the claimant, (including job description(s) and details of the department(s) where the claimant worked), the allegations of fault, causation and of limitation, and if a synopsis or chronology of relevant events has been provided and is disputed, their version of those events;
- if the **claim is not admitted in full**, the defendant should enclose with his letter of reply **documents** in his possession which are **material to the issues** between the parties and which would be likely to be ordered to be disclosed by the court, either on an application for pre-action disclosure, or on disclosure during proceedings. Reference can be made to the documents annexed to the personal injury protocol;
- where more than one defendant receives a letter of claim, the timetable will be activated for each defendant by the date on the letter of claim addressed to them. If any defendant wishes to extend the timetable because the number of defendants will cause complications, they should seek agreement to a different timetable as soon as possible.

7.4 If the parties reach agreement on liability and/or causation, but time is needed to resolve other issues including the value of the claim, they should aim to agree a reasonable period.

7.5 Where it is not practicable for the defendant to complete his investigations within 90 days, the defendant should indicate the difficulties and outline the further time needed. Any request for an extension of time should be made, with reasons, as soon as the defendant becomes aware that an extension is needed and normally before the 90 day period has expired. Such an extension of time should be agreed in circumstances where reasonable justification has been shown. Lapse of many years since the circumstances giving rise to the claim does not, by itself, constitute reasonable justification for further time.

7.6 Where the relevant negligence occurred outside England and Wales and/or where the defendant is outside the jurisdiction, the time periods of 21 days and 90 days should normally be extended up to 42 days and 180 days.

8 Special Damages

8.1 The claimant will send to the defendant as soon as practicable a Schedule of Special Damages with supporting documents, particularly where the defendant has admitted liability.

9 Experts

9.1 In disease claims expert opinions may be needed on one or more of the following –

- knowledge, fault, causation and apportionment;
- condition and prognosis;
- valuing aspects of the claim.

9.2 The civil justice reforms and the Civil Procedure Rules encourage economy in the use of experts and a less adversarial expert culture. It is recognised that in disease claims, the parties and their advisers will require flexibility in their approach to expert evidence. Decisions on whether experts might be instructed jointly, and on whether reports might be disclosed sequentially or by exchange, should rest with the parties and their advisers. Sharing expert evidence may be appropriate on various issues including those relating to the value of the claim. However, this protocol does not attempt to be prescriptive on issues in relation to expert evidence.

9.3 Obtaining expert evidence will often be an expensive step and may take time, especially in specialised areas where there are limited numbers of suitable experts. Claimants, defendants and their advisers, will therefore need to consider carefully how best to obtain any necessary expert help quickly and cost-effectively.

9.4 The protocol recognises that a flexible approach must be adopted in the obtaining of medical reports in claims of this type. There will be very many occasions where the claimant will need to obtain a medical report before writing the letter of claim. In such cases the defendant will be entitled to obtain their own medical report. In some other instances it may be more appropriate to send the letter of claim before the medical report is obtained. Defendants will usually need to see a medical report before they can reach a view on causation.

9.5 Where the parties agree the nomination of a single expert is appropriate, before any party instructs an expert he should give the other party a list of the **name**(s) of **one or more experts** in the relevant speciality whom he considers are suitable to instruct. The parties are encouraged to agree the instruction of a single expert to deal with discrete areas such as cost of care.

9.6 **Within 14 days** the other party may indicate **an objection** to one or more of the named experts. The first party should then instruct a mutually acceptable expert. If the Claimant nominates an expert in the original letter of claim, the 14 days is in addition to the 21 days in paragraph 7.1.

9.7 If the second party objects to all the listed experts, the parties may then instruct **experts of their own choice**. It would be for the court to decide subsequently, if proceedings are issued, whether either party had acted unreasonably.

9.8 If the **second party does not object to an expert nominated**, he shall not be entitled to rely on his own expert evidence within that particular speciality unless:

(a)   the first party agrees,
(b)   the court so directs, or
(c)   the first party's expert report has been amended and the first party is not prepared to disclose the original report.

9.9 **Either party may send to an agreed expert written questions** on the report, relevant to the issues, via the first party's solicitors. The expert should send answers to the questions separately and directly to each party.

9.10 The cost of a report from an agreed expert will usually be paid by the instructing first party: the costs of the expert replying to questions will usually be borne by the party which asks the questions.

9.11 Where the defendant admits liability in whole or in part, before proceedings are issued, any medical report obtained under this protocol which **the claimant** relies upon, should be disclosed to the other party.

9.12 Where the defendant obtains a medical report on which he seeks to rely this should be disclosed to the claimant.

9.13 For further guidance see Part 35 of the CPR, Practice Direction 35 and the Protocol for the Instruction of Experts to give Evidence in Civil Claims which is annexed to that Practice Direction.

10 Resolution of Issues

10.1 The Civil Procedure Rules Part 36 enable claimants and defendants to make formal offers to settle before proceedings are started. Parties should consider making such an offer, since to do so often leads to settlement. If such an offer is made, the party making the offer must always supply sufficient evidence and/or information to enable the offer to be properly considered.

10.2 Where a claim is not resolved when the protocol has been followed, the parties might wish to carry out a 'stocktake' of the issues in dispute, and the evidence that the court is likely to need to decide those issues, before proceedings are started.

10.3 Prior to proceedings it will be usual for all parties to disclose those expert reports relating to liability and causation upon which they propose to rely.

10.4 The claimant should delay issuing proceedings for 21 days from disclosure of reports to enable the parties to consider whether the claim is capable of settlement.

10.5 Where the defendant is insured and the pre-action steps have been conducted by the insurer, the insurer would normally be expected to nominate solicitors to accept service of proceedings and the claimant's solicitor is recommended to invite the insurer to nominate solicitors to accept service of proceedings and to do so 7–14 days before the intended issue date.

11 Limitation

11.1 If by reason of complying with any part of this protocol a claimant's claim may be time-barred under any provision of the Limitation Act 1980, or any other legislation which imposes a time limit for bringing an action, the claimant may commence proceedings without complying with this protocol. In such circumstances, a claimant who commences proceedings without complying with all, or any part, of this protocol may apply to the court on notice for directions as to the timetable and form of procedure to be adopted, at the same time as he requests the court to issue proceedings. The court will consider whether to order a stay of the whole or part of the proceedings pending compliance with this protocol.

Annex A
Letter Requesting Occupational Records including Health Records

Dear Sirs,

We are acting on behalf of the above-named who has developed the following (*insert disease*).We are investigating whether this disease may have been caused: –

- *during the course of his employment with you lname of employer if different*
- *whilst at your premises at (address)*
- *as a result of your product (name)*

We are writing this in accordance with the Protocol for Disease and Illness Claims

We seek the following records: –

(*Insert details e g personnelloccupational health*)

Please note your insurers may require you to advise them of this request.

We enclose a request form and expect to receive the records within 40 days. If you are not able to comply with this request within this time, please advise us of the reason.

Yours faithfully

Annex A1
Application on Behalf of a Potential Claimant for Use where a Disease Claim is Being Investigated

This should be completed as fully as possible

Company Name and Address		
1	(a) Full name of claimant (including previous surnames)	
	(b) Address now	
	(c) Address at date of termination of employment, if different	
	(d) Date of birth (and death, if applicable)	
	(e) National Insurance number, if available	
2	Department(s) where claimant worked	
3	This application is made because the claimant is considering	
	(a) a claim against you as detailed in para 4	YES/NO
	(b) pursuing an action against someone else	YES/NO
4	If the answer to Q3(a) is 'Yes' details of	

	(a) the likely nature of the claim, e g dermatitis	
	(b) grounds for the claim, e g exposure to chemical	
	(c) approximate dates of the events involved	
5	If the answer to Q3(b) is 'Yes' insert	
	(a) the names of the proposed defendants	
	(b) have legal proceedings been started	YES/NO
	(c) if appropriate, details of the claim and action number	
6	Any other relevant information or documents requested	
	Signature of Solicitor	
	Name	
	Address	
	Ref.	
	Telephone number	
	Fax number	

I authorise you to disclose all of your records relating to me/the claimant to my solicitor and to your legal and insurance representatives. Signature of claimant
Signature of personal representative where patient has died

Annex B
Template for Letter of Claim

To: – Defendant

Dear Sirs

Re: **Claimant's full name**

Claimant's full address

Claimant's National Insurance Number

Claimant's Date of Birth

Claimant's Clock or Works Number

Claimant's Employer (name and address)

We are instructed by the above named to claim damages in connection with a claim for: –

Specify occupational disease

We are writing this letter in accordance with the pre-action protocol for disease and illness claims.

Please confirm the identity of your insurers. Please note that your insurers will need to see this letter as soon as possible and it may affect your insurance cover if you do not send this to them.

The Claimant was employed by you (*if the claim arises out of public or occupiers' liability give appropriate details*) as job description from date to date. During the relevant period of his employment he worked: –

description of precisely where the Claimant worked and what he did to include a description of any machines used and details of any exposure to noise or substances

The circumstances leading to the development of this condition are as follows: –

Give chronology of events (and in appropriate cases attach a work history from HM Revenue and Customs)

The reason why we are alleging fault is: –

Details should be given of contemporary and comparable employees who have suffered from similar problems if known; any protective equipment provided; complaints; the supervisors concerned, if known.

Our client's employment history is attached.

We have also made a claim against: –

Insert details

Their insurers' details are: –

Insert if known

We have the following documents in support of our client's claim and will disclose these in confidence to your nominated insurance manager or solicitor when we receive their acknowledgement letter.

eg Occupational health notes; GP notes

We have obtained a medical report from (name)and will disclose this when we receive your acknowledgement of this letter.

(This is optional at this stage)

From the information we presently have: –

(i)   the Claimant first became aware of symptoms on (*insert approximate date*)

(ii)   the Claimant first received medical advice about those symptoms on (*insert date*)(*give details of advice given if appropriate*)

(iii)   the Claimant first believed that those symptoms might be due to exposure leading to this claim on (*insert approximate date*)

A description of our client's condition is as follows:–

This should be sufficiently detailed to allow the Defendant to put a broad value on the claim

(For appropriate cases) Our client is still suffering from the effect of his/her condition. We invite you to participate with us in addressing his/her immediate needs by use of rehabilitation.

He has the following time off work: –

Insert dates

He is presently employed as a *job description* and his average net weekly income is £

If you are our client's employers, please provide us with the usual earnings details, which will enable us to calculate his financial loss.

Please note that we have entered into a conditional fee agreement with our client dated in relation to this claim which provides for a success fee within the meaning of section 58(2) of the Courts and Legal Services Act 1990. Our client has taken out an insurance policy dated with (name and address of insurance company) to which section 29 of the Access to Justice Act 1999 applies in respect of this claim. The policy number is [insert], the policy is dated [insert] and the level of cover is [insert]. The premiums payable under the insurance policy [are not] [are] staged [and the points at which the increase premiums are payable are as follows:].

A copy of this letter is attached for you to send to your insurers. Finally we expect an acknowledgement of this letter within 21 days by yourselves or your insurers.

Yours faithfully

Annex C
Guidance for Cases Involving Mesothelioma – Early Notification Letter

Purpose

1 The purpose of the early notification letter is twofold. First, the intention is to give defendants and their insurers as much advance warning as possible about the possibility of a claim so that they can begin to investigate the matter. This is particularly so where relevant information may be decades old and may take time to locate and retrieve. Second, where the claimant has severely limited life expectancy it gives advance warning to defendants of the need for urgency in locating relevant information.

2 It is intended that the early notification letter will be sent before the letter of claim and will not start the timetable for response as set out in paragraph 7 of this protocol.

3 As soon as sufficient information is available to identify a proposed defendant, the claimant should send to the proposed defendant two copies of the early notification letter. One copy is for the defendant, the second for passing on to the defendant's insurers. The claimant should also send a further copy of the same letter directly to the defendant's insurer, where known. In the case of a defunct company the further copy of the letter should be sent to the relevant insurer or handler of that defunct company.

Content of Early Notification Letter

4 All copies of the early notification letter should be clearly marked 'MESOTHELIOMA CLAIM'.

5 The early notification letter should contain basic information sufficient to identify the claimant, the periods of relevant exposure and the potential defendants. As a minimum, the early notification letter should contain the following information:

    (a)   name and address of the claimant/deceased;

    (b)   national insurance number of the claimant/deceased (if known);

    (c)   claimant/deceased's date of birth;

    (d)   employers, where known, of relevant employment and or exposure;

    (e)   occupiers of premises, where known, of relevant employment and/or exposure;

    (f)   date or approximate dates, where known, of relevant employment and or exposure;

    (g)   direct contact details, including e-mail address, for the claimant's legal representative;

    (h)   marital status;

(i)   details of dependents; and

(j)   date of diagnosis.

6 Solicitors are recommended to use a standard format for the early notification letter. An example is set out in Annex D. This can be amended to suit the particular case.

7 The early notification letter should indicate whether a claim is also being made against any other potential defendant and identify any known insurer involved.

8. The early notification letter is not intended to have the same status as a statement of case in proceedings. Matters may come to light as a result of investigation after the letter of claim has been sent.

Employment and Exposure History

9 In view of the joint and several liability provided for in the Compensation Act 2006 in mesothelioma cases the information set out in paragraph 6.5 of this protocol is particularly relevant.

Defendant's response

10 The defendant should respond within 14 days of the date of the letter confirming that the matter is receiving urgent attention.

Compliance with this protocol

11 Attention is drawn to paragraph 9.1 of Practice Direction 3D (Mesothelioma Claims) which provides that in Living Mesothelioma Claims (normally where the claimant has severely limited life expectancy) strict adherence to this protocol may not be required. The issue of compliance with this protocol in relation to certain mesothelioma claims is also recognised at paragraph 2.7 of this protocol.

Annex D
Early Notification Letter for use in Cases Involving Mesothelioma

URGENT – MESOTHELIOMA CLAIM

YOU MUST DEAL WITH THIS LETTER IMMEDIATELY

Dear Sirs,

We are acting on behalf of the above-named who has developed mesothelioma. We are investigating whether this disease may have been caused:

during the course of his employment with you / name of employer if different whilst at your premises at (address)

between the approximate dates of: (insert relevant dates of employment/at the premises) as a result of your product (name)

Please note your insurers will require you to advise them of this letter. You must pass a copy of this letter to your insurer immediately.

We are writing this letter in accordance with the Pre-Action Protocol for Disease and Illness Claims.

Our client's details are as follows:

Name:

Address:

National Insurance Number (if known)

Date of Birth:

Marital status:

Details of dependents:

Date of diagnosis.

We require a response from you confirming this matter is receiving urgent attention with 14 days of the date of this letter.

The direct e-mail address, which you may use for urgent communications and which should be followed up with paper copies, is: (insert e-mail address)

Yours faithfully

INDEX

References are to paragraph numbers.

Accrual of claim of action   4.6

Apportionment   3.1, 3.10
   basis   3.10.1
   death from asbestos, and   3.10.5
   divisible disease cases   3.10
   expert evidence   3.10.3
   jury question   3.10.1
   occupational stress claims   9.6, 9.8.5
   pleading   3.10.4
   practical application   3.10.2
   proving   3.10.4

Asbestos *see also* Asbestos-related
     illnesses
   1987 Regulations   11.2.3
   2002 Regulations   11.2.4
   amosite   5.1
   anthophyllite   5.1
   breathing apparatus   11.2.1
   carcinogenic substances   11.2.4
   chrysotile   5.1
   cleaning   11.2.1
   containment   11.2.1
   control of exposure   11.2.4
   crocidolite   5.1
   diseases   5.3
   duties of employer   11.2.4
   exhaust drafts   11.2.1
   foreseeability   2.3.1
   health surveillance   11.2.4
   Industry Regulations 1931   11.2.1
   information, instruction and
     training   11.2.4
   lung cancer, and   5.3.5
   monitoring   11.2.4
   persons employed   11.2.1
   protective equipment   11.2.4
   Regulations 1931   11.2.1
     scope   11.2.1
   risk assessment   11.2.4
   secondary exposure   5.2
   storage   11.2.1
   substances hazardous to
     health   11.2.4
   types   5.1
   uses of   5.2

Asbestosis *see* Asbestos-related
     illnesses   5.3.4

Asbestos-related illnesses   5.1
   applicable law   5.5.2
   apportionment of damages   5.5.5

Asbestos-related illnesses—*continued*
   Asbestosis
     death from
       apportionment, and   3.10.5
     general damages   15.3.4
     lung cancer, and   3.7.2
   breach of duty   5.4
     apportionment of damages   5.4.3
     causation   5.4.2
     contributory negligence   5.4.4
     date of knowledge   5.4.1
   causation   5.5.4
   damages   5.5.8
   exposure   5.5.3
   limitation   5.5.6
   medical diagnosis   5.5.1
   medical prognosis   5.5.7
   specific considerations   5.5

Asthma
   general damages   15.4

Asymptomatic asbestos conditions   3.9
   causation   3.9

Audiogram   6.2
   interpretation   6.3

Basic principles   1.4

Bereavement damages   15.1

Breach of duty
   asbestos-related illness   5.4

Buildings
   meaning   10.2.3
   Regulations   10.2.3

Carcinogenic substances
   meaning   10.2.8, 11.2.4

Carpal tunnel syndrome   8.1

Causation   2.4, 3.1
   asymptomatic asbestos
     conditions   3.9
   'but for' test   3.2
   de minimis exposure   3.8
   doubling the risk   3.5
   effective   3.3
   epidemiological evidence   3.5
   increasing the risk   3.4
   lung cancer   3.7
   material cause   3.3

Causation—*continued*
mesothelioma	3.6
duration and intensity of	
exposure	3.6
indivisible nature of	3.6
occupational stress claims	9.6, 9.8.4
pleural plaques	3.9.1
standard test	3.2

Claimant's evidence — 14.2
asbestos	14.3.1
length of exposure	14.3.1
other sources of exposure	14.3.1
protective equipment	14.3.1
protective measures taken,	
whether	14.3.1
type of product or substance	
used	14.3.1
when he worked	14.3.1
where he worked	14.3.1
work done	14.3.1
work done by others in	
proximity	14.3.1
employment history	14.2
noise	14.3.2
length of exposure	14.3.2
other sources of exposure	14.3.2
place of work	14.3.2
protective equipment	14.3.2
protective measures	14.3.2
type of tools and machines	
used	14.3.2
when working	14.3.2
work done	14.3.2
work done by others in	
proximity	14.3.2
required details	14.3
vibration white finger	14.3.4
other sources of exposure	14.3.4
place of work	14.3.4
protective equipment	14.3.4
protective measures	14.3.4
time at work	14.3.4
type of tools or machinery	
used	14.3.4
warnings and instructions	14.3.4
work-related stress	14.3.5
causation	14.3.5
knowledge of defendant	14.3.5
what could have been done to	
avoid stresses	14.3.5
work done	14.3.5
work-related upper limb	
disorders	14.3.3
other sources of exposure	14.3.3
places of work	14.3.3
protective measures	14.3.3
time worked	14.3.3
when working	14.3.3
work done	14.3.3

Common conditions — 1.2

Company
existence of	12.2
receivership	12.4

Company—*continued*
restoration under Companies	
Act 2006	12.3
application	12.3.1
hearing	12.3.3
limitation	12.3.4
order	12.3.3
procedure	12.3.2
retrospective permission to	
sue	12.4.1

Compensation Act 2006
mesothelioma, and	3.6

Construction
1961 Regulations	10.2.6
1966 Regulations	10.2.7

Constructive knowledge — 4.10

Contributory negligence — 3.1, 3.11
knowledge of risks, and	3.11

Control of Substances Hazardous to Health Regulations 1988, 1994, 1999 and 2002 — 10.2.8

Costs
limitation, and	4.28

Date of knowledge
meaning	4.7

De minimis exposure — 3.8
causation, and	3.8

Death, claims following
limitation	4.29, 4.30

Defences — 14.5

Disability
limitation, and	4.31

Disability discrimination
occupational stress claims	9.7.3

Disease
definition	13.1

Dismissal
occupational stress claims,	
and	9.5.3

Display screen equipment
assessment	11.2.7
breaks	11.2.7
overlap with other	
regulations	11.2.7
provision of information	11.2.7
reassessments	11.2.7
self-employed	11.2.7
training	11.2.7
user	11.2.7

Divisible disease — 3.1.1
indivisible disease	
distinguished	3.1.2

Documentary evidence — 14.6

Duty of care — 2.1
employees, and	2.1
extent	2.2
families of workers	2.1
foreseeability	2.2
to whom owed	2.1

Effective cause — 3.3

Employer
existence of — 12.2
which employer to sue — 12.1
worth suing, whether — 12.6
Epidemiological evidence — 3.5
causation, and — 3.5
doubling the risk, and — 3.5
Evidence *see also* Claimant's
evidence
asbestos — 14.3.1
claimant — 14.2
required details — 14.3
defence — 14.5
documentary — 14.6
investigating circumstances of
the claim — 14.4
noise — 14.3.2
vibration white finger — 14.3.4
witness statement — 14.1
work-related stress — 14.3.5
work-related upper limb
disorder — 14.3.3
Exhaust drafts — 11.2.1
Expert evidence
apportionment, and — 3.10.3
foreseeability, and — 2.5
Experts — 13.9
flexibility in approach — 13.9
single — 13.9

Factory
1937 Act
dust, fume and other
impurities — 10.2.2
injurious substance — 10.2.2
1961 Act — 10.2.5
meaning — 10.2.2
Fatal Accidents Act claims
special damages — 16.4
Foreseeability — 2.2
asbestos — 2.3.1
knowledge, development of — 2.3.1
expert evidence, and — 2.5
HSE publication, and — 2.2
knowledge and practices of
particular industry — 2.2
knowledge at date of exposure — 2.2
noise — 2.3.2
date of knowledge — 2.3.2
occupational stress claims — 9.4
real risk — 2.2
specific diseases, in — 2.3
vibration white finger (VWF) — 2.3.4
date of guilty knowledge — 2.3.4
work-related stress — 2.3.5
work-related upper limit
disorders — 2.3.3

General damages — 15.1
asbestosis — 15.3.4

General damages—*continued*
asbestos-related disease — 15.3
pain, suffering and
disability — 15.3.1
asthma — 15.4
handicap on labour
market — 15.4.2
loss of congenial
employer — 15.4.3
pain, suffering and
disability — 15.4.1
bereavement — 15.1
handicap on labour market — 15.3.7
hearing loss — 15.5
handicap on labour
market — 15.5.1
loss of congenial
employment — 15.5.2
loss of congenial
employment — 15.3.8
lung cancer — 15.3.3
mesothelioma — 15.3.2
pleural plaques — 15.3.6
pleural thickening — 15.3.5
provisional — 15.2
vibration white finger — 15.7
handicap on labour
market — 15.7.1
loss of congenial
employment — 15.7.2
work-related stress — 15.8
handicap on labour
market — 15.8.1
loss of congenial
employment — 15.8.2
work-related upper limb
disorders — 15.6
handicap in labour market — 15.6.1
loss of congenial
employment — 15.6.2
medical conditions — 15.6
General statutory duty — 10.1

Handicap on labour market
general damages — 15.3.7, 15.4.2,
15.5.1, 15.6.1, 15.7.1, 15.8.1
HAVS *see also* Vibration white
finger — 8.1
Hearing protection — 6.6

Identifying issues — 1.3
Implied duty of trust and confidence
occupational stress claims,
and — 9.7.2
Increasing the risk
but for test, and — 3.4
Fairchild — 3.4
new tort, whether — 3.4
Indivisible disease — 3.1.1
divisible disease distinguished — 3.1.1

Insurance law *see also* Third Parties
    (Rights Against Insurers) Act
    2010   12.6
Insurance policies   12.6
Insurer
    finding   12.7
Investigating circumstances of
    claim   14.4

Knowledge
    meaning   4.9

Letter of claim   13.6
    defendant's response to   13.7
Limitation   4.1
    accrual of cause of action   4.6
        actionable injury   4.6
    act or omission by person other
        than defendant   4.14
    breach of duty, and   4.3
    claims following death   4.29, 4.30
        Fatal Accidents Act 1976
            claim   4.29.2
        Law Reform (Miscellaneous
            Provisions) Act 1934
            claim   4.29.1
    constructive knowledge   4.10
        meaning   4.10
        objective test   4.10
    disability   4.31
        who is under   4.31.1
    discretion of court under section
        33   4.17
        claims following death   4.30
        considerations in exercising   4.19
        costs   4.28
        duration of disability of
            claimant   4.24
        effect   4.31.2
        extent to which claimant acted
            promptly and reasonably
            after knowledge   4.25
        extent to which evidence likely
            to be less cogent   4.22
        general principles   4.19
        historic sexual abuse cases   4.21,
                                            4.22
        length of delay   4.21
        liability, and   4.19
        onus   4.20
        poor legal advice   4.21
        previous proceedings   4.18
        proportionality   4.19
        reasons for delay   4.21
        setting aside   4.27
        steps taken by claimant to
            obtain expert advice   4.26
    expiry of period   4.15
        effect of   4.4
    extension of period by
        agreement   4.16
    intentional tort, and   4.3

Limitation—*continued*
    knowledge   4.9
    knowledge of identity of
        defendant   4.13
    knowledge that injury was
        attributable to act or
        omission constituting
        negligence, nuisance or
        breach of duty   4.12
        act or omission   4.12
        attributability   4.12
        principles   4.12
    knowledge that injury was
        significant   4.11
        exacerbation of injury   4.11
        personal characteristics of
            claimant   4.1
        three stage test   4.11
    knowledge under section 14   4.7
    occupational stress claims   9.8.6
    onus of proof   4.8
    personal injury claims   4.2
    reasons for   4.1
    when time begins to run   4.5
Loss of congenial employment
    general damages   15.3.8, 15.4.3,
                        15.5.2, 15.6.2, 15.7.2, 15.8.2
Loss of earnings *see also* Special
    damages   16.1
    alternative work   16.1
    future effect on employment   16.2
    prognosis   16.1
Lung cancer   3.7
    asbestos, and   5.3.5
    asbestosis, and   3.7.2
    causation   3.7
    causes   3.7.1
    general damages   15.3.3
    genetic factors   3.7.4
    indivisible nature of   3.7.4
    smoking, and   3.7.4
    without asbestosis   3.7.3

Management of health and safety at
    work
    health surveillance   10.2.9
    Regulations 1992 and 1999   10.2.9
    risk asessment   10.2.9
    training   10.2.9
Manual handling operations
    1992   11.2.9
    duties of employers   11.2.9
    risk assessment   11.2.9
Material cause   3.3
    Bonnington Castings   3.3
    several causes, and   3.3
Medical expenses   16.3
    examples   16.3
Mesothelioma *see also*
    Asbestos-related illnesses   5.3.6
    causation   3.6
    Compensation Act 2006   3.6

Mesothelioma —*continued*
general damages 15.3.2

Noise *see also* Noise-related
conditions
2005 Regulations 11.2.11
foreseeability 2.3.2
Regulations 1989 11.2.6
Noise-related conditions 6.1
applicable law 6.7.2
apportionment of damages 6.7.5
audiogram 6.2
awareness of data collection
methods 6.5
calculating hearing loss 6.4
causation 6.7.4
damages 6.7.8
exposure 6.7.3
hearing loss 6.3
hearing protection 6.6
human ear, and 6.1
interpretation 6.3
limitation 6.7.6
medical diagnosis 6.7.1
medical prognosis 6.7.7
sound waves 6.1
type of noise source 6.7.3
typical audiogram pattern 6.7.1

Occupational health records
obtaining 13.2
Occupational illness
Pre-Action Protocol 1.1
Occupational stress claims *see also*
Stress 9.1
alternative causes of action 9.7
alternatives to common law
claim 9.8.9
applicable law 9.8.2
apportionment 9.6, 9.8.5
breach of duty 9.5
breach of implied duty of trust
and confidence 9.7.2
causation 9.6, 9.8.4
common law 9.2
counselling service, provision
of 9.5.2
damages 9.8.8
definition 1.1
demotion, and 9.5.3
disability discrimination 9.7.3
dismissal, and 9.5.3
evidential value of GP
certificates 9.4.2
exposure 9.8.3
foreseeability 9.4
general principles 9.2
gravity of harm 9.5.1
guidance 9.3
inherently stressful
occupations 9.4.3
knowledge about employee 9.4.1

Occupational stress claims —*continued*
limitation 9.8.6
management standards 9.4.4
medical diagnosis 9.8.1
medical prognosis 9.8.7
occupational health, provision
of 9.5.2
practical propositions 9.3
Protection from Harassment Act
1997 9.7.1
reasonableness test 9.5.1
specific considerations 9.8
statutory duties 9.2
stress, definition 9.1
Sutherland v Hatton 9.3
working time, and 9.2

Part 36 offers *see also* Settlement 17.4
liability, and 17.5
quantum, and 17.6
Pleural effusion 5.3.3
Pleural plaques 3.9.1, 5.3.1
actionable damage 3.9.2
associated anxiety and
psychiatric reaction 3.9.2
causation, and 3.9.1
general damages 15.3.6
Johnston 3.9.2
medical evidence 3.9.2
Pleural thickening 5.3.2, 15.3.5
**Pre-action protocol for disease and
illness claims** 13.1
aim of 13.1
defendant's response to letter of
claim 13.7
disease, definition 13.1
experts 13.9
failure to comply with request
for information 13.4
letter of claim 13.6
obtaining health and
occupational records 13.2
resolution of isssues 13.10
schedule of special damage 13.8
scope 13.1
starting proceedings 13.11
third parties holding records 13.5
timetable 13.1
where defendant has difficulty
providing information 13.3
**Protection from Harassment Act
1997**
occupational stress claims 9.7.1
Provisional damages 15.2
criteria 15.2
Part 36 offer, and 15.2
Psychiatric illness
stress, and 9.1

Real risk
meaning 2.2

Receivership
  companies in   12.4
Regulations with specific
  application   11.1
Resolution of issues   13.10
Risk assessment   10.2.9
  substances hazardous to
    health   10.2.8

Settlement   17.1
  diagnosis, and   17.3
  knowledge of issues   17.3
  negotiations   17.2
  Part 36 offers   17.4
  pre-trial preparations   17.1
  prognosis, and   17.3
  when to negotiate   17.2
Shipbuilding
  1931 Regulations   10.2.1
  1960 Regulations   10.2.4
Significant injury
  meaning   4.11
Smoking
  lung cancer, and   3.7.4
Special damages   16.1
  Fatal Accidents Act claims   16.4
  future effect on employment   16.2
  loss of earnings   16.1
  medical expenses   16.3
  schedule of   13.8
Statutory basis of claim   10.1
Statutory provisions   10.1
Stress *see also* Occupational stress
    claims   2.3.5
    definition   9.1
    foreseeability   2.3.5
    guiding principles   2.3.5
    psychiatric illness, and   9.1
    reaction, as   9.1
    relevant factors   2.3.5
    signs of   2.3.5
    single test   2.3.5
Substances hazardous to health
  carcinogenic substances   10.2.8
  control measures   10.2.8
  exposure limit   10.2.8
  health surveillance   10.2.8
  meaning   10.2.8, 11.2.4
  monitoring   10.2.8
  Regulations   11.2.8
    risk assessment   10.2.8

Third Parties (Rights Against
    Insurers) Act 2010   12.5
  application of   12.5.2
  defences   12.5.4
  functioning of   12.5.1
  insurer's concession   12.5.6
  limitations   12.5.4
  obtaining disclosure from insurer
    and third parties   12.5.5
  relevant person   12.5.3

Transfer of undertakings   12.6
Trigger litigation   12.6

Vibration white finger *see also*
  HAVS   8.1
  applicable law   8.7.2
  apportionment of damages   8.7.5
  awareness of   8.1
  British Standards   8.4, 8.5
  carpal tunnel syndrome   8.1
  categories of damages   15.7
  causation   8.7.4
  causes   8.2
  common law duty   8.4, 8.5
  damages   8.7.8
  diagnosis   8.1
  evidence of symptoms   8.1
  exposure   8.7.3
  foreseeability   2.3.4
  general damages   15.7
  HAVS, and   8.1
  limitation   8.7.6
  long-term exposure   8.1
  medical diagnosis   8.7.1
  medical prognosis   8.7.7
  prescribed disease   8.3
  Regulations   11.2.10
  RMS value   8.4, 8.5
  specific considerations   8.7
  statutory duty   8.6
  Taylor-Pelmear table   15.7
  time of exposure   8.4, 8.5
  type of work and machinery and
    tools used   8.7.3
  vibration dose   8.4, 8.5

Witness statement   14.1
Woodmaking
  1974 Regulations   11.2.5
Work equipment
  meaning   10.2.11
  Regulations 1992 and 1998   10.2.11
Workplace
  1992 Regulations   10.2.10
  ventilation   10.2.10
  workstations   10.2.10
Work-related stress
  form   14.1
  general damages   15.8
Work-related upper limb disorder
  alternative diagnosis   7.5.1
  applicable law   7.5.2
  apportionment of damages   7.5.5
  breach of duty   7.2
  causation   7.2, 7.3, 7.5.4
  damages   7.5.8
  defined medical condition   7.4
  exposure   7.5.3
  foreseeability   2.3.3, 7.2
  general damages   15.6
  limitation   7.5.6
  meaning   7.1
  mechanical basis   7.4

Work-related upper limb disorder—*continued*
medical causation	7.3
medical diagnosis	7.5.1
medical prognosis	7.5.7
nature of work, and	7.2
prescribed conditions	7.4
scope	7.1

Work-related upper limb disorder—*continued*
specific considerations	7.5
symptoms	7.4
tenosynovitis	7.4
type of medical condition	7.5.1
work task	7.4